LIVES OF THE GREAT GARDENERS

LIVES OF THE GREAT GARDENERS

STEPHEN ANDERTON

Thames & Hudson

CONTENTS

Half-title: Illustration from Humphry Repton, *Fragments on the Theory and Practice of Landscape Gardening,* 1816.

Frontispiece: A landscape gardener with the tools, costume and apparatus of his trade, by Martin Engelbrecht, *c.* 1721.

Lives of the Great Gardeners © 2016 Thames & Hudson Ltd

Text © 2016 Stephen Anderton

Designed by Karin Fremer

First published in 2016 in hardcover in the United States of America by Thames & Hudson Inc., 500 Fifth Avenue, New York, New York 10110

thamesandhudsonusa.com

Library of Congress Catalog Card Number 2015959505

ISBN 978-0-500-51856-4

Printed and bound in China by C&C Offset Printing Co. Ltd

INTRODUCTION

I F YOU PERHAPS doubt that gardens are among the most luxurious products of civilization, just consider how many millions of people travel even more millions of miles every year to enjoy them. The greatest gardens are in fact works of art, and the world is their gallery. And, like all great art, they are priceless yet unnecessary (in practical terms); that is the wonder of them.

History is full of gardens, at first vegetable gardens set close to a house and protected against wild animals or domestic livestock, or monastic and physicians' gardens, walled and sometimes even moated to keep their highly valuable stock of plants secure. In the east, gardens were paradises set in desert landscapes, or philosophical and religious retreats with highly symbolic meanings and conventions. Gardens such as these existed even in lean times. In better-off times, modest ornamental gardens flourished around the houses of the rich and even the moderately well-off. Such were the cottage gardens of 19th-century Britain, so admired by Gertrude Jekyll.

But it is when money starts to flow generously – the result of imperial conquest or trade, or from long-standing aristocratic land tenure, or through the rise of a comfortable middle class – that we see truly ambitious ornamental gardens. Real surplus encourages real luxury. And so as the Medici sponsored great artists to paint in Renaissance Florence, so French aristocracy and royalty and then the political classes of 18th-century Britain, rich from trade, employed talented gardeners to create their landscape gardens. Ornamental gardens demonstrated one's wealth and one's taste. But private or not, gardens are a democratic medium: those landscapes

Vita Sackville-West created the famous garden at Sissinghurst, in Kent, in the mid-20th century with her husband, Harold Nicolson, and it is visited by thousands today. Vita's style of planting was one of abundance, always artfully and purposefully untidy, never too pristine.

gave and still give a huge amount of pleasure, not just to their present owners, but also to anyone who sees them, from archduke to tourist to trespasser.

What sort of people make gardens? On the one hand they are people who know how to spend their own or their clients' money in order to see their ideas take three-dimensional form. Some have ended up seriously in debt as a result. But it's one thing to spend money and another to spend it well. Not all gardens require limitless sums, and the great gardeners of this book have the ability to match their talent constructively to their resources in order to produce a garden that is not just a collection of cameos, but somewhere of distinct character. The 18th-century landscaper Lancelot 'Capability' Brown called himself a 'place maker', which might at first sound either rather dull or self-deprecatory, but in fact once you understand the principle that a good garden is a place of a unique nature, a special environment, then 'place maker' becomes a purposeful as well as an ambitious label. It proposes that a gardener can create a place greater than the sum of its parts.

Great gardeners have come from all over the world and all kinds of background. Some have begun life in humble, manual occupations. 'Capability' Brown, perhaps with André Le Nôtre one of most influential gardeners ever, first worked as a garden boy on a small estate in Northumberland, a county which in the 18th century was

André Le Nôtre's immense garden at Versailles, seen here in a 19th-century engraving, incorporated strong symmetry and axes. The garden was a symbol of the order of the rule of Louis XIV; its great central vista started from the king's bedroom.

Henry Hoare's Stourhead: a gravel path encircled the lake, offering views of different buildings alone or in combination. Note the way the tree canopies are kept slim and open textured to the top, to ensure good views.

a place remote from anywhere. Intelligent, ambitious and worldly-wise, in a very few years Brown found himself socially at ease with the greatest politicians in the land. William Robinson, the father of wild, naturalistic gardening, started life as a hands-on gardener in rural Ireland, and, through charm and determination, turned himself into a hugely successful publisher and author. If such elevations as these sound implausible, it is worth knowing that 'the gardening world' – of gardeners, designers, garden owners, botanists, nurserymen, garden historians, journalists, photographers – is a delightfully small and generous one. When occasionally people move into it from high finance or the law, perhaps, looking for a second, more 'real' career, they are amazed at its sense of good fellowship. Perhaps it is because gardeners share the recognition that each one of them will always have more to learn about plants, and that even the best, newly created garden is inescapably at the beginning of its road to decline, as plants develop and die. Gardens are a process as much as a work of art.

It's also worth remembering that gardeners are in part salesmen, for professional designers have businesses to run and families to support. At the turn of the 19th century, Humphry Repton was notorious for the fawning nature of his entreaties for work. Even the most retiring of garden-makers must be, if not a salesman, then something of a showman.

Many great gardeners are of course gifted amateurs rather than trained professionals, such as Henry Hoare, whose lakeside garden at Stourhead is accepted as one of the world's most influential landscape gardens. Rosemary Verey, a *grande dame* of gardening and darling of the American lecture circuit, was a county horsewoman and mother, who turned to gardening and writing when she could no longer easily ride, but her garden at Barnsley House became a place of pilgrimage for gardeners from all over the world. The great Gertrude Jekyll herself, author of so many authoritative books about plants and gardens, and maker of so many brilliant English gardens with the architect Edwin Lutyens, learned all she knew about garden-making from inquisitive observation and hands-on experience.

Often men and women have turned to gardening as a form of artistic expression alongside other media. There have been painters such as Claude Monet at his garden in Giverny, near Paris, and Lelia Caetani at Ninfa outside Rome. Nicole de Vésian came from the world of fashion design. The Scotsman Ian Hamilton Finlay was a leading exponent of concrete poetry. Some garden-makers were polymaths within the arts: William Kent could design a house or a gilded console table or paint a ceiling as easily as he could make a garden; the Brazilian Roberto Burle Marx enjoyed making sculpture, jewellery and paintings every bit as much as gardens.

There have also been gardeners whose pleasure in garden-making has been to express beautifully a social or philosophical idea. At Monticello in Virginia, President Thomas Jefferson wanted to show what would grow well in North America, and how plants and animals could be bred to perform better. Today, the American architectural critic Charles Jencks makes his landscape gardens throughout the world using sculpted, turfed landforms set beside sinuous water bodies. It is the 18th-century landscaper's idiom revisited, but this time arranged to express the latest theories about the nature of the cosmos.

Some gardeners, like William Nesfield, brought experience of soldiery to their gardens, using their practical knowledge of surveying and earth-moving. Brown and Le Nôtre both employed these skills to remodel extraordinarily large landscapes and to handle huge budgets and vast numbers of staff. In Le Nôtre's case, some of those staff were actually soldiers temporarily assigned to the making of Louis XIV's palace of Versailles.

People have also come to garden-making from the study of allied disciplines. In Britain, Edwin Lutyens and Christopher Bradley-Hole first trained and worked

Nicole de Vésian brought her eye for fashion to gardening. Here she supervises the clipping of an upright specimen of the local cypress to create a more stylized pencil shape. Tight but irregular shapes, formally used, were her trademark.

as architects, using as William Nesfield put it, the sweet reason of the straight line. In the USA, Thomas Church trained in landscape architecture, as do professional designers today; landscape design has become an accepted academic discipline at last.

Owning a nursery has been a route to garden-making, too. Alan Bloom, in England, had one of the most ambitious and influential nurseries in post-war Europe, and bred dozens of now mainstream varieties as well as making his own garden at Bressingham. Also in England, Beth Chatto began making a garden with unusual plants and found a demand existed for them, so built up an excellent nursery. In the Netherlands, Piet Oudolf was a nurseryman long before he became a planting designer, but now works with landscape architects making some of the most admired gardens in the world, including New York's High Line. It is no surprise that nurserymen never lose that primary interest in the plants themselves rather than in the spatial aspects of garden-making, and consequently their work leans towards a more informal, naturalistic style. It is popular, highly influential, and accords well with the ecological and conservative preoccupations of our day.

Piet Oudolf's 2-ha (5-acre) Lurie Garden, in the Millennium Park, Chicago, divides into meadow and prairie areas, using native perennials, and is sheltered by huge shoulder hedges. It is a sophisticated reproduction of the wild – a modern rus in urbe, *or country in the city.*

Steve Martino's style of gardening may seem exotic to gardeners from temperate climates, but here in the Sonoran Desert this palette of plants is the vernacular. Martino's skill is to create a kind of desert lushness that seems completely at home.

These, then, are some of the world's great gardeners – plantsmen, lovers of intellectual ideas, of geometry or nature's sinuous curves. Their work, like that of great painters, is completely international – it knows no language barriers and appeals as much to visitors from different cultures as to the person next door. Think of Roberto Burle Marx, used to the flamboyant colours of Brazilian flora, coming to Europe for the first time and still being dazzled by the green landscapes of trees, grass and water; or consider Christopher Lloyd longing to dig up his Edwardian rose garden and replant it with the loud colours of Rio.

Always it is a combination of imagination and determination that makes a good gardener. But what makes a great gardener is the ability, so proudly expressed by 'Capability' Brown, to create a 'place' with a unique flavour of its own, through a particular alchemy of mass and void, of architecture and planting, of earth and water, of light and shadow and reflection, of things static and things motile, of loud and cool colours and perhaps perfume – a coming together of elements that declares this is a very special place. It takes a very special person to make such a garden.

GARDENS OF IDEAS

A MEDIEVAL GARDENER miraculously transported to the present day would be astonished by the range of plants available, as if by magic, to gardeners anywhere in the world. By way of explanation he would hear a tale of British, Spanish, Portuguese and Dutch empires, of the colonization of uncharted continents, of an agricultural and aesthetic hunger that caused plants to leap the seas: grapes and oranges taken from the Old World to California, maize and potatoes brought from the New World to Europe; treasured rhododendrons and tree peonies carried to European gardens from China; Australian eucalyptus trees becoming weeds in South Africa; and Japanese cedars in the Azores. He would find the world a far smaller place – a melting-pot indeed.

He would also be amazed by the speed with which in the 19th century new plants were discovered by Western science and travelled round the globe. No surprise, then, that a desire for novelty then obtained; garden*ing* was more important than gardens, opulence of planting more admired than sophistication of design. But gardens were not always so furiously horticultural. Well before the horticultural Big Bang they were places made as an expression of ideas or of a philosophy, with a far simpler palette of plants. Space and architecture and ornament said everything that mattered, and flowering plants were a lesser, although delightful, gilding of the intellectual lily.

Aristocratic gardens in China date back thousands of years. Their subtle use of rocks and water could represent the abode of the gods or express man's journey through life. In Japan, gardens of ideas reached great heights of sophistication and subtle imagery. Imbued with concepts from Shinto and Zen Buddhism, rocks, moss and gravel were used to represent landscapes, but also to encourage contemplation. And in the highly contrived tea house gardens, every element was there for a particular reason and in its designated position.

In 18th-century Britain the landscape movement first emerged under the hands of men such as William Kent. Old and nouveaux riches gentlemen alike created parks around their country houses that showed off the extent and natural beauty of their estates, and how, with sufficient taste, heaven could be made on earth using only water, trees and green space. Henry Hoare achieved this sublimely at Stourhead. The landscape movement was seized on in Europe and 'English Gardens' sprang up across the world. In Germany, Friedrich Franz of Anhalt-Dessau's landscape garden at Wörlitz combined perfectly the English Garden with Enlightenment philosophy.

To confirm their liberal credentials, the owners of these parks added a layer of Classical allusion through architectural ornament and inscription, with many a reference to the Virgilian ideal of the politician retired to his farm. After a long political career, Thomas Jefferson, third president of the United States and author of the Declaration of Independence, devoted great attention to his estate at Monticello, where he experimented scientifically with what could be grown.

It is not too unkind to say that most of the 19th and 20th centuries belonged to plantsmen gardeners, not to gardeners who wished to express ideas; and yet gradually the principle of a garden with something to say, with an intellectual agenda, a garden that sets out to provoke, has begun to rise once more. Sir Roy Strong's garden in Herefordshire, begun in 1973, marked a return to the garden of allusion and autobiography. To the single-minded plantsman gardener who looks to a garden for benign, trouble-free beauty, this one still comes as a shock and even an affront. 'The gardener who resorts to plants has failed', teases Strong. In Scotland, the concrete poet Ian Hamilton Finlay created a world-famous garden of provocative inscriptions, set among trees around a cottage halfway up a moor. He called it 'an attack' on the senses and the mind. Once again its intellectual agenda frustrates the plantsmen, who fail to enjoy his wit or his considerable humour.

The last 25 years have seen the rise of the 'conceptual garden', a temporary artistic installation made partly using plants. It was pioneered through the Festival of Gardens at Chaumont-sur-Loire in France, and has been emulated in many countries, England included, but nowhere so successfully as at Alexander Reford's festival at Les Jardins de Métis in Quebec Province in Canada.

Perhaps more significant than all of these developments are the landscapes of turf and water made by architectural critic Charles Jencks, not because they mark a return to working with old elemental materials, but because they express concepts of 21st-century cosmography. They leave behind social philosophy and at last tackle current, sometimes unproven scientific theory. They are truly modern.

Plan of Friedrich Franz of Anhalt-Dessau's garden at Wörlitz.

WEN ZHENGMING

Nature gently re-imagined

1470–1559

1470
First major section of the Great Wall of China is
    constructed.
Birth of Michelangelo, sculptor and painter of the Sistine
    Chapel, Rome.
Birth of Albrecht Dürer, German painter and printmaker.
The Ottomans capture the island of Euboea, in Greece.

1559
The coronation of Queen Elizabeth I of England.
Work commences on St Basil's Cathedral, Moscow.
Jean Nicot introduces snuff to the French court.
Work starts on the Villa Farnese and garden, Caprarola,
    Italy.

THE GARDENS OF ancient China, rooted in Taoist and Confucian philosophy, have been a huge influence on both Japanese and European garden traditions. In China, as in many countries, the violent evolution of the ruling dynasties and the almost as violent effects of changing fashions have led to wholesale destruction of gardens, but fortunately painting, so far as we can trust it, has left us an invaluable record of what has been lost. Wen Zhengming was not only a skilled gardener, but also a painter and poet too, and one of those many artists to whom we owe our understanding of ancient Chinese gardens.

Born into a family of successful officials, or as we might call them now, civil servants, it would be expected that Wen Zhengming would aspire to follow the same career. Odd, then, that this man who would go on to become one of the Four Great Masters of the Ming dynasty (1368–1644) because of his work in the Three Perfections – poetry, calligraphy and painting – managed to fail his civil service calligraphy examinations nine times. But Wen Zhengming must have had his saving graces (thereafter all his life he practised his calligraphy before breakfast), because ultimately he did find a post as Hanlin Academician in Waiting at court in Beijing. At the age of 56 he retired, having made next to no money from what should have been a lucrative career as a government official, and returned to his home town of

A moon gate in the Zhuo Zheng Yuan garden, or 'Unsuccessful Politician's Garden'. Moon gates offer a quiet, organically shaped invitation to a prospect, framing it so much less deliberately and controllingly than a rectangular doorway or window. One must also step over a sill into that different world.

Suzhou, in Jiangsu province, where he began in effect a second and far more successful career as an artist.

Through his social connections he became a self-taught connoisseur in the arts, in particular the Three Perfections; a scholar in fact, and, importantly, an amateur. He had begun to paint at 19 and went on to be taught by another of the four Great Masters, Shen Zhou, taking from him a delicacy of technique that would be apparent in his paintings of flowers. But it was in landscape that Wen Zhengming would excel; in this genre his individual style was formed through the study of the paintings from the earlier Yuan dynasty, and in particular the work of the great Buddhist painter and calligrapher, Zhao Mengfu.

Wen Zhengming's retirement to Suzhou fortuitously coincided with that of Wang Xianchen, a public censor, who had led a far more successful official career and become rich. In Suzhou, Wang Xianchen acquired the site of the Dahong Temple, where he built himself a villa and began to make a garden, Zhuo Zheng Yuan, by digging lakes and creating mounds. His friend Wen Zhengming, whose artwork he

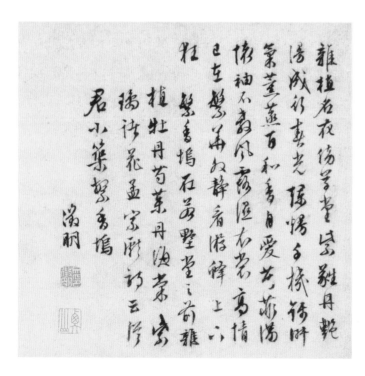

ABOVE Portrait of Wen Zhengming, from a 17th-century album; ink and light colour on silk.

Calligraphy (LEFT) and a scroll painting of a landscape (OPPOSITE) by Wen Zhengming. Calligraphy was considered a great art and, along with poetry and painting, was one of the Three Perfections. Wen Zhengming was a recognized master of scroll painting, sometimes figurative, sometimes of flowers and sometimes of landscapes. He later turned to calligraphic scroll poems.

greatly admired, was given free access to the garden and they worked on it together.

Around 1535, Wen Zhengming painted a series of 31 leaves depicting the garden, each one bearing a different scene and a description of it, with an associated calligraphic poem; it was a combination of all the Three Perfections. Later again, around 1551, when Wen Zhengming was in his 80s and at the height of his powers, he produced a further eight leaves of the garden. It is these that have left us such a distinct record of a garden, and how it was perceived in its day.

In his later years, Wen Zhengming achieved fame for his artistic abilities. His work was copied again and again, both for people to purchase and as an academic exercise, in the same way that 18th-century British artists would go to Rome and Florence to learn to paint by copying the great Italian masters. Many of Wen Zhengming's students (including his sons) went on to become the great painters of the next generation. With his old tutor Shen Zhou, he was regarded as one of the leading artists of the Wu school of painting, which specialized in painting long scrolls.

History has been comparatively kind to the Zhuo Zheng Yuan garden. It was not destroyed by deliberate violence, although it has been changed almost beyond recognition by subsequent developments. In the early 17th century it was divided up to make room for several more villas, and a period of dereliction followed. During the reigns of the Qing emperors Shunzhi (1638–61) and Kangxi (1661–1722) it was repaired, but huge changes were made according to the fashion of the period. The mid-20th century saw a major addition to the east of the garden in historical styles, and Zhuo Zheng Yuan is now a hybrid garden, like so many of the world's most highly respected old gardens. Whether Wen Zhengming would recognize it is another matter. But his paintings tell us so much

*Painting by Wen Zhengming of Zhuo Zheng Yuan, dated 1551, from an album of eight
paintings now in the Metropolitan Museum of Art, New York, showing a great lightness
in both the built structures and in the way the trees are pruned to be open textured.*

about Chinese gardens of his times and what was desired of them. For all their subtleties, they are not scenes of immobile serenity. He shows us domestic scenes of life
being lived, with thatched pavilions enjoyed by their owners, as well as courtyards,
animals and fruit trees; small lakes stretch away towards the mountains. The work
speaks of the good life in a private domain (a wall is seen to enclose the garden),
where a man might retire from the world to devote himself to greater things than the
hurly-burly of politics. It is the Virgilian ideal of the statesman retiring to his farm, a
concept which influenced so many of the great 18th-century English country-house
gardens and estates. And again like those English landscapes, these are scenes not of
flower gardens, but of pavilions, trees, rocks and water, rendered by Wen Zhengming
in the case of his Zhuo Zheng Yuan images in a delicate ink monochrome.

The name of the garden, Zhuo Zheng Yuan, says a great deal. It can be translated two ways, both as the 'Unsuccessful Politician's Garden' and as the 'Artless (or Humble) Administrator's Garden', referring to the Chinese adage that some people may find it easier to administer a garden than to organize public life. The expression 'gardening leave' comes to mind.

Despite containing many buildings, Chinese gardens in general strove to appear natural, employing the basic elements of plants, rocks and water in a manner that was informal, though nothing like the randomness of real nature, and stopping short of being rigid and static. Balanced, yes, but not unwelcoming to the addition of life; one feels invited to walk into the scene without any possibility of spoiling its composition. Urban Chinese gardens were often mazes of spaces for living, many of them roofed in, with interconnecting views offered to other spaces beyond. They were varied and sociable. But the various elements of a garden had particular associations or symbolism. Rocks and water suggested the harmony of nature, its yin and yang, motion and stillness, age and freshness. Individual rocks were chosen

This rectangular, ornamented framing of the view is much more purposeful than the curve of a moon gate. It commands rather than invites the viewer to contemplate the suggested journey over bridges beyond the water.

with extraordinary care, often for their complex shapes, and their selection became a profession in itself. Old trees symbolized the passage of time and, like old people, were to be respected. Thus each tree was encouraged to show all its developing idiosyncrasies of form – hollows, multiple trunks and tilting to one side – and yet to demonstrate a settled, comfortable aspect: equilibrium in nature rather than turbulence. Views of mountains or constructed mountains were always an important part of Chinese gardens. They were used to represent the five holy mountains that were home to the immortals, who might then be tempted to descend to bless the garden and its owners.

How far were Wen Zhengming's paintings a true representation of the garden Zhuo Zheng Yuan? It is impossible to tell. But that conundrum begs a further question: which was the greater, the influence of gardens on painting or the influence of painting on gardens? In the European landscape garden it was the influence of Italian painting that shaped the garden. What we can be certain of is that Wen Zhengming's paintings represented an ideal garden for their times: a refinement, a Perfection.

The sourcing and transporting of wild, craggy rocks to represent China's dramatic natural landscapes, as seen here in the garden Zhuo Zheng Yuan, was a profession in itself. Most desirable were hollowed, water-worn rocks, often grotesque to Western eyes.

HACHIJO TOSHIHITO AND HACHIJO TOSHITADA

Precise control of plants and people

1579–1629 AND 1619–1662

1570s
Sir Francis Drake lands in California and claims it for
    Queen Elizabeth I.
Rudolf II becomes Holy Roman Emperor.
Palladio publishes his *Four Books of Architecture*.
Death of Giorgio Vasari, architect and art historian of the
    Renaissance.

1660s
Work commences on the Palace of Versailles.
Completion of the Pearl Mosque at the Red Fort, Delhi.
The dodo becomes extinct.
Publication of Boyle's Law, concerning pressure in gases.

MOSS, WATER, A GNARLED PINE, Mount Fuji beyond – these must spring to mind in anyone's first ideas about historical Japanese gardens, together with a special stillness, a poise, an elegance, as if they were a frozen composition, which somehow seems lacking in most Western gardens. In the case of some Japanese gardens, that suggested immutability is intended, but others were most definitely gardens for moving through – the Edo period's 'stroll gardens'. In these, the garden was never presented as a whole picture, but rather as a series of contrived views, near or far. Perhaps the best of the extant stroll gardens is Katsura Rikyu, on the edge of Tokyo, made by a father and son, Hachijo Toshihito and Hachijo Toshitada.

The story begins in 1586, when seven-year-old Toshihito, brother of the Emperor Go-Yozei, was adopted by the warrior-politician Toyotomi Hideyoshi in order to strengthen his ties with the imperial family. But only a few years later Toyotomi had a son of his own and the adoption was annulled. By way of compensation, Toshihito was given a generous gift of lands and the opportunity

Formal portrait of Hachijo Toshihito, first generation of Katsura Rikyu's garden-makers.

to establish a family himself, one which, alongside three other families, would be eligible to assume the Chrysanthemum Throne and provide an emperor should the emperor's own line die out.

The old aristocracy, who owed strong allegiance to the emperor, found themselves in an invidious position, deprived of influence by the aggressive Tokugawa shogunate (1603–1868), which was keen to draw all political power to itself. So the aristocracy was left to amuse itself with culture and the arts, not least of which was the creation of gardens. Japan had already passed through several distinct garden styles by this stage in its history. The great gardens of the Heian period (794–1185)

had been theatrical playgrounds where their owners could party on their lakes and admire the scenes planted around them. The Kamakura period (1185–1333) absorbed Zen Buddhism from China and produced smaller, simpler gardens, which eventually led to the refined rock and raked gravel compositions so familiar to the West. In the Muromachi period (1333–1568) gardens became things to look *at*, influenced by the landscape paintings of the earlier Chinese Song dynasty.

In the following Momoyama period (1568–1600), the tea ceremony dominated: aristocrats walked through their gardens to a tea house along a carefully contrived path, lit by stone lanterns at night, stopping to wash their hands along the way. Here they would take part in the elegant ceremony of tea drinking, said to lead to personal and spiritual enlightenment. The stroll gardens of the subsequent Edo period (1600–1868) were of a less religious but more aesthetically ambitious nature. In these the walk and views along the way were as important as the arrival at the garden's pavilions and tea houses. Toshihito's was just such a garden.

But there was more than tea gardens influencing Toshihito. Six hundred years previously, a lady-in-waiting at the emperor's court, Murasaki Shikibu (b. 973), had written what has since been termed the first novel, *The Tale of Genji*, about the life

Illustration from The Tale of Genji, *a story that would be influential for generations.*

Looking outwards from a tea house pavilion over the water at Katsura Rikyu; it is clear why such simple architecture appealed to Le Corbusier and Modernist architects.

and loves of a young nobleman of that name at court. It is known to have been completed, possibly in instalments, by 1021, and was written to entertain the ladies at court. Alongside the main events in the story are long descriptions of landscapes and gardens with flowers, which were real places known to the court. The book was a great success. Early copies still exist today, including scenes on the illustrated scroll Genji Monogatari Emaki made in the 12th century, and a version also in the 12th-century scroll style by Tosa Mitsuoki. In modern times it has been made into films and even an opera. *The Tale of Genji* was well known in the aristocratic circles in which Toshihito moved, prized both because it looked back to Heian times when the aristocracy held more power and also for the sheer romance of its story and setting. And part of the Tale was set, in Murasaki's own words, 'far away, in the country village of Katsura [where the] moon upon the water is clear and tranquil'.

Keen to make a garden, though with limited funds, Toshihito found land by the river at Katsura, as in the *Tale*, and work began around 1619 on a new villa and garden, Katsura Rikyu. Built to Toshihito's own designs, it began as a modest pavilion, no more, on the shore of a small lake or pond, excavated to create hills around it, and to be seen from a long path which snaked its way around the water, offering carefully composed views. As time went by, Toshihito's wealth grew and he was able

ABOVE The gardens of Katsura in spring. The path, as it winds from shore to island, always offers new and varied views of the garden. OPPOSITE *Portrait of Hachijo Toshitada.*

to expand his building programme. In 1624 Katsura Rikyu was said to have the best view in Japan. By 1631 it had been described as a palace.

When Toshihito died aged 50 in 1629 his son Toshitada was just ten years old and was raised elsewhere, visiting only occasionally. The place deteriorated over many years, until Toshitada made an advantageous marriage to the daughter of a wealthy lord. He decided to renovate his father's villa at Katsura, adding more tea houses and designing a new, larger and slightly more ornate villa. Still, the overall manner of the conception was in line with his father's vision.

For six generations after Toshitada his heirs met cruelly early deaths, and Katsura Rikyu again fell into disrepair until, in the seventh generation, it was rescued, also without major changes involved. The family line finally died out in 1881, and two years later Katsura Rikyu passed to the Imperial Household Ministry, which continues to care for it today, allowing highly restricted access to this cultural treasure. In the 1980s a programme of major repairs was undertaken, dismantling and reconstructing the pavilions, reusing most of the original wood.

It has been suggested that the garden itself was the work of Kobori Enshu (1579–1647), a feudal lord and master of the tea ceremony who created many important gardens around Kyoto, but there is no evidence for this. Katsura Rikyu is certainly an archetypal stroll garden. On entering the gate, the main part of the garden is deliberately concealed by a statuesque pine tree; in fact the garden in its entirety is never seen from any one point. Instead, the path forms a circuit around the irregular pond fringed with leaning pines and, at one point, a pebble beach, passing through a series of pavilions to arrive at the villa. Two islets in the pond can be reached by bridges. Sometimes the same view is glimpsed, but always from a different angle.

It is the path that determines how one experiences Katsura Rikyu, and it provides a lesson for any garden designer today in the way its subtleties manipulate the visitor. Sometimes its surface is smooth gravel or paving, so you can look up and enjoy the view. At other times it consists of rough stepping stones or steps, to force you to look down and see the detail there. The path is narrow – not one for walking along side by side in discussions of other things, but for walking alone, absorbing the scenes and planting as they are gradually revealed.

The pavilions each have different characters. There is the Moon-Watching Tower on its mound, the Pine-Lute Pavilion with its chequered blue panels, the Flower Appreciation Pavilion from which to admire flowering cherries, the round-windowed Laughing Thoughts Pavilion and curving-roofed family Shrine. Taking its inspiration from *The Tale of Genji*, the villa has a platform jutting out over the water, specially placed to appreciate the reflection of the full moon in August. The three sections of the villa, the Old, Middle and New Shoin, are miracles of minimalist rectangular simplicity, both indoors and out, and they offer fine views back over the water. It was this cool spareness of the architecture and its modular plan that so appealed to the 20th-century European Modernist architects Walter Gropius and Le Corbusier, who found in it a model for their own un-ornamented, uncluttered style. Since the repairs of the 1980s the parallels with Modernist architecture are even clearer. People are enchanted by Katsura Rikyu, for the clarity of its antique style and its evocation of a lost golden age to which we, with our busy modern lives, might wish to return. There is a sense of timelessness at Katsura Rikyu, which itself was built on images already 600 years old.

WILLIAM KENT

Creator of the painterly picturesque

c. 1685–1748

1685
Death of King Charles II of England.
Birth of George Frederick Handel, composer of the
    Messiah.
Birth of Italian composer Domenico Scarlatti.
Louis XIV approves the use of slaves in French colonies.

1748
The ruins of Pompeii are discovered by Rocque Joaquín
    de Alcubierre.
Philosopher and social reformer Jeremy Bentham born
    in London.
Birth of French painter Jacques-Louis David.
Free-market economist Adam Smith lectures in
    Edinburgh.

IT IS A COMMON CONCEPTION that the 18th-century English land-scape garden was a cool creation, with all the serenity of a mythical Arcadia. And yet it is an image that is quickly dissipated when one looks at the work of William Kent, the ebullient founding father of the Landscape Movement. It was Horace Walpole who said of Kent that he 'leapt the fence, and saw that all nature was a garden' – and leap he did.

Kent was a polymath. He could turn his hand to many areas of artistic endeavour, from painting and architecture to the design of furniture, ceremonial robes and – only part of his work – gardens. He loved glitz, the sparkle of white and gold, to the point that he even advised the owners of some great mansions to gild the outsides of their window frames. He was plump, and a man whose extravagant, attractive, humorous, not to say camp, manner showed in all his work. He was also a careerist, who rose, like Lancelot 'Capability' Brown, from being a clever (if perhaps dyslexic) small-town boy, through the exploitation both of his own considerable talents and of patrons of all political persuasions, to be a wealthy and respected man.

Born on the Yorkshire coast at Bridlington, the son of a joiner, Kent left school with his talent for drawing recognized and an introduction from his schoolmaster to influential friends in London. He never looked back. Working there as a portrait artist, he soon came to the attention John Talman, an antiquary and collector, who took him off, aged 24, to Italy. He worked there for nine years, mostly in Rome, as a copier of great paintings and adviser and dealer for art collectors in England. He even came to paint a fresco at the church of San Giuliano dei Fiamminghi in Rome. Kent had the knack of finding sponsors and this, combined with his commercial enterprises, left him comfortably off and able to travel further afield in Italy to extend his education as an artist. All the while he was meeting influential English aristocrats – Thomas Coke, Earl of Leicester, for whom he would later work, and Richard Boyle, Lord Burlington, as whose protégé Kent would soon prosper meteorically.

Returning to London via the Rococo Parisian art scene, Kent began his career as a painter. Burlington, artistic mover and shaker, soon had Kent working for him

on the interiors of his new Neo-Palladian villa at Chiswick, as well as on its grounds. These had already been developed for Burlington by Charles Bridgeman, Kent's most important predecessor in garden design, who worked in a style of military order, with formal canals, earthworks and woodland wildernesses – large scale but not remotely natural.

For Kent, Burlington and Chiswick led to commissions from King George I at Kensington Palace, including the painting of ceilings, after which enviable public positions followed, and Kent became a wealthy man. He never married, but was involved in a long relationship with a mistress, and they had two children.

Princess Caroline (shortly to become George II's Queen in 1727) scooped up Kent to work for her at Richmond Lodge, on the Thames, where he undertook architectural garden works that brought him even more public attention. All the world tried to get tickets to see the 'Signor' Kent's Hermitage and Merlin's Cave, both buildings with a large intellectual and iconographic subtext, and where extravagant entertainments were staged, for which Kent provided the sets. He also designed the Royal Barge built in 1732, as well as funerary monuments in Westminster Abbey; his Treasury building and Horse Guards can still be seen in Whitehall.

Great country house commissions followed, notably for long-standing British Prime Minister Sir Robert Walpole, at Houghton in Norfolk, where Kent's interiors

Portrait of William Kent, paintbrush in hand, by William Aikman (c. 1723–25).

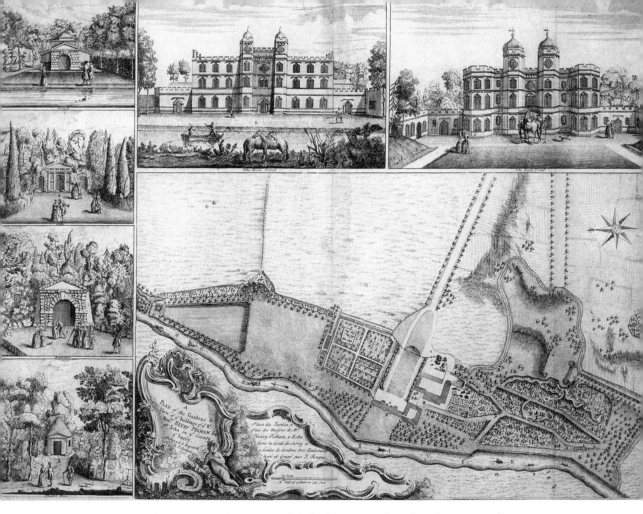

Plan of the gardens, with vignettes of the buildings, at Esher Place, for Henry Pelham. Every woodland vista provided an introduction to some Classical building and a mysterious invitation to step inside. Tall cypresses are a reminder of Kent's beloved Italian landscapes.

were every bit as opulent as those he designed for royalty. For Henry Pelham at Esher Place in Surrey, Kent created a house in the Gothic style, a departure for both him and for the times, which were so firmly pursuing Classicism and the Palladian revival. This was perhaps Kent's first complete foray into garden design, with a series of eye-catching buildings and a 'natural' landscape of open space and trees, so unlike the theatrical blocks and avenues of Bridgeman's time.

Perhaps most famous of Kent's garden designs was for the Elysian Fields at Stowe, in Buckinghamshire, for Lord Cobham. It is a splendidly Kentian composition of water and trees, elegantly placed, and juxtaposing on opposite sides of the river the Temple of Ancient Virtue and the Temple of British Worthies, which contained busts of Lord Cobham's heroes, from Shakespeare to Queen Elizabeth I and Sir Isaac Newton. Here was gardening with a stoutly political agenda, demonstrating Cobham's Whiggish position, as well as setting out the 18th-century view of Britain

TOP *The Rotunda at Stowe (1720–21) was designed by John Vanbrugh and sheltered a copy of the Medici Venus, gilded in the best Kentian manner.* ABOVE *Drawing by Kent showing the front of Chiswick House, depicting himself in the garden in conversation with Lord Burlington.*

as a new Augustan age after the manner of imperial Rome. It was during Kent's involvement with Stowe that the young Lancelot Brown became head gardener, following on from Kent with his own designs elsewhere in the garden.

Less striking than the Elysian Fields, if more surprising, is Kent's Temple of Venus, set in a landform by Bridgeman, in which suggestive scenes of sexual license were on display. Kent enjoyed this kind of game, played between him, his patron Lord Cobham, and those who would come to visit and understand the scheme's philosophical associations. Kent was a lover of games in general, and would often decorate his architectural sketches with figures of himself or people he knew relaxing informally. Important work also came to Kent from Thomas Coke, Earl of Leicester, whom he had met during his Italian sojourn. Coke was revamping Holkham, his home in Norfolk, and Kent was called in to design the garden, extend the house with two vast wings and create some of the most spectacularly opulent interiors in Britain, a truly Roman Marble Hall in particular. Outside, he made the most of the flat Norfolk landscape with a large temple and distant obelisk.

Kent's Temple of British Worthies, in the Elysian Fields at Stowe, contains busts of Lord Cobham's Whiggish, libertarian heroes, including Alexander Pope, Isaac Newton, Walter Ralegh, Elizabeth I, Inigo Jones and Shakespeare.

Apollo stands at the end of a long, winding (and today heavily shaded) path with his back to the garden at Rousham, looking down to the river Cherwell and up to the eye-catcher on the horizon.

In 1738 Kent began work at Rousham in Oxfordshire, to create what, although small, is perhaps the finest early 18th-century landscape garden. Here, Kent was able to perform his magic and prove that, in his eyes, all the world was indeed a garden. Working as so often on a previous layout by Bridgeman, Kent softened the line of the river and developed idyllic Virgilian views over the water meadows to a Gothicized water mill. Within the garden, a series of tableaux explored the trials of life as expressed through Classical allusion. Venus' Vale, with cascades and water jets once 15.25 m (50 ft) high and glorious male nudes, proposed the life of pleasure, while the Dying Gladiator suggested the situation of Kent's mortally ill client, General James Dormer, whom he had known for many years as a friend of Burlington. Elegant seats were designed for significant viewpoints, and a long arcade of arches, reminiscent of the Temple of British Worthies at Stowe and known as Praeneste, provided a gallery from which to enjoy an idealized pastoral landscape. The garden at Rousham remains largely unaltered since Kent's day, although the theft of statuary has left its messages much obscured, even for those who have the necessary Classical terms of reference. The intriguing serpentine rill that runs (unusually – what had Kent in mind?) along the centre of a curving woodland path remains one of the best-known images of 18th-century gardens. Kent died at Burlington House, aged 62, and was buried in the Burlington family vault at Chiswick.

HENRY HOARE

Stourhead and the Claudian idyll

1705–1785

H ENRY HOARE is known for only one garden, but what a garden it is: Stourhead, in Wiltshire, possibly the most famous landscape garden in the world. The miracle of Stourhead is that it has been so little altered in the last 250 years, and such changes as there have been are decorative, not structural, Hoare's successors having dressed his landscape with brightly coloured trees and shrubs. Henry Hoare may not have have approved, since he much preferred the subtle interplay of different greens, but he might well have been pleased with the success of his garden in the popular imagination. Even in his day gardens were meant to be seen, and if not by the masses then by interested groups and wealthy tourists visiting the fashionable and cultural sights of the county, either out of curiosity or perhaps because they themselves were making a garden. If the owner was not in residence, the head gardener could give a tour; and often this was precisely what was necessary so that the visitor would make the correct circuit of the garden in order to appreciate its narrative and symbolism.

The story of Stourhead is full of promise and of sadness – promise, certainly, in the resources that Henry Hoare possessed. His grandfather, Richard, had been a successful London goldsmith and founder of the private bank, now C. Hoare & Co. Henry's father (also a Henry) continued the business and made a fortune as a result of the 1719 collapse in stock values known as the South Sea Bubble. It seemed a suitable moment to prove himself a gentleman by acquiring a country estate and building himself a mansion. Land in the Stour valley was bought from

Pastel portrait of Henry Hoare, 'the Magnificent' (artist unknown). OVERLEAF *A plan of Stourhead, 1779, by a Swede, Frederik Magnus Piper, which shows important sight lines at eye-level.*

Plan
...park vid Stourton i Wiltshire

Utsigt
af Casino Sedt ifrån Landsvägen

L. Lawn eller gräsplan som sluttar och widgar sig åt
landsvägen med en bra ha t. emellan de närmaste
planteställene —

Z. Obelisque af samma dimensioner med den wid Porta
del Popolo i Rom —

X. Apollo Belvederes Staten på en upphöjning i slutet
af en 128 fot bred och 4 ggr så lång Pelouse på den
sidan —

Y.Y. Terasse, den 2:dra sats eller samma sköld ifrån Apol-
los Staten och Obelisken och hwarifrån är en bred
präckt utsigt öfver de nedre anläggningarne, samt af
Solens Tempel N. Hermitagen O. m.m.

P. Hwälfd uppgång öfver landsvägen emellan artificiella
klippor, för att komma till hermitagen —

R. Souterrain eller grotta som går under landsvägen —

S. Fördämning som med dess convexa sida uppehåll-
ler en watten massa af 28 fot djup och hwarigenom en
triangel formig artificielle basin eller sjö erhålles,
mellan de omgifwande höjderne —

T. Pantheon eller rotunda med en portique af 6 colonner fram-
före och som med 4 antique Staten kostat 12000 pund Sterl.

W. Grotta anlagd emot sluttningen af den bakom warande
höjden, bestående af flere cavernes och af ...ningar med
tillhörande ...olen, smärre cascades, badcisterner och Statuer

K. Bro...äge af ek, af 100 fots öpning, med trappsteg från båda
land...asten och ... midt uppå och hwarifrån en
gång slingrar sig uppföre backen till tältet P.

D. Chinesisk Alcove; E. Floras tempel; F. Orangerie —

G. Trägårdsmästarens byggning. — H. Portique —

m. Lägre watten, hwartill den tillförne genom dålden
löpande bäcken hade sitt utlopp och det genom för-
dämningen 3:m aflopps kammer leda saltut ifrån
den öfre sjön när den behöfver uttappas, och som
Skedde wid anläggningen af Grottan W.

Obs. Ifrån Z till Y är Allien /: som är 32 fot bred :/ belagd
med den finaste torf och på båda sider 10 a 15 fot
gröna gläser ... sluttningar, hwaruppå är en hög och
tät plantering af cedrar, bokar och Americanske så
kallade Silver Furar ... se alldeles ut som de wor...
fortsättas på andra sidan)

Engraved View of Stourhead, 1777, looking across the water, as do all Stourhead's prospects, to the boathouse, Palladian bridge, church and village cross. Most of these views work just as dramatically in reverse.

Lord Stourton, and the Neo-Palladian architect Colen Campbell employed to build the new house, which Hoare named Stourhead.

Henry the father died in 1725, and Henry the son, now aged 19 and back from his Grand Tour of Europe, found himself suddenly the master of a great estate with a freshly completed mansion, and a partner in a successful London bank. He married in 1726, but his wife died a year later, leaving a daughter who also died. In 1728 he took a second wife, Susan Colt, and they had five children. One daughter, Anne, married her cousin Richard Hoare before she herself died, but not before she had given birth to a son, Richard Colt Hoare, Henry's grandson. It was this grandson who would inherit Stourhead after Henry's death in 1785.

During his second marriage Hoare lived at Wilbury House, a fine Palladian building in Wiltshire, and was for a time Member of Parliament for Salisbury. He took seriously to the study of painting, travelled abroad and began to collect works of art. On his mother's death in 1741 Hoare finally moved into Stourhead, but it was only after his second wife's death in 1743 that he turned to gardening. His new landscape, which provided work for 50 gardeners, would be in the Classical style. It was also an opportunity to demonstrate his knowledge of Greco-Roman civilization by creating a landscape of antiquity as seen through the work of painters such as Claude Lorrain, Nicolas Poussin and Gaspard Dughet: it would be a product of the Enlightenment and of its politically free spirit.

Stourhead, like Friedrich Franz of Anhalt-Dessau's landscape Wörlitz that followed it, centred on water. A small river was dammed at great expense to make a three-pronged, 12-ha (30-acre) lake around which a circuit walk was created. After crossing an open lawn from the house, and descending through a grove of firs, it only remained to brave a slender and rather alarming wooden bridge (later a ferry) across one arm of the lake before the journey was begun. Today, the need for car parking means that the circuit of the garden starts elsewhere.

Hoare's fantastic landscape was designed to represent episodes from Virgil's *Aeneid*, specifically Aeneas' descent into the Underworld, with its 'innavigable lake'. These scenes would be evoked through carefully positioned architectural tableaux. Visually compelling close-to, they were always seen to greater advantage across the water. But the landscape was intended to make its meanings felt as much as seen, and so light and shade, cold and heat would all be part of the gardener's tool-kit.

Watercolour of 'The Grotto, or Cave, interior', by Francis Nicholson, with (right) sleeping nymph and (left) the river god. Lighting comes from above and from 'windows' on to the lake.

The circuit began with an arrangement of lakeshore grottoes in cold shade, where a nymph and river god sculpted by John Cheere recline on plinths in subterranean gloom amidst mossy tufa and the sound of trickling water. From here could be seen the perfect, rock-framed view of the Temple of Flora (1745) on the opposite bank, created after Pliny the Younger's description in his *Letters* of a temple at Spoleto, Italy, dedicated to the river god Clitumnus. The Temple was designed by the architect Henry Flitcroft, who worked for Hoare at Stourhead and in London. A cluster of a few houses, a church and village cross could also be glimpsed behind a five-arched Palladian bridge.

From the grottoes the circuit climbed through the trees and into the sun to find the Pantheon (1753), the greatest of Hoare's garden buildings and again designed by Flitcroft (Hoare's uncle died in 1750, making Henry senior partner at the bank and well able to invest in his garden). A large, domed temple, it is dedicated to the god Hercules, whose statue stands inside, carved in 1776 by John Rysbrack. The Pantheon is situated on a grassy mound, visible in all its grandeur from the village across the water; it is a classic image of an Arcadian landscape, and one remarkably reminiscent of Claude's *Landscape with Aeneas at Delos* (1672), well known to Hoare.

As the circuit of the lake continues, another major monument appears, the Temple of Apollo (1765), set suitably high for a sun god. It was based on the temple of Venus at Baalbek in Lebanon, illustrated a few years previously in Robert Wood's *Ruins of Baalbek* (1757), a copy of which was in Hoare's library. With the construction of these three temples and an Egyptian obelisk, the garden was largely complete, but Hoare continued to make further additions. The largest is Alfred's Tower, a 49-m (160-ft) brick tower designed by Flitcroft as an eye-catcher for the whole estate, and commemorating King Alfred's defeat of the Danes in AD 879, the end of the Seven Years War with France and the accession of King George III. The tower stands to this day, despite an aircraft crashing into its upper storeys in 1944, killing five aircrew. Other additions included a Convent, a Chinese alcove, a Venetian seat, and a Turkish Tent like the one made by Charles Hamilton at that other great garden of the time, Painshill, in Surrey.

Meanwhile Hoare's grandson Richard was being trained to enter the family firm. In 1783 he married Hester Lyttleton, but she died in 1785, followed a month later by Henry Hoare himself. Stourhead was left to Richard, on the condition that he leave the bank and concentrate on Stourhead, safely separated from the uncertain fortunes of commerce. Like his grandfather, Richard was an earnest antiquarian and keen tourist of Classical antiquities, and he spent the next four years travelling in Europe, sketching and keeping diaries for later publication.

The classic view from the village, past the Palladian bridge to the Pantheon. It is perhaps the best-known and most widely published view of any English landscape garden.

On his return to England, Richard removed some of his grandfather's more outré additions to the garden such as the Turkish Tent, to keep it closer to its Classical inspiration, and added a boathouse and a lodge in strict Greek fashion by William Wilkins, architect of London's National Gallery. Perhaps more significant are his changes that resulted from the collecting and planting of more exotic and colourful trees and shrubs: tulip trees and swamp cypresses, and purple rhododendrons. For his work at Stourhead he was elected a fellow of the Linnaean Society. Through the later 19th and early 20th centuries yet more exotic planting was added: new giant conifers from America, copper beeches, and flowering small trees and shrubs including purple maples and brightly coloured rhododendron hybrids.

In 1946 the latest Henry Hoare gave Stourhead to the newly formed National Trust, having lost his son and heir in the First World War. The Trust continues to make vital repairs, and its Gardens Adviser Graham Stuart Thomas (p. 244) was responsible for taming the wilder colour schemes and reopening views obscured by seedling rhododendrons. Today the vista from the village to the Pantheon is an image known across the world, reproduced anywhere from academic journals to biscuit tins, and if the public are not seeing Henry Hoare's intended garden of soft greens, still they love what they see.

FRIEDRICH FRANZ
OF ANHALT-DESSAU

Enlightenment ruler and passionate gardener

1740–1817

1740

Annual British iron production reaches 17,000 tons a year.

Birth of the Marquis de Sade, French aristocrat, philosopher and author.

Invention of a device to cut clock wheels.

Jews expelled from Little Russia.

1817

Invention of the velocipede by Karl Drain in Mannheim, Germany.

Mississippi becomes the 20th State of the USA.

Death of British novelist Jane Austen.

Birth of British botanist Joseph Dalton Hooker.

PRINCE LEOPOLD III, Friedrich Franz of Anhalt-Dessau is the perfect example of an Enlightenment leader: brave, cultured, creative, travelled, liberal and wise. Fortunately for us, he was from a remarkably young age also passionate about gardens, so much so that despite world wars and Communist neglect, his life's work was designated a World Heritage Site in 2000.

Anhalt-Dessau is a tiny German princedom centred on the town of Dessau (later the home of the Bauhaus), created from 46 even smaller states pulled together by Franz's forebears, a family of artistic and military distinction who had once been patrons of the great composer J. S. Bach. This tiny princedom lies on the river Elbe, which constantly threatened to flood the fertile plains, so great works were undertaken to build a system of dykes to protect the rural economy.

Franz was steered toward a military life even as a child, and joined the Prussian army aged 16 to fight the Saxons in the Seven Years War. His parents were already dead, and he was in the guardianship of his uncle until he came of age. But a year later, he thought better of the military life and requested an honourable discharge from the Emperor, allowing him to return home to rule his 700 square kilometres (around 270 square miles) and 30,000 subjects. The boy already had plans.

Franz's lifelong friend, kindred spirit and collaborator was Baron Wilhelm von Erdmannsdorff, who, after spending time in Italy as a painter, had set up home in Dessau. When Franz was 23 the two of them set off on a Grand Tour – not to Italy, as was the norm, but to the Netherlands and England, where, with the creation in mind of a new palace and garden at Wörlitz outside Dessau, they studied the architecture of Inigo Jones and vast English landscape gardens such as Stourhead and Stowe, as well as Alexander Pope's tiny garden at his villa in Twickenham. As a scion of the Dutch House of Orange-Nassau, which had produced King William III of England, Franz was feted by all. England was then rapidly industrializing, and Franz admired the wonders of Progress at every turn. To this lover of Enlightenment thinking, England demonstrated clearly how beauty and utility could be combined for the greater good of human-ity, and he came home even more determined to turn his princedom into a model state.

Further trips followed, to France and Switzerland, and to England again. In 1764 he and Erdmannsdorff travelled to Italy, becoming friends of Sir William Hamilton, the English ambassador at Naples and art collector. Together they climbed Vesuvius in a spirit of scientific enquiry. There was just time in 1767 to marry his cousin, Luise of Brandenburg-Schwedt, before beginning work in 1769 on his new house and garden at Wörlitz, with Erdmannsdorff as architect. It was to be a symbol of progress in the world, a combination of art and social improvement, and it was also Germany's first Neoclassical house, inspired by Palladianism in England. Its interior decoration would take years to complete, with Erdmannsdorff making many further trips to Italy to secure paintings and sculpture. It was also, like the English country houses, a retreat, while the centre of workaday government remained the Schloss in Dessau.

Many an English landscape garden focuses on a green bowl of grassland, encircled by trees, lying before the house, perhaps with a river running through

Portrait of Friedrich Franz of Anhalt-Dessau, the original by Anton von Maron.

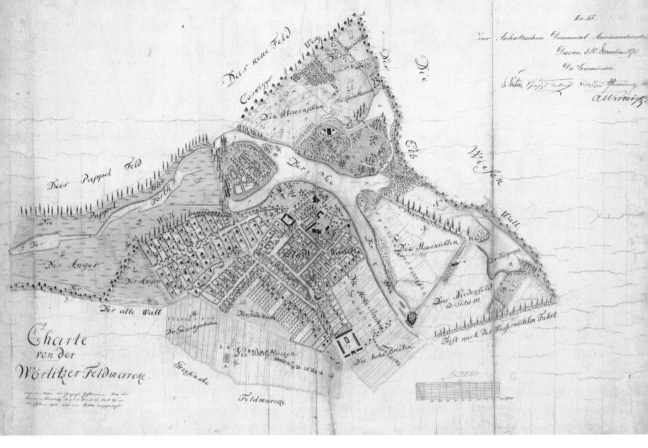

Plan of the garden at Wörlitz, of 1789/91, showing the many-limbed lake at its centre. It is interesting to compare it with the lake which forms the core of the garden at Stourhead, as seen in the plan on pages 36–37.

it. At Wörlitz, Franz made his central open space of water itself, rather like Henry Hoare had done at Stourhead. The lake had arms leading off in various directions, interconnected by paths and 30 bridges; its boundaries (if such they can be called) were the great dykes that protected against flooding, from which one could look out over scenes of Virgilian pastoral beauty. It was a democratic landscape without perimeter walls. Temples sprang up in various styles.

One whole island was dedicated to the French Enlightenment thinker Jean-Jacques Rousseau. Another, 17 m (56 ft) high, was created in the shape of Vesuvius, with subterranean temples and, on its slopes, a huge amphitheatre and an exquisite pavilion known as the Villa Hamilton. The volcano even erupted smoke and flame-illuminated water during grand outdoor entertainments. The gardener's house became a dramatic essay in the Gothic style and eventually Franz's own retreat *within* a retreat, where he could extend his library and collection of paintings and spend time with his mistress, the gardener's daughter. His wife Luise now had her personal retreat, too, the Luisium, again designed by Franz and Erdmannsdorff – a perfect chocolate-box house set in its own miniature landscape garden.

Other, older palaces and gardens already existed within the state of Anhalt-Dessau, and Franz incorporated them into his grand improvements. Oranienbaum, in the Dutch style, was given a Chinese garden, inspired by the 1757 *Designs of Chinese Buildings, Furniture, Dresses, Machines and Utensils* by the Englishman Sir William Chambers, whose great Pagoda at Kew Gardens of 1762 closely resembles Franz's later Pagoda at Oranienbaum. Franz's benevolence extended to his citizens. He made Anhalt-Dessau famous for its religious tolerance, and one of Wörlitz's 'temples' was in fact a synagogue built for the Jewish community. He sent his head gardeners on extended training visits to England, and improved systems for education and public health. The roads through his princedom were lined with fruit trees and tall poplars suggestive of the landscape of Italy, and there were experiments to create improved lines of livestock and fruit trees.

All of this was achieved in a state which, when Franz inherited it, had been physically and financially broken by the Seven Years War. He had an unquenchable

Night scene of fireworks, imitating the eruption of Vesuvius. The flow of lava was simulated by huge volumes of water released from storage tanks hidden in the body of the 'volcano' and lit by coloured lights; creating smoke was easier.

The synagogue at Wörlitz, with church and town close by. The arrangement was intended to demonstrate the state's cultural enlightenment: 15 per cent of the state's population was Jewish, with 130 living here in the town.

optimism concerning the perfectibility of mankind and never ceased to modernize his princedom. Railways were made, and lucrative potash mines established. The Junkers engineering company was founded, which would go on to build aeroplanes for the Third Reich.

World wars and Communist poverty did little to help preserve Franz's masterpiece at Wörlitz, although the synagogue survived being torched thanks to the fearlessness of its then garden director. Ironically it was the 2002 floods of the Elbe valley that brought funding to the area and facilitated the restoration of his garden. Where else today can one sit in a gondola at midnight while watching the eruption of Vesuvius?

THOMAS JEFFERSON

President and scientific plant pioneer

1743–1826

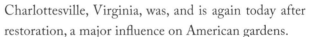

1743
Birth of Sir Joseph Banks, British botanist and naturalist.
French physicist Jean-Pierre Christin publishes the design
   of a mercury thermometer with a centigrade scale
   running from the freezing point of water to its boiling
   point.
Handel's *Messiah* receives its London premiere.

1826
First publication of French newspaper *Le Figaro*.
Death of Stamford Raffles, founder of Singapore.
Sir John Soane's Bank of England completed in London.
Franz Schubert writes his 'Great' 9th Symphony.

THOMAS JEFFERSON, third President of the United States of America and principal author of the Declaration of Independence, stands also as one of the founding fathers of American horticulture. Not only was he a politician, he was also a farmer, lawyer, inventor, architect, musician, botanist, linguist, bibliophile, gourmet, philosopher, scientist and gentleman: a true product of the Enlightenment. His garden at Monticello, near Charlottesville, Virginia, was, and is again today after restoration, a major influence on American gardens.

Several things mark out Monticello as different from other gardens of the period. It was as much a botanical collection as a garden, thanks to Jefferson's worldwide connections and active encouragement of botanical exploration. More than that, it was a garden with its roots in the English landscape style, examples of which he had seen on his European travels. And it was a garden made around a new house placed not in a sheltered valley but on a hilltop, where views and vistas were as important as the plants. If Jefferson had been influenced during his student years by the formal gardens of the College of William and Mary, developed in the formal French and Dutch manner with clipped shapes the order of the day, Monticello was an informal landscape garden in a naturalistic manner, with sinuous walks and woodlands.

Portrait of Jefferson by Rembrandt Peale (1800).

View of the west front and garden at Monticello, 1825, by Jane Braddick Peticolas. House and garden combined Jefferson's vision of agricultural virtue with Neoclassical ideals.

Jefferson's father was a successful Virginian planter and surveyor, and on his death left the 14-year-old Jefferson 2,025 ha (5,000 acres) and a number of slaves, an inheritance he gained control of when he came of age at 21. After graduating from the college in Williamsburg in 1762, he was admitted to the Virginian bar. He later married a wealthy widow, Martha Wayles Skelton, who brought more land and slaves, and the couple proceeded to have six children, most of whom died in childhood. In the weeks after their marriage they left the family estate at Shadwell, near Richmond, and moved to Monticello. It was a new house, built to Jefferson's own designs, though it was still a construction site at the time.

Aged 26, Jefferson's political career began as a Representative in the Virginian House of Burgesses. In 1775, at the start of the American Revolutionary War, he was a member of the second Continental Congress, and was a friend and ally of John Adams, who became the US President after George Washington. Adams asked him to head a five-man committee to work on a Declaration of Independence. Jefferson himself drafted it, and after adjustments by Congress, it was approved. After two years as Governor of Virginia, he was sent to Paris as trade commissioner and then succeeded Benjamin Franklin as Minister of State to France. Here he spent five years, absorbing European culture, gardens and architecture, and learning to admire things French and to despise Britain, from whom his homeland was so newly independent. He did, however, visit London in 1786, and he and his old friend John Adams, now US ambassador, made a short tour from the city, including Blenheim Palace and Stowe. The French Revolution erupted shortly after Jefferson departed from Paris for home in 1789.

On Jefferson's return to America, the newly elected President Washington made him Secretary of State, a role he fulfilled until he retired to Monticello in 1793 and began with skilled slave labour to rebuild the house, based around the theories of Palladio's *Four Books of Architecture* (1570), which in turn celebrated the buildings of ancient Rome. But 1796 saw him returning to politics as Vice President to John Adams. From 1801 to 1809 he was himself President, residing at the new capitol in Washington, DC. Jefferson's time in office was notable for several things, including the 1803 Louisiana Purchase from Napoleon, thereby virtually doubling the size of the USA. Close to his own heart was the expedition he dispatched, under Lewis and Clark, to explore the lands west to the Pacific, establishing a claim for the USA on those still uncharted territories. It was a journey of enormous geographic, scientific and political importance, and, to his great satisfaction, the source of many botanical introductions to Monticello. In order to prepare for the expedition Jefferson sent Lewis to seek advice from the botanist and physician Benjamin Smith Barton, who had earlier named a genus of small wild flower *Jeffersonia* in his honour.

In 1809 Jefferson left politics for good and spent the last seventeen years of his life as elder statesman at Monticello, developing the house and garden while at the same time setting up and designing the principal buildings and campus for the University of Virginia, which was to be managed without church influence; Jefferson was Christian but favoured independence in all things. (His attitude toward slavery was mixed; he was in favour of emancipation, more so in his younger life, but felt

Herbarium sheet of Balsamorhiza saggittata, *the arrowleaf balsamroot, a pressed specimen from the Lewis and Clark expedition. After the expedition, Lewis sent plants to Thomas Jefferson, and they were later worked on by Benjamin Smith Barton.*

1812.   Arrangement of the Garden.   N.W. Border.   45.

7. beds of asparagus. at S.W. end.

Fruits. — on the Upper Platform — **Pulse** / **other Fruits**

- I. square. Peas. Hotspur.
- II. Peas. Leadman's dwarfs. — Frame Peas.
- III. do
- IV. do
- V. Beans. Snap.
- VI. do — Snaps.
- VII. Haricots. red — Windsors
- VIII. Cucumbers Gherkins. — Cucumbers
- IX. 1.2.3. Nasturtium. 4.5.6. Melons. 7.8.9. Melongena. 10.11.12. Capsicum. — Capsicum.
- X. Tomatas. Okra. — Tomatas.
- XI. Artichokes.
- XII. Squashes. — Strawberries.

Roots. — middle Platform to the Walk G.

- XIII. Carrots. — Radish
- XIV. Salsafia Beets Garlic. Leeks. — Lettuce Endive Corn sallad Terragon
- XV. Onions.

Leaves. — Lower Platform — **Sallads. Raw.** / **Dressed.**

- XVI. Scallions. Shalots
- XVII. Radish Lettuce Endive Corn sallad. Terragon.
- XVIII. Celery.
- XIX. Spinach.
- XX. Sorrel Mustard.
- XXI. Sea kale. Cauliflower. Broccoli — Spinach.
- XXII. Cabbage early.
- XXIII. Savoy
- XXIV Kale Sprout. — Brassica plants

A page from Jefferson's Garden Book, 1812, listing crops and their arrangement in the beds in the vegetable garden He maintained this practice for many years.

unable as a slave-owning farmer to accept its virtues.) He died, aged 83, on 4 July 1826, the 50th anniversary of the Declaration of Independence. Debt had troubled him all his life and the estate was sold and its botanical treasures dispersed.

The principal elements of the garden at Monticello were simple enough: around the domed Palladian hilltop house was an oval lawn bordered by a winding walk, itself flanked by oval beds and by Jefferson's collection of rare trees. Jefferson was mostly vegetarian, and on the lower slope was his terraced vegetable garden, which functioned as an experimental laboratory for growing an astonishing range of crops and assessing their worth and viability in the American climate. He also had a fruit garden where he grew 170 varieties. Under the cool shade of the surrounding woodlands he developed the kind of vistas and open spaces that he had seen under the wide skies of the English landscape garden. His vast collection of flowers, vegetables, shrubs, fruit trees and forest trees was constantly topped up by species new to science and by cultivated varieties, coming to him from gardeners and nurserymen as far afield as Europe.

Not until the late 20th century was Monticello restored, using as a source of information his autobiography, his lifetime of letter-writing and the careful notes he had always made in such personal journals as his Garden Book, in which he meticulously recorded precise details of what he planted and when, the weather, and his successes and failures. It was and remains a remarkable place.

Aerial view of Monticello showing the fruit and vegetable plots, the oval lawn before the house, and woodlands, today probably enclosing the house more than in the garden's heyday.

IAN HAMILTON FINLAY

Poet, artist and literary gardener

1925–2006

1925	2006
The Exposition Internationale des Arts Décoratifs et Industriels Modernes is held in Paris.	Launch of first space mission to Pluto.
Hitler publishes volume I of *Mein Kampf.*	Launch of Twitter.
Chrysler Corporation founded.	The Human Genome Project publishes the last chromosome sequence.
F. Scott Fitzgerald publishes *The Great Gatsby.*	Saddam Hussein, former President of Iraq, executed.

AN INFLUENTIAL POET, author and artist, Ian Hamilton Finlay may be remembered by many as much for his moorland garden at Stonypath in the Pentland hills south of Edinburgh as for his writings. Stonypath, otherwise known as Little Sparta, is one of the most remarkable gardens of the 20th century and, like that other avant-garde Scottish garden, Portrack near Dumfries (p. 66), it bears a transatlantic influence.

Finlay's life was all one might expect for a Romantic poet. Born in Nassau in the Bahamas, he spent his infancy there on his Scottish father's schooner, used for pearl fishing and carrying bootleg liquor into America. At six the boy was sent to

boarding school in Scotland, where his teachers included the poet W. H. Auden. The end of Prohibition saw his father growing oranges in Florida, but when frosts ruined his business he retreated to penury in Glasgow, where the Finlay family huddled under the kitchen table as the Luftwaffe blitzed the dockyards on the Clyde.

Hamilton Finlay, poet, gardener, roadman, shepherd and lover of the hands-on life. OPPOSITE *Little Sparta's manifesto: 'All the noble sentiments of my heart, all its most praiseworthy impulses – I could give them free rein, in the midst of this solitary wood.'*

All the noble sentiments of my heart, all its most praiseworthy impulses – *I could give them free rein, in the midst of this solitary wood.*

Even as a teenager, Finlay assumed he would become an artist, and briefly took up a place at the Glasgow School of Art, where his rebellious spirit led him to organize a student strike. He then abandoned college and hitched a ride to London with his future wife, the artist Marion Fletcher, and they tasted the artistic life of Soho. In 1942 he was called up to join the Non-Combatant Corps and, although he did not see active service, he later spent some time in Germany.

Now married, Finlay set off with his wife to live the artistic life in the Orkney Islands. Over the next decade, he worked as a shepherd and roadman, while painting and writing stories for the *Glasgow Herald* and radio plays for the BBC, sometimes living in Edinburgh, sometimes Orkney. In 1961 he co-founded with Jessie Sheeler the Wild Hawthorn Press, to publish his and others' poetry, having abandoned prose following his collection of stories, *The Sea-Bed, and Other Stories*, of 1958. His paintings had been committed to the fire and his medium now was to be words, but especially words arranged in a meaningfully visual way – as concrete poetry, which he was instrumental in introducing into the UK.

OPPOSITE *If a garden is an attack as much as a retreat then here is the warning, in hand-grenade finials at the garden entrance, exquisitely crafted as were all Finlay's works.*
BELOW *An icon of 20th-century gardening, Finlay's monumentally expressed quotation from the philosopher Saint-Just:* THE PRESENT ORDER / IS THE DISORDER / OF THE FUTURE.

With his second wife, Sue Swan, he had two children. Stonypath, a gift from her parents, became their home in 1966. It was a poor, ruinous farmstead, 300 m (1,000 ft) up on a bleak, rolling hillside graced then by a single ash tree. Undaunted, they dug and planted by day and wrote and edited by night, until, as the 1970s passed, a garden emerged, all created by their own hands. It became a private domain, sacred to ideas pastoral, Classical, Neoclassical and polemical. The life for which Finlay is well known now began.

Stonypath covers only a few acres, an open-textured pattern of low copse, pools, long and short grass and a modest amount of perennial planting. Most of the plants are quiet, native or northern cottage garden species – birch, alder, pine, iris and geranium. Into this matrix, which was at first mostly Sue's creation, Finlay inserted his inscriptions and allusive sculptures, pieces that were illuminated by, and themselves illuminated, their particular surroundings. It might be a group of massive stone slabs inscribed with a quotation from the French Revolutionary Saint-Just, a pair of gate pillars topped not with stone pineapples but with stone handgrenades, a giant gilded head of Apollo labelled 'TERRORISTE' emerging from the land, or wooden red-and-grey 'camouflaged' stakes helping to protect the raspberries from the birds.

At first glance some people may find Finlay's aphoristic 'poem-objects' ponderous, baffling or simply too numerous; but they are not there to be glanced at lightly. Their many and equally valid layers of meaning are in themselves an engaging use of wit. Finlay hated self-indulgent 'confessional' poetry, or work that simply set out to be different. 'I am not interested in "experiment" but in avant-garde work which can take the creative step backwards to join with the past', he wrote. He felt gardens deserved to be the carriers of ideas just as much as horticulture, and

Finlay's Temple at Little Sparta, the taxable status of which saw him embroiled in a public row with local government and made national news. It became a battle of intellectual gamesmanship.

that good aphorisms could be the philosopher's 'hand-grenade'. And so alongside allusions to Virgil and old Classical values, of a kind favoured in the 18th-century English landscape garden, there appeared questioning references to Nazi and French Revolutionary ideals, making it a place where passionately held values of whatever kind were fought for and prized.

Finlay himself had many a battle at Stonypath, most notably with local government, which wanted to charge him rates on a converted byre which he used to display his and others' art, and which he regarded as a Temple, inscribed TO APOLLO, HIS MUSIC, HIS MISSILES, HIS MUSES. The ensuing intellectual and physical stand-off made national news, and his friends formed the Saint-Just Vigilantes to protect it; Stonypath became 'Little Sparta', setting out to resist Edinburgh's secular bureaucracy, that city famous as the 'Athens of the North'. The sentence for which Finlay is best known will always be 'Certain gardens are described as retreats when they are really attacks.'

Was it all too clever by half? No. As Finlay wrote to Sir Roy Strong, 'It never seems to occur to certain people that what seems elitist to them, can seem quite ORDINARY and NATURAL to others. Of course it is only educated people who accuse other people of being elitist (alas); the word is unknown to ordinary people, some of whom in spite of everything still think it a good idea to make an effort.'

In his later years, following his installation *The View to the Temple* at the 1987 Documenta exhibition in Kassel, he began to achieve some financial stability at last. He worked on the garden Fleur de l'Air in Provence, advising on planting and installing 40 of his artworks. He was ever reluctant to travel far from home, but none the less his installations were sought out abroad, usually collaborations between Finlay's poetic skills and the sculptural skills of others. As well as Little Sparta, where his last artwork was transforming a barn into a 'Hortus Conclusus', completed after his death, he left behind 76 permanent installations in Europe and North America, incorporating almost 190 artworks. Notable locations are the Max Planck Institute, Stuttgart, Germany, and the Stockwood Discovery Centre, Luton, England. Little Sparta can still be visited.

While reaction to most of Finlay's artworks may be predominantly cerebral, there is no escaping a visceral shock from this huge gilded head of Apollo, sternly rising from the woodland floor amidst the greenery.

SIR ROY STRONG

Allusion and autobiography at the Laskett

BORN 1935

1935
Hitler announces German re-armament in violation of
the 1919 Treaty of Versailles.
Development of Prontosil, the first effective antibiotic.
The first television programme is transmitted in Berlin.
Porgy and Bess by George Gershwin opens on Broadway.

A LTHOUGH SIR ROY STRONG, eminent art historian, critic, museum director, gardener and dandy, has been called on to advise on the making of many ambitious gardens, he has lavished the greatest care and attention on his own garden, the Laskett, set in rural Herefordshire, which he created from 1973 with his wife, the theatre designer Julia Trevelyan Oman. It is a garden loved and disliked in equal measure because it has swum so valiantly against the tide of popular fashion. Neither polarized viewpoint can stop the Laskett being a truly remarkable garden, and the product of a provocatively independent mind.

What is it about the Laskett that is so controversial? Laskett-lovers will declare it an admirable return to the 18th-century idea of a garden as a symbolic narrative, representing the maker's life and preoccupations. The Laskett also dares to be busily rectilinear and labour-intensive in an age when the desire for low-input natural gardening is supreme. Laskett-loathers will reply that it is egotistically self-referential, elitist, out of touch with the democratic, ecologically aware spirit of the times and overcrowded with clichéd architectural ornament.

What both sides miss is first that the Laskett is fun, that it is a kind of game, albeit a serious and ambitious one, played by its makers over many years, as were those 18th-century gardens of ideas such as Stowe. Serious things are said, but the touch is light. Secondly, it is private; it has not been made for public consumption or approval, even though the public's desire to see it persuaded Strong eventually to allow limited access for groups.

Part of its *joie de vivre* comes from having so much packed into it. There is no stately progress of long vistas unfolding grandly and symmetrically from the house.

Instead its vistas are joined at irregular angles because of the constraints of the site, and they unfold one after another, with barely a pause for rest. Yet the element of surprise as one passes from one to the next is as great as one finds on encountering any theatrical *bosquet* at Versailles. Strong happily pays tribute to those grand designs of past centuries and has the nerve to play with them in miniature.

Roy Strong was born into a small suburban household in Winchmore Hill, north London. His ambition matched his academic abilities and he went on to read history at the University of London, followed by a PhD at the Warburg Institute.

The London boy recreated himself as a man of a wider intellectual and social world. In 1959 he became assistant keeper at the National Portrait Gallery, and thereafter was its Director (1967–73). In this role he revivified what had previously been a valuable but neglected gallery; it now drew huge crowds, especially for the exhibition of portraits by the society photographer Cecil Beaton.

In 1971 Strong married the theatre designer Dr Julia Trevelyan Oman, fresh from her success at the Royal Ballet working with choreographer Frederick Ashton on his *Enigma Variations*. Strong has always loved to tell how little he was paid (£9,000) as the hugely successful Director of the National Portrait Gallery (he was in fact the first director not to have a private income), so it was with a small budget that he and his wife began looking to buy a country retreat, purchasing the Laskett and its 1.6 ha (4 acres) in 1973. Described by Oman as 'rural Regency of an undistinguished kind', it was a reasonably blank sheet on which to make a home and garden.

Strong became the youngest ever Director of the Victoria & Albert Museum in South Kensington in 1974, where, once again, he brought a new freshness to an infamously staid institution. Two major exhibitions demonstrated Strong's growing preoccupation with gardens. His first, in 1974, *The Destruction of the English Country*

Strong with his wife Julia Trevelyan Oman, theatre designer, in her beloved orchard; she hated to be called Lady Strong.

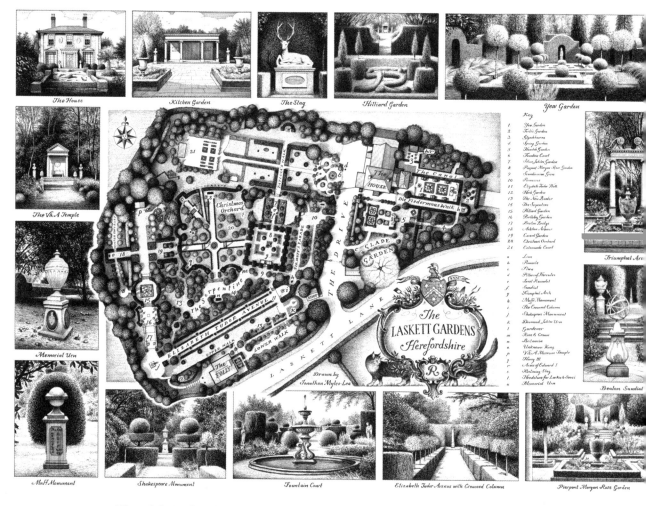

The House   Kitchen Garden   The Stag   Hilliard Garden   Yew Garden

The V&A Temple

Memorial Urn

Muff Monument   Shakespeare Monument   Fountain Court   Elizabeth Tudor Avenue with Crowned Column   Pierpont Morgan Rose Garden

Triumphal Arch

Beaton Sundial

Plan of the Laskett, by Jonathan Myles-Lea, making a nod to the 18th-century manner of illustrating gardens as seen in the plan of William Kent's Esher illustrated on page 30.

House 1875–1975, flagged up the sad plight of the thousand or so great houses and estates lost over that period to high taxes and increasing urbanization. What he learned from staging the exhibition set him his own challenge: to defy 'the times and ideology of the age' he would plant a formal country garden at the Laskett, 'idiosyncratic and English', of topiary and roses and fruit trees. It would be 'a garden of vista and surprise, private and mysterious, but also celebratory, a garden of memory about two people, their lives and their friends'. He called their garden 'a world of allusion'. Its layout was largely completed during his directorship of the V&A (1974–87).

In 1979 another major V&A exhibition, *The Garden: A Celebration of a Thousand Years of British Gardening*, reflected both the rich heritage of British gardening and also its problems at that time, most significantly a lack of funding for large, ambitious gardens of all periods. It was coincidentally a moment when the study of garden history, as a respected discipline, was coming of age. The Garden History Society had begun in 1966, first as a charity funded only by membership, but which was to be given the statutory role of advising government on planning applications related to gardens on the Register of Historic Parks and Gardens of Special Interest in England, set up in 1983. Strong would later be its President.

His inspiration to garden with the 'order and visual excitement' of formal geometry had been in part informed by Reginald Blomfield's *The Formal Garden in England* (1892) and H. Inigo Triggs's *Formal Gardens in England and Scotland* (1902). Triggs's inspiration in turn was the great 17th-century French gardener André Le Nôtre (p. 84). And for advice on the skills of handling formal clipped shapes, Strong looked to *Garden Craftsmanship in Yew and Box* (1925) by Nathaniel Lloyd, father of Christopher Lloyd (p. 264). The simple geometry of Levens Hall, Cumbria, laid out in the late 17th century, embodied what Strong most admired. Twentieth-century sources of inspiration were found in the enclosed and individually characterized 'garden rooms' to be seen at Vita Sackville-West's Sissinghurst in Kent (p. 230) and Lawrence Johnston's Hidcote Manor, Gloucestershire (p. 104).

But Strong's ideas came not only from English gardens. In Italy in 1973 he had admired da Vignola's formal Renaissance gardens at Caprarola and the Villa

The Laskett, complete with monograms: it is a more playful version of Hamilton Finlay's pilastered Temple at Little Sparta. The box parterre was later ravaged by blight and replaced by heather.

OPPOSITE *The Silver Jubilee Garden.* ABOVE *The Elizabeth Tudor Avenue. Nothing is simple at the Laskett: multi-layered, shadow-playing hedges flank a vista of complex tiling that leads to a polychrome, gilded and crowned column.*

Lante, and in 1979 he visited the newly begun restoration of the great Dutch formal garden of Het Loo. This was also the year he published his book *The Renaissance Garden in England.*

Having met the *grand dame* of English gardening, Rosemary Verey (p. 258), in the 1980s, he appreciated her garden at Barnsley House in Gloucestershire for its collection of fine cameo features, many of which followed the ideas of Tudor and Stuart gardens – the knot garden, the tunnel, the pleached lime walk, the potager. Of the Laskett, Verey announced to Strong that his sequence of vistas and focal sculptures was 'just like the V&A … all corridors with things at the end of them'. And so the Laskett's structure developed, its features memorializing the lives and friendships of its makers and even their cats: the Hilliard Garden, the Ashton Arbour, the Die Fledermaus Walk, Covent Garden and the V&A Museum Temple, inscribed appropriately in Greek (by Simon Verity, Rosemary Verey's favoured sculptor) 'Memory, Mother of the Muses'.

A visit in 1995 to Little Sparta, Ian Hamilton Finlay's heavily allusive garden in the Scottish Borders (p. 52), inspired Strong to employ more inscription within the Laskett, and never mind who understood it; it was simply for the pleasure of those who could.

Julia Trevelyan Oman's orchard, a formal composition of apples and roses. With arches smothered in romantic climbers, it was one of the areas that were opened up and revitalized after her death, to make a fresher impression. Age takes gardens as well as people.

Through Rosemary Verey, Strong became a player in Gloucestershire aristocratic circles, and it was she who introduced him to Prince Charles, for whom in 1989 he designed profiles cut into the yew hedges in the Prince's private garden at Highgrove, Tetbury, which is gardened organically. Strong even went along occasionally to clip them himself. He was knighted in 1983.

For all Strong's leading position in the world of the arts, the Laskett continues to be made on a relatively small budget, its architectural features formed not of carved stone, but mostly of moulded, reconstituted stone, somehow confirming (or is it cementing?) the idea that the garden is a source of personal enjoyment, not a *folie de grandeur*. Well aware of the unfashionable formality in which he deals, Strong has always been wickedly happy to throw bones of contention to gardeners of a more naturalistic bent. Thus he says: 'The gardener who resorts to plants has failed!' and 'One cannot have too much gold in a garden!' – this of his penchant for gilded finials on Classical urns and the much-photographed antlers belonging to a stone stag couchant. William Kent would have loved it.

In 1987 Strong retired from the V&A and has since pursued a life as a scholar and author on art history, a garden writer and a presenter of popular television programmes. He has gone on to publish numerous books, including diaries, and holds honorary positions in many arts-related organizations.

Julia Trevelyan Oman, plantswoman, lover of privacy and the greater romantic of the couple, died in 2003, prompting Strong to make major revisions to the garden, cutting back clipped vistas to their original widths and taking out smothering climbers and redundant evergreen trees originally planted for shelter. It has been a new lease of life for both garden and gardener, and the great game of making the Laskett continues. Strong has bequeathed it to the gardening charity Perennial, and, though he acknowledges that gardens change and develop, he hopes the Laskett will in some measure survive, as what Rosemary Verey called 'the largest formal garden to be made in England since 1945'.

Strong is a great admirer of the practical skills of gardening and has left the Laskett on his death to the organization Perennial, formerly the Royal Gardeners' Benevolent Society. The kitchen garden forms a sizeable part of the garden.

CHARLES JENCKS

Interpreter in landforms of theories of the cosmos

BORN 1939

1939
J. Robert Oppenheimer and Hartland Snyder predict the existence of black holes.
Discovery of nuclear fission.
Alan Turing starts work on codes and cyphers at Bletchley Park.
Nylon fabric introduced at the New York World Fair.

CHARLES JENCKS'S MISSION is to make metaphors of science and cosmology in the form of landscape. According to him it's nothing new – examples can be found in ancient Persian and Egyptian gardens – although he admits that symbolic gardens of any kind have always been very much scarcer than gardens made in a simply aesthetic tradition.

But perhaps Jencks's foray into cosmological gardens is important because it brings something new to the powerful Western European tradition of garden design. When Charles Darwin published *On the Origin of Species* in 1859, it freed people, through reason and science, to question established views on existence and divine creation. The idea that man and the universe were evolving phenomena rather than the result of divine intervention began to be explored and even became commonplace in literature and the arts. Yet not until Jencks in the 1990s did this way of thinking find its way visibly into the art of garden-making. It represents a great leap forward.

Charles Alexander Jencks was born in in Baltimore, USA. After an MA in architecture at Harvard, he came to Britain to study for his PhD in architectural history at University College, London, in 1970. He stayed in Britain and went on to make an international career as an architectural critic, best known for naming and defining Post-Modern architecture. He has published numerous books, mostly on architecture, some on landscape, and taught at over 40 universities. His development as a maker of landscapes grew alongside his architectural interests.

In 1978 Jencks married Maggie Keswick, an architect, designer of gardens, expert on Chinese gardens and daughter of Sir John Keswick, head of Jardine Matheson, the trading conglomerate. At her family home, Portrack House in

ABOVE *Charles Jencks at Portrack, his home in Scotland. He is a great provocateur of the horticultural establishment, which responds to his intellectually absorbed work with pleasure or dismissal.* BELOW *Maggie Keswick, Jencks's wife, with whom he began the garden.*

Dumfries and Galloway, the two of them began to develop from 1989 a symbolic garden that would reveal the principles of nature rather than simply imitate natural scenery. Known as the Garden of Cosmic Speculation, its largest feature, the Snail Mound with crescent lakes, has become an icon of 20th-century gardens, just as Thomas Church's 1948 swimming pool in the Donnell Garden did in California (p. 176). Maggie Keswick Jencks died of cancer in 1995, and at her instigation the Maggie Keswick Jencks Cancer Caring Centres Trust was established to offer social and emotional support to cancer sufferers. New Maggie's Centres continue to be built, employing the world's most renowned architects and landscape architects.

Since that first landform at Portrack, Jencks has followed the path of symbolic gardening, and in particular the use of green landforms, creating almost 40 of them to date. Each one aims to express something of the underlying physical and social landscape, combined with contemporary ideas about how we and the landscape fit into current scientific theories about the universe.

It is ironic that so many images of the Portrack mounds simply offer the aesthetic beauty of sculpted greensward, water and shadow, whereas to Jencks, the precise meaning of such a landscape – expressing ideas about everything from DNA to black holes to the multiverse – is as important as its beauty. Work which at first uninformed glance may seem to be a landscape of mounds and perhaps stones will on closer inspection quickly be seen to contain a great deal of sculptural hardware and inscription, which Jencks insists is not decoration but is absolutely integral to the landscape. People whose tastes run only to the aesthetic may find the work compromised by this determined physical expression of meaning. Jencks finds that some clients are seeking to create a landscape that is more purely aesthetic than symbolic.

Snake and Snail Mounds at Jencks's home, the Garden of Cosmic Speculation, Portrack, Scotland. It shares the same ingredients as the 18th-century landscape garden – trees, lawn, water and reflection.

ABOVE *The Symmetry Break Terrace, Garden of Cosmic Speculation. Some people find only aesthetic pleasure in Jencks's work, others love to engage with its intellectual agenda.* OVERLEAF *Black Hole, at the Crawick Multiverse, Scotland. Jencks's overlaid image shows how the reality on the ground is based on ideas of cosmology and science.*

His reply is simple: 'If you will accept a polemic, I will work for you.' He requires intellectual vigour in the conception of a landscape to make it worthwhile, and occasionally that conception is a polemic. 'People have to break through that *barrier*, rise above a purely aesthetic approach, for new things to happen.'

Jencks is, however, happy for people to bring their own meanings to his landscapes, because after all they are already co-creations, interventions between man and the earth. But he insists that meaning, symbolism, significance are vital if a designed landscape is to have any value. To him the big questions about the universe matter; he considers the discoveries of science to be one of the shining achievements of our times, and where better to express their significance than in a garden, where one is physically set down, exposed, among living things under an open sky. If in former times a garden provoked feelings and questions about one's existence and proximity to God, today a Jencksian garden is free to explore just what it is that we exist *in*.

Eco-Geo Festival, Suncheon, Korea. Jencks's landforms usually allow people a degree of access, so they can have physical experience of the 3D scientific simile. The grand opening involved dancers, music and motorcycles.

Jencks is not in the business of providing answers, of telling people what to think. He sees an artist's job, obligation even, as responding to new, mind-stretching ideas and offering them as symbol or metaphor, so that people can reach their own conclusions. The work is a discussion, and it should come as no surprise to find that in his book about Portrack, *The Garden of Cosmic Speculation* (2003), Jencks uses the mechanism of Platonic dialogues – usually between himself and an eminent scientist – as a means of elucidating a difficult idea by stages, in order to make it memorably understood.

At least half of Jencks's work has been made for public spaces, and virtually all of it is regularly accessible. A park for the Eco-Geo Festival at Suncheon City, Korea, the landscape outside the Scottish National Gallery of Modern Art in Edinburgh, and the work at CERN, Geneva, for the Large Hadron Collider project, were all made with public footfall in mind. Jupiter Artland, also outside Edinburgh, is a private initiative and in effect an elegant form of sculpture park. Northumberlandia, just north of Newcastle upon Tyne, is a 19-ha (46-acre), 34-m (112-ft) tall community park in the form of a sleeping woman, but it is also, like several of Jencks's projects, a piece of industrial land reclamation, here following coal extraction. At the Parco Portello in Milan, Jencks created a landscape on the site of the polluted former Alfa Romeo works, and a recent project, the Crawick Multiverse, in Scotland, with eight landforms and several other features, was built on a vast area scarred by opencast coal mining.

Time will tell whether Jencks's highly relevant and well-respected scientific symbolism will become a regular element of modern gardens. But whatever the verdict of contemporary garden-makers and garden-watchers, his projects will survive, like the pyramids and other burial tumuli too large to be easily removed, as viscerally attractive mysteries.

Northumberlandia, Newcastle upon Tyne, is a public park in the form of a figurative landscape, created from mining waste and only recognizable from the air. Below is the head of the reclining goddess, above the Eye of the Universe, a feature on her forehead.

ALEXANDER REFORD

Champion of the conceptual

BORN 1962

1962
The Beatles audition for Decca and are rejected.
The Cuban missile crisis takes place.
Algeria gains independence from France.
Telstar 1 communications satellite is launched and relays
    the first live transatlantic television.

A T THE END of the 20th century the garden world started to tire of opulent, plant-rich gardens in the Arts and Crafts tradition. The question began to be asked: what is a garden? Further questions followed. Does a garden have to be all about horticulture? Could it be more about ideas? Could a garden not raise issues like any other piece of art? Could a piece of outdoor installation art be called a garden?

Responses to this debate began to emerge at the Festival of Gardens at Chaumont, in the French Loire valley. It was a festival of gardens such as had never been seen before, and it inspired Canadian historian Alexander Reford to set up a similar festival in the Reford Gardens, or Les Jardins de Métis, at Grand-Métis, in deep-rural Canada. This annual event would go on to become an international icon of Canadian gardening, and one of the leading garden festivals in the world. Reford's quiet intent worked wonders.

Reford's father was a geophysicist, who later turned to farming outside Ottawa. Reford grew up on the farm, but school led him to a degree in philosophy and thereafter to the study of history at the universities of Toronto and Oxford. An academic career beckoned and, with particular interests in Canadian and business history, he began work at the University of Toronto, until a foray into the family archives pushed his life in a totally different direction.

The story now travels back a hundred years. In 1894, Reford's great-grandmother Elsie married Robert Reford, whose family wealth lay in shipping. The

ABOVE Elsie Reford in the romantic waterside garden, around 1935, with her beloved lilies.
OPPOSITE Alexander Reford.

couple built a house in Montreal and developed a riverside summer retreat, Estevan Lodge, which Elsie had inherited from her uncle, 480 km (300 miles) to the east in Quebec Province, at the confluence of the Métis and St Lawrence rivers. Here the summers were cooler, even if snow lay 3 m (10 ft) deep from November to May, and winds could blow off the St Lawrence River, at this point 65 km (40 miles) wide, that plunged temperatures down to -35°C (-31°F).

It was a sporting estate, for fishing, hunting and skiing, but, from 1926, when she was 54 and convalescing from an operation for appendicitis, until her death in 1967, Elsie Reford transformed it into a 8-ha (20-acre) garden, completely self-taught. The garden took ten years to construct and provided welcome employment for local people during the depression. She began to collect particular plants that would perform well in that limited summer season – lilies, gentians, peonies, delphiniums, primulas and crab apples. Having been finished in Dresden and Paris, Elsie had a feeling for European traditions and she had read Gertrude Jekyll (p. 222) and William Robinson (p. 208), whose ideas on wild gardening matched her own. The garden contained only one straight line, but that consisted of a herbaceous border 90 m (300 ft) long and 3 m (10 ft) deep, in the front row of which grew literally thousands of perfumed lilies.

The house and garden at Métis then passed to Reford's grandfather, a career soldier in the Irish Guards, who soon realized the place was more than his energies

Traditional gardening alongside the modern festival of garden installations has proved a huge tourist success, even so far from major conurbations.

could maintain. In 1961 the Canadian government bravely stepped in and bought it as an aid to developing the busy summer tourist trail that winds around the peninsula, and it was opened to the public in 1962. It became an attraction, with food and a craft shop, but the income was never sufficient for it to be a self-sustaining enterprise, and after 30 years of trying, the government decided in 1994 that it must be privatized or close.

Meanwhile, Alexander Reford had come across Elsie's lifelong diaries and Robert's huge archive of photographs in the Montreal house, and he became fascinated. In 1995 the Reford family set up Les Amis des Jardins de Métis, a non-profit-making corporation for the development and restoration of the garden. There followed summer schools, held with the landscape department of the University of Montreal, and Elsie's collections of plants began to be recreated and then expanded in line with her horticultural ambitions, rather than the precise condition of the garden at her death. The fashion at that time was for accurate historical garden restorations, and it was splendidly common-sensical of Reford, himself no plantsman, to take this freer approach to the restoration of a garden that would have to work

ABOVE Camouflage View, 2005. Reflective fins invisibly obstruct the path to the sea, by showing light, shade, wood and water – anything but what lies beyond.

Rotunda, 2014, a steel dish of water, intended to pull the sky and wooded landscape and variable rainfall into itself. Filled only once, it also reflects the development of life in water, as animal and vegetable organisms colonize it naturally.

so hard to make ends meet. Reford, tiring of the 1,300-km (800-mile) trip from Toronto, finally gave up teaching and moved to Métis.

He read with professional interest and envy the press coverage given to a project in France begun in 1992, the Festival of Gardens at Chaumont-sur-Loire, the brainchild of Jean-Paul Pigeat. Reford visited Chaumont in 1998, realized its brand of summer-only installation gardens could help revivify Les Jardins de Métis, and secured funds in Canada for a similar festival there, a project to celebrate the Millennium. Support came from Philippe Poullaouec-Gonidec, professor in landscape architecture at the University of Montreal, and Denis Lemieux, architect with the Ministère de la Culture and the initial festival director. The International Garden Festival was the first of its kind in North America and remains one of a handful worldwide.

From the beginning, the Festival's installation gardens were the antithesis of traditional show gardens as seen at the Royal Horticultural Society's Chelsea Flower Show, where perfect horticulture and cultivation reign supreme and gardens are

OPPOSITE *Réflexions Colorées, 2003. A tinted glass triangle creates deceptive reflections of the woodland, and of the viewer.* BELOW *Jardin des Hespérides, 2006. A huge silk lantern floats in a woodland pool surrounded by perfumed floating orange trees.*

viewed frozen in time from behind a rope. At Métis, visitors can walk through the gardens – they are boxes of ideas rather than framed arrangements of landscaping and flowers. The setting, with installations scattered through woodland in pockets of open space, some of them with views down to the St Lawrence, provides the designers with great natural opportunities. And whereas at Chaumont the gardens rub together like paintings in a gallery, several visible at once, at the Jardins de Métis they can be separate and have a more individual atmosphere.

Exhibitors may already have successful careers in their own right or go on to develop them. Claude Cormier's celebrated Blue Stick Garden (2006) worked brilliantly with the use of colour and materials to evoke the mixed border so successfully propounded by Gertrude Jekyll. He has won many awards for his subsequent work in Montreal, Toronto and elsewhere in North America. The Aranda\Lasch architectural studio, which presented Camouflage View (2005), is recognized as being at the cutting edge of American architecture.

Ha!Ha!, 2009. A sinuous sunken walkway with sitting spaces is hidden by a ha-ha and surrounded by the luminous colours of tropical gardening. Not all the installations at Métis are serious.

Blue Stick Garden, 2006. Sticks all painted a different colour on one side demonstrate how colours change, as one walks around. It also celebrates the blue poppies that grow at Métis.

The festival has gone from strength to strength, as has Elsie's original garden, and has now become an event attracting people in their 30s and 40s, as well as the over 50s who are the traditional garden-visiting constituency. From an initial annual offering of around 20 gardens, many retained for two to three years, the festival has grown. For the currently available half dozen places per year there are 300 proposals, from landscape architects, garden designers, architects, and graphic and sculptural artists the world over, which are carefully selected by an expert jury. The gardens are funded and built by the Festival, and unlike at Chaumont there is no annual theme – the meaning of the garden is entirely up to its designer. There are also no prizes. In its four-month season, 60,000 visitors come to the Reford Gardens, no small achievement for a place 360 km (225 miles) from major conurbations (Chaumont, 200 km/125 miles from Paris, attracts 150,000 visitors over six months).

If Reford's project has a problem now, it is that Métis's installation art has begun to be copied and emulated in other Canadian cities, stealing a little of the festival's thunder; but then imitation is the sincerest form of flattery.

GARDENS OF STRAIGHT LINES

MANY PEOPLE, it seems, dislike straight lines in a garden. A better word might be resent, because they regard perfectly straight lines in the outdoor environment as an infliction on nature, and indeed on themselves – an attempt by the garden-maker to control and corral people who visit the garden.

In a way they are right, of course. It is a form of control, but it is a benign one, and if one steps far enough back to gain perspective, the use of lines and three-dimensional rectilinear geometry is simply a discipline within which to work, in the same way that the geometrical (or some would say mathematical) musical structures of Bach are seen as an artistic discipline in themselves, showpieces of what the human intellect can do.

It might be said of gardeners who make straight lines that what they do is a response to the vagaries of nature – to harsh weather, to hunger and disease, to losing one's way in the featureless wild wood. So began the ancient paradise gardens of Persia, where the shelter of high walls and the presence of water in shining canals and fountains was a welcome relief from nature's ruthless power over us. It is too easy now, in times of antibiotics, air-conditioning and reduced child mortality, to forget that nature has until very recently been a cruel master.

That Persian tradition found its way into the Moorish gardens of North Africa and thence into works such as the Generalife garden in Granada in Spain; from there it moved again into the great Renaissance villa gardens of Italy. Here the formal control of water reached new heights, in pools and cascades and fountains, mastering a three-dimensional complexity that Bach would surely have admired.

The same love of geometric pools can be clearly seen in gardens of the modern era. Lutyens's circular basins and long rills at Hestercombe are clearly in the Moorish tradition, as is the long pond used by Penelope Hobhouse at Walmer Castle. At Hidcote, Lawrence Johnston created simple vistas with his extensive use of straight hedges contrasting with his more exuberantly planted enclosures. The trunks of his pleached and stilted hedges have rhythm in their spacing like a great avenue, demonstrating another pleasure of formal geometry and a further parallel with music.

There have been gardens of course where formal geometry has genuinely been used as a means to control people. The supreme example will always be Louis XIV's vast 17th-century garden at Versailles, made for him by André Le Nôtre. Here, in the grand canals and radiating vistas where members of the court were obliged to pass their time, was nature tamed to impress; in its *bosquets* – ornate, highly architectural gardens set each on its own among the trees – was an invitation to magnificent shows of theatre or fireworks that no one could refuse. Versailles was an expression on the landscape of Louis's iron control of his court. If there was a certain amount of ornamental, trilling geometry between the grander straight vistas, it was the vistas that counted most.

Others have then taken elements from that French precedent and used them in their own way. In late 19th-century England, ex-soldier William Nesfield became famous for his great parterres, where, to the horror of gardeners such as William Robinson who promoted naturalistic planting, formal curlicued patterns of coloured gravels could riot between straight paths.

Some gardeners have enjoyed using rectilinear geometry for the way it can express proportion. Russell Page designed terraces, avenues and pools with a great sensitivity to the relationships between them and with the house. Christopher Bradley-Hole's imaginative and modernist garden architecture is often based on the proportions of the Golden Section, not out of a sense of correctness but out of the desire to make things invisibly right and satisfactory; it is used as a tool, not an end in itself. Others again have taken their use of straight lines in gardens from agriculture, as an echo of the lines made by ploughing or crops in a field, to give a garden a sense of belonging in its local environment and thereby gain a feeling of age, of being long-settled in its location and so more comfortable to be in. In France, Nicole de Vésian created a parterre of lavender that echoed the lavender fields of Provence where she lived. In Spain, Fernando Caruncho in his early work recreated a kind of elegant, idealized agriculture around his houses, to settle them into their rural surroundings.

It is telling that however much a person may resent the controlling nature of a vigorously geometric garden, almost everyone enjoys a blend of geometry allied to romantic planting. To a considerable extent, the sweet reason of the straight line is, it seems, irresistible.

Plan of Vaux-le-Vicomte, designed by André Le Nôtre.

ANDRÉ LE NÔTRE

Arranger of exquisite geometric illusions

1613–1700

1613
Shakespeare's Globe theatre is destroyed by fire.
The Romanov dynasty is founded in Russia.
The Ottoman Empire invades Hungary.
Monteverdi becomes Chapel Master at St Mark's, Venice.

1700
Death of poet John Dryden.
The Russian army invades Swedish Estonia.
The Cascadia earthquake runs for 1,000 miles (600 miles)
    along the coast of North America.
Edinburgh substantially destroyed by fire.

NO NEW ARTISTIC ENDEAVOUR emerges with absolute originality from the mind of its creator, it is always a product of its own times and a response to what has preceded it. Today, André Le Nôtre is credited with being the originator of the grand French tradition of formal gardening, and yet he had contemporaries such as Claude Mollet and Jacques Boyceau who had been developing the same style. What makes Le Nôtre so special, what gives him such importance in the history of garden design, is that he was gardener to the Sun King, Louis XIV of France, at Versailles, and he worked with a budget that has never been equalled. Versailles went on to influence formal gardens across Europe for the next 300 years, at Drottningholm Palace in Sweden, at Hampton Court in England, at Het Loo in the Netherlands, through the great formal revival in 19th-century England with such figures as Charles Barry and William Nesfield (p. 90), and on into late 20th-century domestic gardens.

Le Nôtre's inspiration came, in turn, from the great formal Renaissance gardens of Italy, where plants and landscape and especially water were subjected to the ruthless power of human engineering, where symmetry reigned, where an owner could survey the garden and landscape from a palace at its centre, where ornament and myth were woven into the fabric of the garden, and where surprise led on to more surprises. And yet Le Nôtre's gardens were different in one major aspect: where so many of the Italian villas were built on eminences, either for safety or cooler air, Le Nôtre's gardens were built on flat land. The patterns of his gardens were more two-dimensional, and his stretching of that third, vertical dimension came through deep reflecting pools and soaring water jets. He made the most of the contrasts between solid geometry and open space, between the grand, open, rectilinear vistas and the winding woodlands where *bosquets* – semi-formal, often hedged and highly stylized enclosures – were the setting for musical and dramatic performances.

In an age when patronage was the key to success, Le Nôtre was a man who, fortunately, managed to get on with everybody. He was apolitical, but more than this, he was a great collaborator. Le Nôtre would work happily with his client's ideas, turning them into something wonderful on the ground, through feats of landscape engineering as much as horticulture. His father was also a royal gardener, at Les Tuileries in Paris, and Le Nôtre himself set out on a similar career, with all the benefits of family connections. He became known as a maker of parterres, and by 1635 he was working for the Duc d'Orleans at the Luxembourg palace. He was also a skilled interior painter, like William Kent (p. 28), and favoured by fashionable architects of the time. In 1643, the year Louis XIV became king, he was appointed to a part-time administrative role with especial involvement in gardens, but still undertaking his own garden contracts for others, and generally making a name for himself.

His greatest feat was the creation of the garden at Vaux-le-Vicomte for Nicolas Fouquet, the King's finance minister. This was Le Nôtre at the height of his powers (when work began in 1657 he was 44). Magnificent in scale and with a mastery of perspective, even today Vaux remains one of France's great – if not its greatest – historic gardens, for its breathtaking symmetry, its grand canals and its elaborate waterworks. Fouquet lavished huge sums on the chateau and the garden, and in 1661 launched it with the party to end all parties, at which the young King Louis was guest of honour. Ever the shrewd and jealous politician, Louis saw hubris here, not to say embezzlement. Fouquet was stripped of office and Vaux stripped of its wonders. Among the spoils was Le Nôtre himself, who, managing to remain untainted by his collaboration with

Portrait of Le Nôtre by Carlo Maratta, 1679.

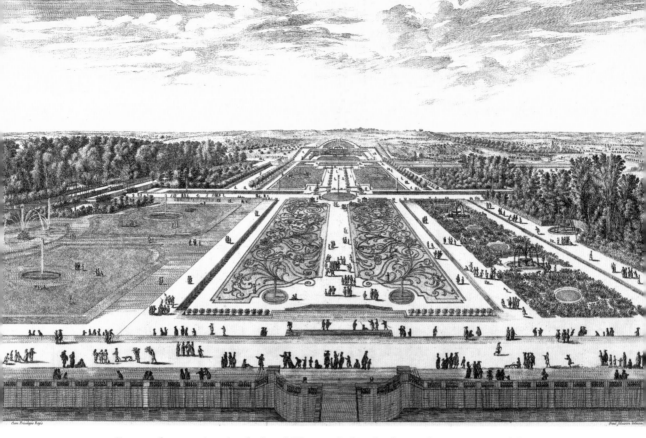

Engraved perspective view by Israel Silvestre, looking back over the greater part of the garden at Vaux-le-Vicomte; water gardens follow.

Fouquet, was taken to Versailles, 20 km (12 miles) from Paris, to create something even more magnificent. Work on this extraordinary garden was still continuing when Le Nôtre died in 1700.

The whole purpose of the palace of Versailles was to impress the world with Louis's power – but more particularly the fractious French nobles who, now required to live at court rather than in the provinces, were safely under the eye of the king. Versailles was his means of ensuring order, and the garden was a symbol of that order on the ground; its great central vista started from the king's bedroom itself.

Once a mere hunting lodge, Versailles was transformed over the decades into the greatest palace on earth, with its own new town and smaller, subsidiary mansions. Crossing the unpromising, low-lying, swampy malarial ground, there appeared a Grand Canal, 1,500 m (1,640 yd) long and 62 m (203 ft) wide, forming the spine of a landscape of vast basins, fountains, formal woodlands and parterres. Once again it was all created with terrifying symmetry. The work was done by blasting or by hand, often employing soldiers more accustomed to making military fortifications. There were landslips and the casualty rate among the workforce was appalling. The planting was also stupendous: 42,000 elms and 600 walnut trees were shipped from as far afield as Flanders, and 2,600 orange trees perfumed the garden, arranged in the cuboid 'Versailles planters' that feature in many a garden today.

Louis would make tours of the garden with Le Nôtre, just as he made military inspections, planning extensions or looking at entire new houses and estates nearby. He would sometimes come out and do a little clipping himself and would take important visitors around the garden personally; he even wrote a guidebook. For many a designer Louis would have been the ultimate interfering, nightmare client, but Le Nôtre made the most of it. If the garden at Vaux had been a unified work of art, Versailles was a great experiment, forever expanding and reinventing itself.

Le Nôtre of course did not work alone, and the garden was a collaborative project. In its early years the financial and logistical hand was Jean-Baptiste Colbert's, and architects Louis Le Vau and later Jules Hardouin-Mansart were also involved. Great sculptors, playwrights such as Molière and Racine, and composers such as Lully and Couperin produced work for the extravagant, week-long entertainments in the garden, with sea battles, monumental firework displays and wild beasts. The canals had their own fleet, complete with an admiral and 262 officers. The whole garden was effectively a stage set, managed by Le Nôtre and created to show off Louis's power and talent. Scarcely a picture of Versailles exists which is not densely populated with courtiers out to see and be seen.

Aerial view of Vaux-le-Vicomte today, but lacking that great population of strutting courtiers who made gardens like Vaux places of such social and political importance.

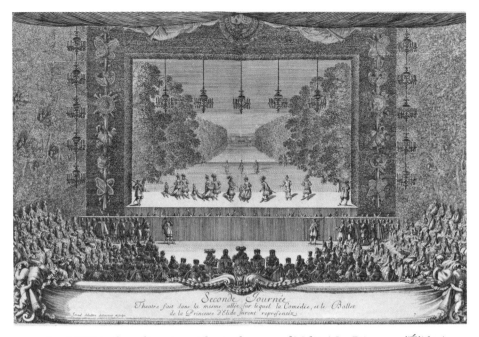

ABOVE Louis XIV in the audience to watch a performance of Molière's La Princesse d'Élide *in the garden at Versailles, 1673.* OPPOSITE *Versailles, a perspective view with fountains and* bosquets, *with putti sweeping and watering, by Jean Cotelle, 17th century – an impossible view, since the land was flat.*

During his long career, Le Nôtre's work was never confined only to Versailles, and he developed great gardens for other royalty and influential aristocrats. Best known are the chateaus at Chantilly, Fontainebleau, Saint-Germain-en-Laye, Saint-Cloud and Sceaux. At the Tuileries he made a grand avenue that is today the Champs-Élysées. He was no great traveller, having more than enough to do in Paris, but he was consulted by Nicodemus Tessin, the important Swedish designer, and provided plans for English royalty at Greenwich and Windsor; he did travel to Italy where, ever the French diplomat, he met the Pope. He retired in 1693, aged 80, on a generous state pension, and enjoyed a healthy old age in comfortable but not grand circumstances, with a fine personal collection of paintings. Versailles continued to develop under Jules Hardouin-Mansart, with particular emphasis on architectural and sculptural elements, but it had been under Le Nôtre that it had taken on its substance as a garden.

Today, little of Le Nôtre's work remains unaltered by subsequent generations intent on saving money or pursuing more naturalistic fashions, and it is all too easy to assume that any remaining formal elements date from his time when in fact they were made much later. Like 'Capability' Brown, Le Nôtre was no writer and, to our great loss, left little behind except a few plans. And, of course, Versailles.

WILLIAM NESFIELD

The military approach to vistas and avenues

1794–1881

1794
Erasmus Darwin, in his *Zoonomia*, proposes that all living organisms have a common ancestor.
Robespierre establishes the Cult of the Supreme Being as the new State Religion of France.
William Blake's *The Ancient of Days* published as the frontispiece to his *Europe a Prophecy*.

1881
Assassination of US President James A. Garfield.
The First Boer War ends.
Birth of Pablo Picasso and Stefan Zweig.
Gunfight at the OK Corral, Tombstone, Arizona.

I N THE 18th and 19th centuries, unlike today when originality is all, the revival of older artistic styles was acceptable and even laudable. Neoclassical, Neo-Palladian, Gothic Revival, Pre-Raphaelite – all of them were highly fashionable in their day; their practitioners took great pride in the principle of reviving older styles and had the confidence to acknowledge their debt to the past and imitate or develop it. Such a man was William Andrews Nesfield, soldier turned landscape architect, whose revival of Tudor and 17th-century French garden idioms made such an impact on mid-19th-century British gardens.

Born the son of a clergyman at Lumley Park near Chester-le-Street, County Durham, in the north of England, even as a boy Nesfield could draw with remarkable skill. Having narrowly avoided a career in the church he joined the army, which trained him in engineering, draughtsmanship and map-making – skills that were useful later – and packed him off as a 2nd Lieutenant to fight in the Peninsular War under Wellington. He then served as an aide-de-camp to the British Commander of the North West Army in Upper Canada, Sir Gordon Drummond, painting dramatic landscapes such as Niagara Falls as he went.

Pencil drawing of Nesfield by James Duffield Harding, c. 1840.

Watercolour by William Nesfield of his house and garden at Fortis Green, north London. It may seem informal (if smart) by Nesfield's standards, with no parterre to be seen, but then this is the carriage entrance only.

In the end it was painting that commanded his greater loyalty, and after a brief period in England again, at Sandhurst, he left the army aged 25 to paint professionally, taking up residence in County Durham once more. He joined the Old Water-Colour Society and remained an active member until 1851, when he resigned to devote his attention to an expanding career as a landscape architect. Romantic landscapes were his speciality and he travelled to paint dramatic scenery from the Highlands of Scotland to the European Alps, often in the company of well-known watercolourists such as John Varley and David Cox. John Ruskin admired Nesfield's work in his *Modern Painting*.

Nesfield's career as a landscape architect was encouraged by his brother-in-law, Anthony Salvin, a Gothic Revival architect, who employed Nesfield's skills as a military draughtsman to set out the gardens around his buildings. With work for government and the royal family in Salvin's portfolio, the association with him gave Nesfield an invaluable introduction to wealthy clients, and he collaborated further with other important architects including Edward Blore and William Burn. Nesfield's own garden at his villa designed by Salvin at Fortis Green in north London was admired by the popular garden journalist John Claudius Loudon in his *Gardener's Magazine*.

If Humphry Repton civilized the expansive landscape gardens of 'Capability' Brown by adding a modicum of formality and terracing close to the house, Nesfield was to reinforce that formality with military enthusiasm. His method was to level the land in front of the house for terraces or grand complicated parterres, decorated with intricate, box-edged beds, often featuring the owner's initials and sometimes in-filled with coloured gravels. Architectural highlights would come in the form of carved stone vases and clipped evergreens. There might be a central fountain, and always a heavy balustrade marking the change from high formality to more informal gardening beyond, with ultimately a view to the horizon. Again like Repton, Nesfield liked to offer his clients before-and-after illustrations when submitting his proposals to them.

During thirty years in the middle of the 19th century Nesfield undertook over 260 projects, and shared dominion of the world of garden design with Sir Charles Barry, architect of the Houses of Parliament and creator of Italianate parterres at

Broughton Hall, Yorkshire: this intricate sloping parterre to the side of the house had its scrollwork infilled with coloured minerals and gravels.

The scheme Nesfield overlaid on the 18th-century landscape garden at Castle Howard, Yorkshire, became ever more formal as it approached the house, ending in a vast parterre.

Dunrobin Castle in Scotland, Harewood House in Yorkshire and Trentham Hall in Staffordshire, all three still well maintained today. There was a confidence about their work, the unselfconscious parterre thrusting out into the landscape like the prow of a ship, which appealed to the owners of great houses who were ready to spend on their gardens.

Important commissions came Nesfield's way. At Kew he designed the Syon Vista, Pagoda Vista and Broad Walk, all extant, and a great parterre, which is much simplified today (as are most of his remaining parterres). Perhaps the best of his parterres in unaltered condition is that at Broughton Hall in Yorkshire, which slopes gently upwards from the house like a drawing laid out on a lectern, separated from the park by a robust balustrade and leading to an Italianate pavilion which looks back over both house and park. He designed the garden of the Horticultural Society (later the Royal Horticultural Society) in Kensington, and the Avenue Garden in Regent's Park, close to where he lived in later life.

For 20 years Nesfield worked at Castle Howard, near York, creating lakes and a truly massive parterre centred on a spherical fountain depicting Atlas holding

ABOVE AND OPPOSITE *Witley Court was an enormous but relatively simple scheme, centred on the monumental Perseus fountain (above hidden by the garden pavilion). Note the great glass conservatory.*

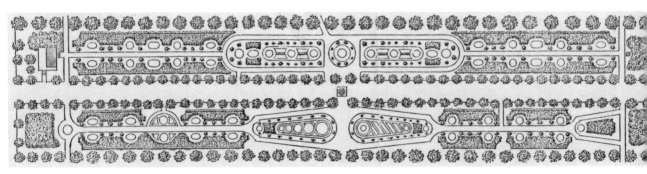

ABOVE *Design for a parterre in Regent's Park. It is now restored, though not in all its finer detail since labour was so much cheaper in Nesfield's day and public parks were better respected.*

up the world. This can still be seen today, as can the maze at Somerleyton Hall in Suffolk, one of several he made. Other commissions included Highgrove House, now home of the Prince of Wales, Holkham Hall and Alton Towers.

His work at Witley Court in Worcestershire has fared less well. Here was an Italianate mansion, before which Nesfield set out a huge sloping parterre that centres on his 'monster work', the steam-powered Perseus and Andromeda Fountain, which shot water 36 m (120 ft) into the air and was said to be as loud as an express train. Sadly, the mansion was extensively damaged by fire in 1937 and remains a shell, while the garden was stripped of much of its ornament and most of its plants, though two parterres have now been reinstated. Little but the vast fountain remained, a great mass of carved stone that only escaped being shipped to America for Bing Crosby's Hollywood home by virtue of impracticality: its central block weighs 20 tons. It has now been restored to working order.

Just as the formal gardens of the Tudor and Stuart period gave way to the naturalistic 18th-century landscape gardens of Kent and Brown, so after only a few decades, Nesfield's and Barry's formal grandeur and the whole system of bedding out summer flowers gave way to the desire for less ostentatious and more domesticated gardening, in the manner of William Robinson (p. 208) and Gertrude Jekyll (p. 222). Part of the reasoning (as had also been pleaded in the 18th century) was the cost of maintaining a complex formal garden. If only a few of these grand Victorian designs remain today, eclipsed by naturalistic or ecologically inclined gardening, still the British public admire their vigour; the designs perhaps speak more satisfactorily to gardeners from Belgium and the Netherlands, who continue to find pleasure in geometry.

SIR EDWIN LUTYENS

'By measure we must live'

1869–1944

1869
In Germany Friedrich Miescher discovers DNA.
Inauguration of the Suez Canal.
War and Peace published in book form.
Birth of Neville Chamberlain, British Prime Minister.

1944
Paris liberated from Nazi occupation.
Hitler survives an assassination attempt by Claus von
    Stauffenberg.
Soviet troops liberate Crimea and change Turkish place
    names to Russian.
Casablanca awarded Best Picture at the Oscars.

THE GREATEST ARCHITECT of his generation? The principal architect and master planner of New Delhi? Designer of the Cenotaph in Whitehall and the man who, had he lived longer, might have completed a British cathedral bigger than St Peter's in Rome? Edwin Lutyens was all these, and undoubtedly was one of the leading architects of the British Empire. But in a smaller way, through his more modest country houses, he was also responsible for establishing a style of garden that would last for a hundred years. His name has become a byword for Edwardian gardening.

Edwin Landseer Lutyens was the son of Captain Charles Lutyens, society horse painter and man of independent means, whose wealth had been created through government trading by his forebears, Dutch immigrants from Hamburg. In a highly religious household the young Lutyens grew to be a studious boy, unable to take part in vigorous sports due to an early bout of rheumatic fever, but instead making himself master of playing the fool and of verbal as well as visual punning. The family spent their time between London and a house at Thursley in rural Surrey, where young Lutyens gladly absorbed the country ways. His numerous brothers went away to school, but Lutyens was educated at home with his sisters until at 15 he was enrolled at the South Kensington School of Art. Here he fell headlong in love with the disciplines of architectural history and construction. He sketched obsessively, and indeed all his life his letters were dotted with cartoons of people and places and comical ideas, presented with a childlike pleasure. No surprise that he later designed the stage sets for J. M. Barrie's *Peter Pan*.

Lutyens at his drawing board, where he loved to work long hours and well into the night. The pipe was ever present, and smoking doubtless contributed to his death.

Following art school, he was a pupil for 18 months in the office of the great Victorian architects Ernest George and Harold Peto, after which, in 1888, the precocious Lutyens decided he was fit to practise on his own. There was never a time in his career, even at its busiest, when Lutyens was not hungry for work, and over the decades he found himself a sequence of admiring friends, often female, who promoted his skills in affluent society and brought him suitable work. His most famous and productive association was with the Surrey painter, craftswoman and gardener Gertrude Jekyll (p. 222), a blue-stocking spinster 26 years his senior, with whom he struck up the warmest of friendships, based initially on a love of English vernacular architecture. In 1897 he married Emily Lytton of Knebworth House, the daughter of an earl and a former Viceroy of India, and children followed. Later, in middle age, he found himself allied to Victoria Sackville-West, mother of Vita Sackville-West (p. 230), with whom it was rumoured there was more than just friendship.

It was in his early years that his style as a garden designer crystallized. On many of his commissions he would work with Jekyll, she the master plantswoman who would employ her skills in the use of colour and naturalistic gardening to put flesh on the bones of Lutyens's formal layouts. His plans were rarely fussy. His preference was for a strong, simple, unified design centred on the house, with generous inclusion of yew hedges and walls, and with paving delicately detailed in places where it would be effective – perhaps tile-on-edge or flint patterns set into doorways and steps. He loved low-sweeping roofs supported on pillars, large, solid pergolas fit for a painting by Alma-Tadema, and formal, moving water contained in sunken pools, tanks and rills; it is no surprise that his unfinished Liverpool Cathedral was to have contained a sunken altar and organ and running holy water.

Lutyens was taken up by Edward Hudson, the founder of *Country Life* magazine, which featured his work with great enthusiasm. It is instructive to look at the black-and-white *Country Life* photographs in Lawrence Weaver's accounts of Lutyens's gardens when they were brand new. There you can see the way in which, with his intuitive architect's eye, he knew how to be generous with paving, and how when, as today, the planting had softened it and flowed over its edges, the paving would still seem generous and inviting. The boldness, the vigour of those designs has now succumbed unnoticed to the romance of its planting, until its strength is entirely taken for granted.

Commissions for Lutyens's country houses and gardens waxed and waned according to the economic climate. During the First World War work fell away, but revived in the 1920s, only to fall away again in the slump of the 1930s. Those early gardens read like a catalogue of 20th-century greats: Munstead Wood (Jekyll's

TOP *Drawing by Lutyens of a preliminary design for his friend Gertrude Jekyll's house, Munstead Wood, a relatively modest building buried in its garden.* ABOVE Country Life *photograph of the loggia and tank at Folly Farm, Berkshire, a 17th-century house enlarged by Lutyens. Lutyens loved long roofs, and how modern this looks, even today.*

own house), Orchards, Goddards, Abbotswood, Marsh Court, Folly Farm, and both Lindisfarne and the Deanery for Edward Hudson. As the 20th century arrived, Lutyens embraced a more Classical manner – his 'Wrenaissance' period – of which the great example is Heathcote in Yorkshire. Houses further afield followed: Le Bois des Moutiers near Dieppe and Lambay in Ireland. Great Dixter, home of Nathaniel Lloyd, father of Christopher (p. 264), was a brief return to his previous vernacular style. Castle Drogo, on its Devon hilltop, was literally the size and shape of a castle, but built from scratch and with a garden.

After the First World War, Lutyens began to receive more commissions for civic work, in the form of banks and corporate London headquarters, the great monument to the dead at Thiepval on the Somme, and the Cenotaph in Whitehall. It was now that his marriage almost fell apart. It was a sexually frustrating union for

Hestercombe, in Somerset: a Victorian terrace parterre looks down over the grand plat designed by Lutyens and planted by Jekyll. The garden's rills (far right) and semicircular tanks have become icons of 20th-century garden design.

The Thiepval Memorial to the Missing of the Somme (1932), familiar to many people across the world. Lutyens designed many hauntingly beautiful cemeteries in France.

ABOVE The west front of the Viceroy's House. Between his visits to Delhi, Lutyens despaired of the local project management and craftsmanship. The planting in all Lutyens's gardens, even with Jekyll, was relatively simple and blocky. OPPOSITE *Looking west from the Viceroy's House, New Delhi, across the water garden, a modern Versailles. The fountains of red sandstone were based on lilies and built in three tiers.*

Lutyens, and Emily withdrew from the marriage to be an activist in the Suffragette movement and then in Theosophy after she had become besotted with the company of Krishnamurti, the charismatic young Indian who was thought to be the future World Teacher. She was also a supporter of Indian home rule, and became a beloved embarrassment, to Lutyens and to his career.

His greatest project in scale and scope, begun in 1912 and inaugurated in 1931, was his work at New Delhi, for the seat of government of the British Empire in India. It was a project involving town planning as well as monumental architecture in an Anglo-Indian style, which he himself invented, with the Viceroy's House and garden as its centrepiece. At its peak the project employed 3,000 masons and was larger than Versailles. Its garden, grand in the Versailles manner, covered 1.8 ha (4.5 acres).

During the Second World War Lutyens remained in London, hard at work on his abortive cathedral, and in Emily's care died of lung cancer in 1944, brought on no doubt by his ever present pipe of tobacco.

LAWRENCE JOHNSTON

Designing with vistas and enclosed spaces

1871–1958

<table>
<tr><td>

1871

The Paris Commune controls the French capital from March to May.

Verdi's opera *Aida* receives its premiere in Cairo.

Italy unified under King Emmanuele II.

Henry Morton Stanley finds Dr David Livingstone in Africa.

</td><td>

1958

Nikita Khrushchev becomes premier of the Soviet Union.

Bertrand Russell launches the Campaign for Nuclear Disarmament.

USS *Nautilus* becomes the first vessel to travel under the North Pole.

Pius XII declares St Clare the patron saint of television.

</td></tr>
</table>

LAWRENCE JOHNSTON was an enigma. No one claimed to know him well and most people found him reserved, and yet he managed to make a garden, Hidcote Manor, which is regarded as one of the most remarkable of its kind in the world. Johnston was also – and this is highly unusual indeed – a person in whom the two differing skills of garden design and plantsmanship were combined. It is the skill of a great plantsman to be able to put plants together well and to decorate a space with them brilliantly, but to be able to create those spaces in the first place, and to arrange them coherently to make a garden, is a different skill altogether. Johnston, like few others, was a master of both.

Johnston's gravestone carries a contrived coat of arms that illustrates nicely his desire to be an honorary Englishman. He was born in Paris in 1871, to a Baltimore banker father and an heiress mother, and spent much of his childhood between Europe and New York – Europe being then considered by well-to-do Anglo-Saxons as the place where cheap living and a rich culture could happily be found together. When still young, Lawrence lived alone with his mother, Gertrude, who held hard and fast to him. She later remarried, to Charles Winthrop, in London; when he died in 1898, she became the mistress of her own and two inherited fortunes.

In 1897 Johnston graduated from Trinity College, Cambridge, with a second class degree in history. So at home was he in England that in 1900 he took British citizenship and enlisted as a private to fight in the second Boer War in South Africa. He rose quickly through the ranks to be an officer, though found himself curiously out of place: he was to all intents and purposes an American, a short, sandy-haired, stiff little man, with none of the common appurtenances of an officer – no land and no pedigree – even if he was a willing sportsman. Still, by 1913 he was a Major, a title

Hidcote is renowned for the way it is divided into separate 'rooms' of different character. Here a large formal garden with geometric hedges leads through topiary pieces to a small, simpler and circular water garden, followed by a hedge clipped to imitate the gable of a building.

he used for the rest of his life. When the First World War broke out in 1914 he was nearly 43 and back on active service; he was twice wounded and once left for dead.

Gertrude enjoyed the English life just as much as her son, and in 1907 she bought the manor house at Hidcote Bartrim in the Cotswolds, together with its farm and hamlet of cottages, high on an escarpment overlooking the Vale of Evesham, with only a huge cedar and a few rose beds for a garden. Johnston, living on a strict allowance from his mother, was at that time farming in Northumberland, and if Hidcote was intended as a temptation for him to come south again and be near Gertrude, it worked. A separate wing was built for his own use, where he could paint, collect antiques, practise the piano and, in a converted barn, play squash.

In combination with his army life, Johnston took up the running of Hidcote estate, though without great success, before transferring his attentions to making a garden. While Gertrude played her part dutifully as local lady of the manor, Johnston made his firsts forays into garden design, based on his experience of European gardens which he had been accumulating throughout his life. His schemes were lavish, although Gertrude's tight financial leash meant he could never do quite as he pleased; she, like others, was well aware of his lack of financial acumen.

ABOVE Johnston and his team of gardeners; he relied on his staff to execute his plans for Hidcote while he was away at his French garden. OPPOSITE Red borders, steps and pavilion lead to stilted hedges and a view out to the landscape below.

When Johnston returned from the First World War the garden was neglected and in need of rejuvenation, a task he set about with great relish. Realizing he needed some serious, thoughtful help with his project, he employed a head gardener, Frank Adams, who had worked at Windsor Castle and who would stay until his death in 1939 and be Johnston's right-hand man through the creation of Hidcote.

Hidcote grew outwards from the house, even if the house itself did not particularly address the garden in any deliberate way. Johnston's genius, as he developed the garden between the wars, was to create a sequence of hedged garden rooms, one leading to another, the planting in each always specialized in some way to create a contrast between them: a simple pool garden, a garden with a complex pattern of dwarf box hedges, or a garden for phlox. And the planting was sophisticated – a white garden, a peony garden, or a pair of red borders. There were vistas leading to viewpoints over the landscape below and, most significantly, there were calm, simply planted spaces as well as busy, thickly planted ones; some of those simple spaces, like the theatre lawn, were truly enormous. And yet all the time there was a sense of domesticity about the garden as a whole.

For all his reserve, Johnston was not an antisocial creature, so long as the conversation stuck to gardens, and he would often play host to weekend parties. A close friendship developed with the gardener Norah Lindsay, another skilled amateur like himself, who made designs for Blickling Hall in Norfolk, Cliveden in Buckinghamshire, and at Long Barn for Vita Sackville-West (p. 230) before she bought Sissinghurst. He made good friendships with Bobby James and Major Edward Compton, both with fine developing gardens in Yorkshire, at St Nicholas and Newby Hall. He also took part in plant-hunting expeditions, to the amusement and sometimes dismay of his travelling companions, famous collectors such as Frank Kingdon Ward and George Forrest, who were exasperated by Johnston's fussiness and desire to take his domestic staff on trips into wild, uncharted country. Yet good things came out of his involvement; new-found plants such as *Hypericum* 'Hidcote' and *Mahonia lomariifolia*, championed and distributed by him, became stalwarts of modern gardens. The lavender 'Hidcote', which he introduced, is one of the best known and favourite varieties of this popular plant.

Gertrude, meanwhile, like many of her contemporaries, was spending her winters on the French Riviera, away from Hidcote's cold, windy ridge. By the early 1920s she was suffering from dementia and was installed in a nursing home there. Johnston, now not without his own physical infirmities, decided to buy a property nearby. He chose a farmhouse, Serre de la Madone, near Menton. Naturally, given a few months there every year, he set about making a garden. This was a far less sophisticated affair than Hidcote, more a set of terraces of carefully coloured plant-ing, where he could grow all those more tender plants for which Hidcote was not a suitable home. From mid-October to May, Johnston was in France, and for the rest of the year at Hidcote, busily developing the garden and then leaving it to Adams to continue his great projects – the pillar garden, the woodland garden – during the winter. Johnston's mother died in 1926, but to his great chagrin, rather than inherit-ing her capital and investments, he was left only an annual income from interest, and so any plans for greater things in either garden were never realized.

Johnston remained in France when the German army occupied the country in the Second World War, but when the Italians entered the war in 1940 he was evacu-ated by ship to Britain. Hidcote had been requisitioned for military use, and its large kitchen garden was producing vegetables to supply local hospitals. It cannot have fitted in with Johnston's inclinations: he always preferred Hidcote to be thoroughly private, for him and his friends, and he was reluctant ever to open it to the public.

By 1942 the dementia that had stricken his mother was beginning to trouble Johnston, mostly in the form of extended lapses of memory. The garden began to be an old man's garden, a little shabby, his favoured dense planting never properly thinned as it developed. Adams was no longer there to be the practical guiding force, and Johnston himself was acting as his own rather tired head gardener.

Some of Hidcote's garden rooms are very simple and spare of detail. How French this looks, with clean trunks rising from gravel, bright light and hard shadow, as if in a village square.

Single or childless makers of great gardens almost invariably seek at the last to ensure the future of their gardens after their death; for Hidcote, being a garden of great structure, largely in the form of hedges, this made sense. The late 1940s, with Europe still impoverished by the war, was not a time for the luxury of garden visiting by the public. Cars were few and the tradition of popular garden tourism had not emerged. Still, after much dithering on Johnston's part, Hidcote was finally handed to the National Trust in 1948. It was the Trust's first garden for visiting independently (the house was retained for summer use by Johnston, then let) and it ran at a loss. It marked a precedent for the National Trust, which today owns and opens more great gardens, and in better condition, than any other organization in the world.

After only rare return visits to Hidcote, Johnston settled permanently at Serre de la Madone, where he lived for a further eight years. There is a satisfying logic to the fact that, ten years after Johnston left Hidcote to the Trust, the first guidebook to the garden was written by Vita Sackville-West, whose garden at Sissinghurst could never have been made without the precedent of Hidcote.

OPPOSITE AND ABOVE In Johnston's day, Serre de la Madone was a rural retreat with a garden of terraces looking out across a small valley. Today the setting is suburban and trees must provide privacy. The garden is undergoing restoration.

Serre de la Madone was left not to the Trust to help finance Hidcote, but to Nancy Lindsay, daughter of his friend Norah. The upkeep proved too much for her, however, and it was sold, some of its plants being sent to the Cambridge University Botanic Garden. Thereafter its fortunes sank, until in the 1980s moves were made to restore it, but by then Johnston's 'country' retreat was in a green suburb and its views were ruined. It inevitably remains an interesting shadow of its former self, while Hidcote is in fine form, even if the popularity of gardening today has made it inordinately busy (Johnston would have been appalled). And yet he himself was never able to fund it properly. He would surely see that the maintenance of a large, intensive garden is expensive, and far more so now than in his day.

Perhaps compared with today's fashion for ever more naturalistic planting, Hidcote may seem a rather stolid affair, everything carefully arranged within its enclosing hedges; and yet the variety of those garden rooms, the loving care expended on those hedges, the sweep of its open spaces and the vistas with which they conclude, never fail to dazzle everybody. Johnston's creative brilliance was to combine that flair for planting with the ability to create spaces, and all from one pair of hands.

RUSSELL PAGE

Master of scale and composition

1906–1985

<table>
<tr><td>

1906

RMS *Lusitania* is launched by the Cunard Line in
    Glasgow and is briefly the world's largest ship.
Alois Alzheimer presents the pathology and symptoms of
    pre-senile dementia.
Birth of the English poet John Betjeman.
Rachmaninov's Second Symphony completed.

</td><td>

1985

Mikhail Gorbachev comes to power in Russia.
The British Antarctic Survey identifies a hole in the
    ozone layer.
DNA first used in a criminal case.
South Africa ends the ban on interracial marriage.

</td></tr>
</table>

RUSSELL PAGE was one of the few gardeners to keep alive the tradition of formal gardens in Europe after the Second World War. His work, which could be large or small, private or corporate, was almost always quiet, elegant, understated and often undertaken for rich clients, although he himself was not primarily interested in the financial rewards for his work. As many of his projects were for private clients, and Page was quiet and reserved, he was perhaps not widely known outside such circles. But he was highly regarded and in great demand in his lifetime. Today the quality of his work is once again beginning to be recognized.

Page was the son of a Lincoln solicitor and was schooled at Charterhouse. Like Graham Stuart Thomas (p. 244) and Christopher Lloyd (p. 264), he showed a precocious interest in plants and gardening, which undoubtedly gave him a head start when he finally began his career as a garden designer. The man himself was and would remain lean, spare, angular, rarely without a cigarette. After Charterhouse there followed three years' study at the Slade School of Art in London, then five years studying art in Paris, during which time he met several people, including André de Vilmorin, son of the famous French horticultural firm, who would be influential; his career took off. Jobs in France came his way, at Melun and at Boussy St Antoine, where he recounted that a fine library did wonders for his aesthetic education. His Paris years also gave him the chance to look at French architecture and the great French formal gardens of the 17th century; it was here he came to realize

*The Frick Collection Garden, New York (see p. 116 for Page's drawing). Page was a master
of simple, formal pools set beside plain lawns, a cool arrangement as good in shade as in sun.*

that, when making a garden, form and structure are so much more important than plants – and this is from an able plantsman. Page became a true son of Le Nôtre; his initial approach to a garden design, he said, was as an artist, preoccupied with the relationship between objects – planting came later.

Back in England in 1932, he was employed by the landscape architect Richard Sudell and began work at Longleat in Somerset, a project that would continue into the 1950s. Longleat had lost its formal gardens around the house long before, when a 'Capability' Brown park had been created over older geometric gardens. Page's plan was to put back some formal, more invitingly liveable gardening around the house, removing some trees and planting hedges, colourful flowering trees and shrubs.

Gradually his reputation began to grow. Between 1934 and 1938 he was invited to

contribute to the magazine *Landscape and Gardening*, and in 1935–39 he worked with Geoffrey Jellicoe, the most highly respected British landscape architect of the day. Page worked alongside architects and decorators on prestigious projects such as the Royal Lodge, Windsor, Ditchley Park in Oxfordshire, Leeds Castle in Kent and around the brave new architecture of the Caveman Restaurant at the Cheddar Gorge in Somerset. Projects continued in France and Belgium, and for two years he lectured at the University of Reading.

Then came the war. Page spent his time working for the political warfare executive, posted in France, the USA, Egypt and Ceylon (Sri Lanka), and no doubt becoming familiar with different climates and floras along the way. When the war ended, he set up home in Paris and found plenty of clients in France and Belgium, and occasionally in Switzerland. In 1947 he married Lida Gurdjieff, niece of the spiritual philosopher George Gurdjieff, whom Page greatly admired. A son, David, was born, but the couple divorced in 1954. Page immediately remarried, to Vera Milanova Daumal, widow of the poet René Daumal.

Britain was a drab place in those post-war years; food and clothing were rationed and the public purse was empty. And so it was decided by the government that in 1951 there would be a Festival of Britain, centred on the south bank of the Thames in London. It would be a celebration of recovery, a return to colour and a reminder

Drawing by Page for a pavilion in the garden at Battersea for the Festival of Britain. Everything about the event was to be light and bright, to relieve the post-war blues.
Photograph of a young Russell Page.

that things were at last looking up, and was to be, in effect, a giant fairground and showcase for innovation. Page was called in to landscape the Festival Gardens in Battersea Park. His central formal space became celebrated for its massive blocks of brightly coloured tulips donated from Holland and for the sheets of colourful bedding plants that followed, creating a succession of colour for the length of the Festival. It may not have been subtle but it was joyful – a whole generation remembers it – and it cost Page eighteen months' work, for which he was awarded the OBE.

Page moved permanently back to London in 1962, the year his second wife died, and he took a small flat in Cadogan Square in Chelsea, where his one indulgence was a collection of Persian carpets. It was to be an important year, marking the publication of his artistic manifesto and manual, *The Education of a Gardener*. Along with Thomas Church's *Gardens Are for People* and John Brookes's *Room Outside*, it must fall into that small list of 20th-century books that have shaped the views of all subsequent garden-makers. But if those other two books took a more practical approach to teaching design, Page's book was aesthetically aimed, partly autobiographical, not remotely difficult to read or understand, but still more philo-sophical in its approach. It had a touching universality that has ensured its place in the canon of important garden books.

Page remained in London for the rest of his life, travelling to clients through-out Europe, his style perhaps in general becoming rather more plant-rich as the 1970s went by. In the USA he worked at the Frick Collection in New York, Washington's United States National Arboretum and on the sculpture park at PepsiCo's headquarters in upstate New York. In Britain he worked at Badminton House for Lady Caroline Somerset, creating a garden rich in roses, low box hedges and white-painted trellis. At Port Lympne in Kent, famous for its temple-topped Great Staircase which Philip Tilden designed for Sir Philip Sassoon, Page replanted a 124-m (406-ft) long border for the new owner John Aspinall. In Italy he worked at La Landriana outside Rome and at La Mortella on the island of Ischia for the English composer Sir William Walton and Lady Walton.

The wonder of Page's work is its simplicity, which, for him, had a spiritual purpose. He knew how to make fine but not grandiose terraces and lily pools

Page's drawing for the Frick Garden, New York, designed to be looked at but not entered. With its screen gateway and the delicate false windows it looks very Mediterranean.

The Orange Garden, La Landriana, south of Rome. Although perhaps somewhat busy for Page, the plain, ground-hugging greenery is a fine setting for the perfumed lollipops of orange blossom.

(swimming pools, too), using the best quality materials and workmanship. His planting never required more maintenance than his clients could understand or pay for, and he often revisited projects to check on their development. His blueprint for hot climates – clipped hedges and evergreens highlighted by massed bedding plants and roses – was elegant and discreet. How ironic it is that those same plants, as seen in post-war suburban gardens without Page's wonderful structure to rest on, have been so derided as boring and kitsch. But looked at in the longer view, Page's planting was in a sense always old-fashioned; it had a degree of High Victorian formality about it, but it was made fresh by transporting it into smaller, more glamorous gardens and more welcoming spaces. It was aristocratic and domestic, and perfectly in tune with the contemporary approach to the great country houses as expressed by hostess and

View looking down on to the pool at La Mortella, Ischia, designed by Page for Sir William and Lady Walton. It was a new venture for Page to concentrate on a palette of exotic plants.

decorator Nancy Tree (later Lancaster) at Ditchley Park – to make beautiful but bleak old houses modern and comfortable, as well as timelessly elegant.

For all his ability to resist the temptation to overplant a garden, when a client was open to a richer planting he could and would provide it. His first work at La Mortella was a pool below the house surrounded by plants that would survive in the dry, inhospitable conditions. He knew from experience what would thrive there. Later, when water was generously on offer, he created a lush planting of exotics instead, a tropical jungle of a totally different nature, with plants from all over the world. He also included a formal rill in the Moorish style, which he had come to admire through following the writings of the spiritual philosopher Idries Shah.

Page hated to see his work diluted or changed by his clients or their successors and he would no doubt be sad today to see how few of his gardens remain unaltered; but such is the fate of all garden-makers. Among the best surviving examples of his work is the Villa Silvio Pellico in the Po valley near Turin, made in the 1950s. It has his signature falling terraces, on the lowest of which is a simple rectangular pool.

There are hedges aplenty for separating the various spaces of the garden (Lawrence Johnston's Hidcote was a huge influence on Page) and for making patterns on the ground. His La Landriana has another rectangular lily pool on a lower terrace, serene but with gentle surface jets and protected by tall evergreen trees.

Page's papers were left to his friends Robert and Jelena de Belder, makers of the famous arboretum at Kalmthout in Belgium, and are now held by the Garden Museum in London; drawings and photographs also went to the Royal Horticultural Society library. He is buried at Badminton, Gloucestershire, in an unmarked grave.

Villa Silvio Pellico, near Turin, made just after the war, must have been a great gesture of optimism, so fresh and bright and open, pushing out into the landscape with all the thrust of an Italian Renaissance villa garden.

NICOLE DE VÉSIAN

Topiary Mediterranean style

1916–1996

1916
On the first day of the battle of the Somme, the British
    suffer 57,470 casualties.
Composer Gustav Holst writes *The Planets*.
The Easter Rising declares an Irish Republic.
The car manufacturer BMW founded in Munich.

1996
An Irish Republican Army bomb injures 200 in
    Manchester, England.
In Afghanistan the Taliban capture Kabul.
Birth of Dolly the sheep, the first cloned mammal.
Death of jazz singer Ella Fitzgerald.

GREAT GARDEN-MAKING is a multi-disciplinary art. It demands that a maker should have a strong aesthetic sense, a profound awareness of space and a good grasp of practical matters, as well as the ability to anticipate a garden's fourth dimension: the passage of time. Into this mixture, makers bring their own particular skills and specialisms, perhaps from other disciplines – geometry and proportion from architecture, the use of colour and light from painting, a desire to express in gardening ideas that have come from politics or science or history.

Nicole de Vésian's personal magic came from the world of fashion, in particular the elegant, Parisian chic for which, as a designer and stylist for Hermès, she became legendary. She was born Nicole Llewellyn, the daughter of a Parisian banker of Welsh descent. Her French mother was from Avignon, in Provence, the region where Nicole would spend the last ten years of her life making her garden.

When the Second World War came and the Germans were about to take Paris, she fled south like so many others, short of money and trying to make ends meet with two small children in tow. Always practical and resourceful, she grew vegetables and managed to make the kind of stylish, attractive clothes she enjoyed from whatever came

OPPOSITE *Nicole de Vésian in later years, as chic and tanned as ever.* ABOVE *Lines of clipped lavenders below the house at La Louve remind one of resting chess pieces.*

to hand. She even took a job delivering letters. But the glamorous life was never far from Nicole de Vésian, and she found her own artistically sympathetic company, including the avant-garde writer Gertrude Stein and her partner Alice B. Toklas.

After the war the family moved back to the wealthy Auteuil district of Paris, where they bought a fine 1920s house in the style of a Roman villa. By the 1960s she was able to set up an advertising agency, and soon after established her own company, Nouvelle Vision, in the basement of what had once been a coal depot in the Rue de l'Élysée, close to the presidential palace. From here she travelled regularly to New York to advise her many international clients on modern styles in all things, from fabrics to shoes to table linen. Life was a race and she relished it. If the logo for Nouvelle Vision also spelled her initials, well, it was her life, glamorous and rigorous. She dressed with real elegance as her career demanded, but simply, in her favourite beiges, chignon swept high as she drove to work in her beloved green Austin Princess, the sunroof open to let in every drop of sunshine.

The lavender terrace undergoing its annual clipping. The combination of grey-green foliage planted together with darkest evergreens is a constant ground-note of de Vésian's gardens.

At 60 she reduced her workload and began to work solely for Hermès. Fabrics were her speciality, but she applied her stylist's eye to every product, always favouring a look that was simple and stylish. Then aged 69 she retired completely, to live a quieter life in the south of France, where the sun shone more reliably. For a year she and her husband lived in the Luberon village of Bonnieux, in an old chapel which had been converted into a cinema; it was the kind of challenge that appealed to de Vésian. But when her husband died in 1986 she made yet another fresh start.

In one of the streets at the edge of Bonnieux, looking south across a narrow valley, was a ruined property known as La Louve, so called because the last she-wolf in the region was said to have been killed there in 1957. It appealed to her instantly. With privacy and yet with good views, the house sat at the centre of its plot, sufficiently derelict to permit a major rearrangement of the interior spaces. She bought it and spent the next ten years making one of France's most influential gardens – small, but admired by everyone who saw it and establishing a contemporary idiom for Provençal gardens. It has since been designated a 'Garden of Significance' by the French government.

The garden continues today in the spirit in which it was made, largely unaltered except for a pool, and still in private hands. De Vésian sold it a year before her death, since osteoporosis and crutches made life in such a steep garden too difficult for her. It was then bought by Judy Pillsbury, an American dealer in prints living in Paris, who went on to marry William Waterfield, himself the owner of the famous Menton garden, Le Clos du Peyronnet.

La Louve is a garden made from the land on which it lies. Stone walls support its terraces just as they do those for vines across the region. Stone troughs and stone balls are used as punctuation among the planting and open spaces. The trees – pine, arbutus, cypress, juniper – all belong to the local agricultural landscape, and are part of the way that the landscape has been used and intensively managed for thousands of years. De Vésian chose to look after her shrubs in a similarly manipulative way, clipping and pruning them spring and autumn, not into perfect geometrical forms but as individuals, making the best of their particular trunks and stems, though never relinquishing that directing agricultural hand. Her shapes became characters, not

De Vésian had the ability to mass a multitude of clipped shapes and yet still manage not to make them look hectic, setting them at rest by ensuring some shapes were large enough to be anchors for the smaller ones.

extravagant but quietly cooperative, and her great skill was to group these cubes and balls, domes, discs and dolmens in a way that was comfortable and balanced, varied but still calm, and (which is the greatest skill) to do so without making an effect that was spotty. Moreover, she could do it in a way that made a satisfying composition from all sides and also create a happy frame for the landscape beyond. Some of her more curiously shaped plants, including the signature flat-topped pencil cypresses, were encouraged to take those forms because de Vésian had thriftily bought cheap, damaged stock in the first place.

The garden has regular rhythms in its shapes. A parterre is the focus of the main terrace, for example, but one consisting of clipped lavender, which owes its manner more to the rows of Provençal lavender farmed for oil than it does to Renaissance garden style. Light in the Luberon is strong, and it creates a scene that changes hourly in a garden as full as this one is of firm, rhythmical shapes. Curiously for a scheme that sets out to involve the vernacular, de Vésian used no potted plants. She always had a gardener helping her, and she herself worked long hours in the garden, so it was not for lack of labour to water them. Rather it was part of her desire to have simplicity of line; flowers, yes, but in the ground, not dancing in pots drawing attention to themselves. And yet it was not severe or unwelcoming – there were plenty of places to sit, in sun or shade, alone to enjoy the view, or socially around a table.

De Vésian was no paper designer, although she did collect snippets from magazines to help define her ideas. She liked to see things set out on the ground and move them around until by trial and error they seemed 'right', and it worked. She used the same technique when she was helping others with their gardens, something she did with great success. Her notable clients included the film director Ridley Scott and French Minister of Culture Jack Lang. She also encouraged the careers of other garden-makers in the region, such as the sculptor Marc Nucera and designer Alain David Idoux.

After ten years creating La Louve, she lost interest in it, as well as finding its many different levels troublesome, so she sold it and bought an area of scrub on flat land above the village, Les Blayons, where she could make a new house and garden. Great outcrops of exposed rock and scrubby trees under which truffles grew promised an even simpler, more elemental garden, perhaps in line with concepts of Japanese gardens that she had come to admire. Sadly, she died before it could be achieved, but La Louve lives on much as she left it.

La Louve in winter, composed of nothing but natural, local plants and materials. De Vésian's gardens regularly used paths or tracks that swept across a terrace before rising or dropping down a level at the end.

PENELOPE HOBHOUSE

Renaissance principles in a modern idiom

BORN 1929

1929
The Wall Street Crash sets off the Great Depression.
Stalin sends Trotsky into exile.
Mussolini signs the Lateran Treaty recognizing Vatican
    City as a sovereign state.
Mies van der Rohe designs the Barcelona chair.

PENELOPE HOBHOUSE is perhaps the last of a particularly British breed of lady gardeners who have successfully found their way into the world of garden design and emerged triumphant on the international stage. Indeed, in the last years of the 20th century, along with Rosemary Verey (p. 258), she became synonymous with glamorous English country gardens and was in demand internationally.

Born Penelope Chichester-Clark, her family home was the 18th-century mansion Moyola Park, near Castledawson in Northern Ireland. Her father had been a Member of Parliament, as would be her brother Robin; her brother James became Prime Minister of Northern Ireland. At Girton College, Cambridge (women only) she became a good friend of the botanist and Classics don John Raven, while her various academic relatives in the university meant she mixed in the company of the great and good. She graduated in Economics in 1951, and a year later was married.

Her husband, Paul Hobhouse, was a farmer and son of Sir Arthur Hobhouse, of Hadspen House in Somerset. Three children arrived during the first years of the marriage and at their home on the Hadspen estate Hobhouse had a cottage garden in which she was able to teach herself about plants and the practicalities of gardening. When she was left the money to buy a farmhouse near Florence she began to spend time there, visiting the Italian Renaissance villa gardens. From these, she learned about structure and proportion, and how a garden should relate to its house. She led garden tours in Italy, France and Germany.

On the death of Paul's father in 1967 the couple moved into Hadspen House itself. Its garden had been made by Paul's grandmother in Edwardian times and had not been well cared for since before the Second World War. Now was the time to make it sing again. This would be a lesson in far larger-scale and more sophisticated

Penelope Hobhouse is always happy to be in gardening clothes, although she has spent much of her time addressing international audiences of gardeners.

Pink double borders at Tintinhull. Hobhouse developed a romantic English style far less heavy than Jekyll's and far more sophisticated than that of a traditional cottage garden.

gardening, using a much broader range of plants, and formed the basis of her book *The Country Gardener* (1976). Generous encouragement came from the gardening world, especially from the gardener and author Margery Fish at East Lambrook Manor, Somerset, and from the Heathcoat-Amorys of Knightshayes Court, Devon. But after 28 years, the marriage foundered and she left Hadspen in 1983, determined to earn her own living. (The garden was subsequently leased by a Canadian couple, Nori and Sandra Pope, whose colour schemes in the borders of the walled garden made Hadspen famous. Later, and to her disappointment, Hobhouse's son Niall had the walled garden bulldozed and held a competition for a design for its replanting, which never materialized. The house was then sold.)

On leaving Hadspen, and with her children grown up, Hobhouse moved not far away to Tintinhull, a substantial 18th-century house owned by the National Trust. The 3-ha (7-acre) garden had been established in the 1930s and 1940s by Phyllis Reiss, who had given it a fine series of formal garden rooms after the manner of its contemporaries at Hidcote and Sissinghurst. For Hobhouse, the tenancy was a chance to garden on an ambitiously conceived layout, somewhere she could apply her own ebullient but carefully coloured planting schemes. It was a rare opportunity, made financially possible through her remarriage to John Malins, a passionate gardener and retired Professor of Medicine at Birmingham University. They employed one gardener and gardened full-time themselves.

Tintinhull was a garden of vistas linking progressions of rectilinear spaces along their way, some of which were defined by the colour of their planting and others by a fountain or topiary. The pool garden is a familiar image of Tintinhull, with its broad, stone-edged canal running down the centre of a lawn flanked by gloriously colourful borders, leading to a Classical open loggia. It has a flavour of Islamic and Moorish gardens, something the landscape architect Sylvia Crowe pointed out, and this axial canal was a motif Hobhouse would use in several of her later garden designs, most publicly at the walled garden she made for the government agency English Heritage at Walmer Castle in Kent, to celebrate the 95th birthday of The Queen Mother.

Formally arranged and flamboyantly planted pots were a feature of Tintinhull, providing punctuation to the conversation between the garden's various rooms. But it was the dominance of the house that set Tintinhull apart from Hidcote and Sissinghurst. Hidcote was a muddle of a house that cast a minimal and rather backward glance on its garden. Sissinghurst lacked a significant house; it comprised a

The pool garden and loggia at Tintinhull. Lawrence Johnston might have kept this simpler and flower free, but Hobhouse always includes the softness of flower borders somewhere nearby.

ABOVE *The gravel garden at the Coach House, Bettiscombe, is modern in style and without any lawn.* OPPOSITE *The herb garden at the New York Botanical Garden; America loved the gently old-fashioned Englishness of both Hobhouse and Rosemary Verey.*

series of converted buildings scattered around the garden. Tintinhull, on the other hand, was undoubtedly a house of dignity, substantial but not grand, and sitting responsibly at the end of a main vista in a golden glow of stone. It became famous for the image of the house, taken square on, flanked by eagle-topped pillars and an avenue of low topiary. More Classical, more old-fashioned, more aristocratic than the other two, Tintinhull was just as capable of carrying the same rich planting. Hobhouse could certainly provide that, and she admits she was unquestionably Tintinhull's decorator rather than its designer; that credit falls to Phyllis Reiss (Hobhouse had met her, briefly, twice).

Tintinhull became nationally and internationally known, and after the publication of *Colour in Your Garden* (1985), Hobhouse began to be consulted on gardens by the rich and famous in city and country. She fitted in well to affluent circles and at that time Englishness in gardens was highly desirable and exportable. Never one to turn down a challenge, and forging her career, Hobhouse welcomed these consultations and gradually they became a business. She was aware that her skills were principally as a planting designer, so she found professional associates such as Stuart Grey, trained in landscape architecture, whose technical command of design and construction complemented her own artistic and horticultural abilities. America loved her, both as a gardener and lecturer, and the cable and satellite channel House and Garden Television commissioned her to host a series of programmes called *The Art and Practice of Gardening*.

Hobhouse went on to make gardens for the New York Botanical Garden, the Philadelphia Flower Show and a host of private clients including Steve Jobs, co-founder of the Apple Corporation. In Britain there were commissions for a garden for the ruins of a 14th-century priory on Oronsay, Scotland, a country garden in the Royal Horticultural Society's garden, Wisley, and a garden at Aberglasney in Wales.

John Malins died in 1992 and Hobhouse gave up Tintinhull the following year. The book which reviewed her work there was *On Gardens* (1994). Unlike *The Country Gardener*, it arrived in the age of glamorous garden photography that gave books a previously undreamt of attractiveness; they could be coffee-table books as well as instruction for gardeners. Hobhouse's numerous books always repay study, and several, such as *Plants in Garden History* (1992), are thoroughly educational in nature.

After Tintinhull, she moved to a 0.4-ha (1-acre) garden of her own, at Bettiscombe, in Somerset, where she found herself having to design her own garden for the first time. The house was a conversion of old farm buildings with a walled garden to the rear, and she experimented with a more natural planting, taking a cue from the gardens of Beth Chatto (p. 272) and John Brookes (p. 194). It was while at Bettiscombe that she got to know the gardens of Iran and began to lead tours there. *The Gardens of Persia* was published in 2003. She eventually had to give up Bettiscombe and moved to a flat in the stables at Hadspen, near to her son, but when he decided to sell Hadspen, she moved yet again, to a small house in a village nearby with a garden of 17 x 17 m (56 x 56 ft), where she still happily gardens. She was awarded the MBE for services to horticulture in 2014.

CHRISTOPHER BRADLEY-HOLE

Harmony through order and pure proportions

BORN 1951

1951
Opening of the Royal Festival Hall and Festival of Britain
    in London.
Death of philosopher Ludwig Wittgenstein.
First experimental nuclear power plant, in Idaho.
Publication of J. D. Salinger's *The Catcher in the Rye*.

WITH THE INCREASING power of television to influence popular attitudes to garden design, recent decades have often witnessed the triumph of style over idea. Increasingly gardens began to be regarded not as places to cultivate plants in the post-war tradition, but, like the 1950s gardens of Thomas Church (p. 176), as places requiring minimal maintenance in which to relax, eat, drink and admire a few fashionable plants of the moment. The days of grand designs were drawing to a close, and the size of gardens was rapidly shrinking. Imaginative, provocative garden installations became popular, but were a puzzle to the public eye, which confused them with real, usable gardens.

Into this stylistic muddle came one of the great proponents of modern garden design, Christopher Bradley-Hole. Here at last was a designer working with an awareness of proportion and sensitivity to detail that Lutyens (p. 96) had shown; both were architects, but the earlier working in a Classical idiom, the other a Modernist one, and with a much greater interest in decorative planting than his predecessor.

Bradley-Hole enjoyed gardening even as a teenager, yet his precise nature was lining him up for accountancy until the desire to do something more creative led him to study architecture at the University of Brighton. An ambitious career in commercial architecture followed, progressing from a job in a London office to a partnership. But then he caught the gardening bug. Evenings and weekends were spent visiting gardens and garden centres and buying plants simply to get to know them. He admired John Brookes's seminal book *Room Outside*, and a visit to the garden at Great Dixter found him appreciating Christopher Lloyd's planting almost as much as the spaces designed by Lutyens.

Christopher Bradley-Hole is as careful and enthusiastic a plantsman as he is a lover of architectural precision and proportion. The two do not often go together.

A course in the conservation of historic landscapes, parks and gardens at the Architectural Association put gardens in context, but made him wonder why there was no real Modernism in British gardens. It left him desperate to find like minds – people who agreed that the end of the era of Arts and Crafts-inspired gardens was fast approaching, that in many ways English gardening was a 'cultural desert' eclipsed by new, modern work in Germany and Denmark, and that the last real attempt at Modernism in English gardens had come from Christopher Tunnard in the 1930s (he then left for America) and to some extent from John Brookes (p. 194).

ABOVE The Latin Garden, Chelsea, 1997, which Bradley-Hole described as 'an exploration of the relationship between Nature, culture, and cultivation'. BELOW A London roof garden is surrounded by grasses, which move in the wind, cast little shade and contrast with the solid roofscape of the surrounding Victorian terraces.

Bradley-Hole's transition from architect to garden designer came in his 40s. The first issue of *Gardens Illustrated* magazine included a competition to design a garden for the 1994 Chelsea Flower Show. He entered it speculatively and won. As a result of this success commissions came for a garden and some writing in the *Telegraph* newspaper about clients and contracts. (He has currently made seven Chelsea gardens, and far from finding the present show too much of a media jamboree, sees it still as an unparalleled opportunity to showcase new things: 'it's a perk of the profession – someone else pays and you get the publicity.')

In 1997 the *Telegraph* asked him to design a Chelsea garden. For inspiration his 'Latin Garden' took the life and verses of the Roman poet Virgil, and it won Best in Show. He was then commissioned to write the highly successful *The Minimalist Garden*. Since 2000 he has been able to concentrate solely on gardens rather than architecture. 'Landscape is all about the detail,' he says, 'and architecture about distance. Gardens should have an idea behind them, there should be rigour.' *Making the Modern Garden* followed in 2007.

With Piet Oudolf (p. 280), Rob Leopold and others, he became part of the Perennial Perspectives group, which arose out of a seminal conference of that name at Kew in 1994 led by Brita von Schoenaich and Tim Rees. This promoted the public use of massed perennials that had begun in Germany in the early 20th century under Karl Foerster and later under Richard Hansen. It was a looser, more modern approach to planting, which accompanied perfectly Bradley-Hole's rigorous and harmonious Golden Mean-inspired geometry.

Among Bradley-Hole's best-known gardens is that for John Coke at Bury Court, Hampshire, which displays exactly his pleasure in geometry – here in the form of an actual grid – softened by loose planting and grasses. And it is all the more telling since it is partnered by a garden from Piet Oudolf on the other side of the house. This has echoes of that great 19th-century contrast of garden aesthetics between naturalist William Robinson (p. 208) and the geometric gardener Reginald Blomfield. Bradley-Hole is a great admirer of Oudolf's approach to gardens and planting; further praise goes to John Brookes as the pioneer of modern gardens and to Fernando Caruncho (p. 138) in Spain for the energy of his work.

Alongside Bradley-Hole's enjoyment of clean, spacious planting is a love of plants which have been given sculptural forms through a respectful refining of shape that living has given to each individual specimen or species. He travels a great deal to nurseries; German tree nurserymen remain an object of great admiration, providing him with 'a university education without the university'. Visits to Japan's gardens ancient and modern have been a revelation in the way they manipulate plants and

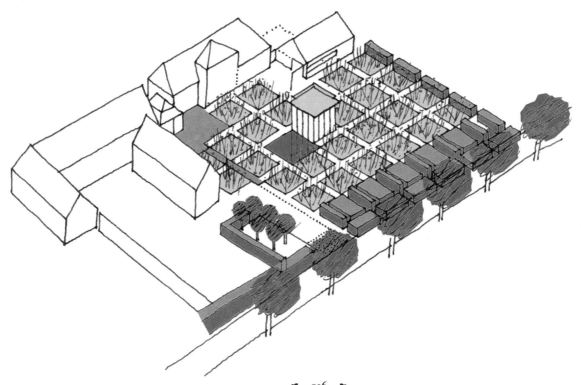

relate to the wider landscape. In Bradley-Hole's own gardens, the refined, sculptural forms of trees are a telling part of the architecture. Today he is working as far afield as Sweden, Germany and Singapore.

Yet however much Bradley-Hole is an architect who loves plants and planting, for him spaces are what garden-making is all about, for it is in the relationship between spaces, and the rigour with which that is thought through, that make a garden an intellectually and emotionally satisfying whole. Currently his fascination is in making gardens which in their design and planting represent a microcosm of the surrounding landscape or are sculpted out of the landscape itself. It would be good to see Bradley-Hole making a mark in larger-scale public spaces, but perhaps his manner is too intimate for the purpose. His office remains small and he likes it that way.

OPPOSITE *Bury Court (photograph and 3D visualization) is a garden with determined geometry centred on the pool and pavilion, but whose grid is disguised by lush summer planting.* BELOW *The Old Rectory: once again, an underlying grid is conspicuous from above but largely invisible on the ground because of generous planting.*

FERNANDO CARUNCHO

Light, water and the language of geometry

BORN 1957

1957
In the USA Gordon Gould invents the laser.
Leonard Bernstein's *West Side Story* opens on Broadway.
The Cavern Club opens in Liverpool
The Treaty of Rome establishes the European Economic
    Community (later EU).

FERNANDO CARUNCHO is commonly referred to as a minimalist working on a grand scale. There is some truth in this, but it is slightly to miss the point, for some elements of his gardens and landscapes are used in great profusion – water, trees and clipped evergreens. What matters most in Caruncho's designs, no matter what the scale, is simplicity. Always, he wonders what he can take away that will strengthen the garden. It is his greatest skill to know exactly how far one can go down the road of Less Is More to produce something shockingly beautiful, before reaching the point of aridness, where some minimalists have foundered.

There is so much that is Spanish about Caruncho's work. He was born in Madrid and he remembers well spending the summer holidays surrounded by the scents of boxwood and jasmine in the houses of his grandparents in Galicia, where the climate is mild and moist, and at Ronda in baking Andalucía, where the family could walk under Judas trees to look out at that stupendous valley far below. Even as a boy he came away moved by the effect of light on that view, the way its 'vibration' can bring the world to life.

Philosophy has always been Caruncho's abiding love and it is no surprise that it was philosophy that he studied at Madrid University and philosophy that brought him to gardens. Had not Plato taught in a garden? In the ancient world were not gardens respected as a link between the physical and metaphysical? Man and nature, said his hero the playwright Euripides, are all one. Making gardens would, for

Clipped, asymmetrically placed evergreens anchor a house comfortably and less competitively than symmetry would do. The scene is saved from stiffness by slender rising cypresses and the implied motion of the clipped shapes.

Camp Sarch, Minorca: pillows of clipped evergreens soften the power of the grid (compare Bradley-Hole's blocks of grasses), as well as distracting from a sloping change of levels.

Caruncho, be a way of defining that vision of nature, and so, with confidence, he changed course and went to study landscape design at the Castillo de Batres School, Madrid, graduating in 1979.

Everyone needs a lucky start in life and Caruncho was indeed lucky. He made a garden for his uncle around a house in Madrid designed by the Austrian-American Modernist architect Richard Neutra as part of a post-war development for the US Air Force, then still present in Spain. A feature followed in the French magazine *Vogue* and Caruncho found himself in the public gaze. The garden owed much to Japanese influence in its use of gravel, standing stones and ferns, but it also displayed many of Caruncho's future trademarks: the abstract formality of escallonia clipped into rolling organic shapes, simple pergolas and reflecting geometric pools.

The Japanese garden Ryoan-ji, simple and refined to the last degree, was a favourite of Caruncho, and he admires English landscape architects William Kent, 'Capability' Brown and Russell Page, who knew how to use space well. But he also loved the highly formal European tradition and its masterpieces at Vaux-le-Vicomte,

France, the Boboli gardens in Italy and in Spain the gardens of Aranjuez and La Granja and the Alhambra, which incorporated the Moorish tradition of rills, fountains and cruciform paths. The makers of all these gardens knew how to manipulate and harmonize the three elements of water, plants and architecture, although crucially, to Caruncho's mind, a gardener must also manipulate a fourth element – light.

Crisp-edged, rectilinear geometry is a major element in all he does, in particular in the form of grids, which appeared increasingly in his gardens. But Caruncho has also always used those sinuously clipped evergreens in idealized natural curves to contrast with the straight lines – vegetable, three-dimensional volumes as a counterpoint to the flat geometric planes of walls, water and paving. And contrast in all art forms is what engages the eye. Caruncho himself does not see the use of a grid form as a rigid imposition on his gardens, even if he recognizes that the straight line must always be an unnatural thing, a rational construct of man. Rather, he sees a grid as 'a net thrown over the space', to help him understand it, just as the ancient Assyrians used geometry to measure the stars. For him, geometry is not the object of a garden, but simply a means to creating harmony.

A grid of fourteen pools at S'Agaro, Catalonia, is softened by the water being brought up almost level with the paving. Thus the complex pattern is confined virtually to the horizontal plane, a labyrinth rather than a maze.

At Mas de les Voltes, Catalonia, an idealized agriculture is guarded by sentinel cypresses and protected by ancient olives. As the season progresses there is a constantly changing relationship of colour and texture between the crop and the mown paths, sometimes matching, sometimes contrasting. OPPOSITE *Fernando Caruncho.*

Nor are his grids always hard-textured; frequently spaces within are filled with water. His garden at S'Agaro, Catalonia, included fourteen contiguous squares filled to the brim with water, some containing water jets, others white water lilies. These liquid grids have more in common with formal Italian gardens such as Villa Lante or Villa Gamberaia than they do with a chess board. At Camp Sarch, Minorca, he even filled some of the squares of a water parterre with low pillows of clipped evergreens, right up to the water's edge, to make extraordinary contrasts of shadow and reflection, flat geometry versus bulging volumes, stillness versus motion.

No garden shows off better his use of grids than that at Mas de les Voltes in Catalonia. The vast grid in this 10-ha (25-acre) garden takes its tenor from agricultural field systems. Stretching down a gentle slope from the house is a parterre of wheat that sways in the wind between broad grass roads lined with tall Italian cypresses. One month it is ablaze with red field poppies, at another green with young shoots, then rough with stubble. It puts the rhythms, motions and colours of nature directly into a formal grid. And if all that is taking place along the plane that is the ground, the cypresses stretch the eye in the opposite direction, towards the sky, and in a regular man-made rhythm. That attention to the vertical is never far from Caruncho's thoughts and he has called gravel 'the floor' of a garden and the sky 'the ceiling'. In his own studio in Madrid, the room at the

centre of the building is partially subterranean so that concrete pillars can rise a remarkable 11 m (36 ft) to support the ceiling, as slender as his signature cypresses.

Circular shapes have always been present to a degree in his gardens. The studio garden ends in a round pool centred on a small fountain, around which is a wide circle of gravel, raked into a spiral every morning by one of his ten assistants. Vistas in other gardens have ended in circular labyrinths set out on the ground, another means of finding mystery and contemplation for the mind. A garden at Boca Raton in Florida descends through three sunken circular spaces (two lawns, one pool) that brush briefly together where they connect, like wheels in a clock. More recently his gardens have moved towards a broader use of circles and to the sinuous shapes that

Vineyard at Amastuola, where the curves of the landform have been exaggerated by the planting. The sinuous volumes of the vine rows allow for an ever-changing expression of light and shade.

the gardener Roberto Burle Marx (p. 188) was inspired to make after seeing the work of the Catalan painter Joan Miró.

At the Amastuola vineyard in Puglia, in Italy, Caruncho spent four years making another of his agricultural landscape gardens. Following but exaggerating the natural lie of the land, he planted curved rows of vines that extended 2 km (1¼ miles), striping the landscape. Two thousand olive trees, some thought to date from the 13th century, were brought in over a two-year period to define the roads through the vineyard. Alongside these, dry stone walls put a crisper line on the land. The result is a landscape of extraordinary beauty, valuable not least because this was a project intended to bring life to neglected land in a poor area. It is a landscape that has been made using the elements that have always formed the landscape there, restoring people's contact with the cycles of nature. And it is mysteriously beautiful, or as Caruncho would perhaps prefer, 'true'.

Today he has received commissions from countries well beyond his native Spain, which absorbed his first ten years as a designer. He has worked for the Spanish Embassy in Tokyo, made gardens in Greece and France and Maine in the US and even in the English Cotswold hills. But no matter where he works, he is always at pains to bring out the spiritual nature of the place, 'to make the light vibrate', or, in an age of science, to reconnect people with philosophy, to put them in touch once more with the elements of water, earth, wind and fire. On seeing Caruncho's gardens such justifications make sense. After all, many a garden-maker has declared the need for gardeners to be in touch with painting and sculpture and music, so why not Plato, Goethe, Mallarmé, Heraclitus and Epimenides of Knossos? Caruncho is clear: 'In all cultures the garden represents the spiritual values of man.'

BELOW *Nature's rougher curves are idealized in this garden at Boca Raton to become circular sunken lawns and a pool, with stepped banks. Light and shade on the steps is suggested all day by running seams of clipped evergreens which contrast with the pale stonework.*

GARDENS OF CURVES

GEOMETRY DOES NOT have to mean straight lines and right angles; it can be curvilinear too. It can mean the precise circle of the compass, the delicate path of a parabola, the sinuous curve of a sine wave. There are precise curves in nature, of course: the spiral of a snail's shell expanding according to the proportions of the Fibonacci Series, the ripples around the pebble dropped in water, the snaking route of a river estuary seen from space. But nature tends to be more irregular, more erratic, more varied. Real nature, in most cases, is flux. The precise curve, used again and again, is a man-made construct and over the centuries some gardeners have made it their theme – a refined, crystallized imitation of nature, but still something not commonly natural. Curvilinear geometry, in fact.

Idealized curves are one of the great features of the English landscape park, as practised by Lancelot 'Capability' Brown and Humphry Repton. Their apparently natural landscapes, developed in reaction to the rectilinear gardens of the 16th, 17th and early 18th centuries, had woodland belts that curved gracefully across the horizon, green grazing-land that swept through a prospect, and lakes and rivers that snaked smoothly through a valley bottom with a simplicity and cleanness of line that have no part in real nature. They were not without incident of course – the occasional clump of trees, a shrubby island in the lake, but the incident that mattered most was architectural: the distant Classical temple, mausoleum or obelisk. If the designed landscape was a stylized refinement of nature, it was also intended as an expression and display of the refinement of its owner's aesthetic sensibilities, of his familiarity with Classical learning and fashionable thought. In other words, the curvilinear landscape was a form of power landscape, as had been the great rectilinear formal gardens of France and Italy. Edna Walling took some of this European tradition, more particularly in her case the English Arts and Crafts style, with her to Australia, and along with her more structured features always included wilder areas with native planting.

The faux-natural curve has also been used as a more democratic proposition. The urban public parks of the 19th century absorbed and incorporated it into their urban sanctuaries for the common man. Joseph Paxton designed such parks in England, and his example was followed by Frederick Law Olmsted in Central Park in New York. Pools, shrubberies, flower-beds and woodland edges swept firmly around, a relief from the straight lines of the city. There was much more gardening going on within these parks than in aristocratic landscapes, but still this was nature refined by the human mind.

Curves have also found their way into gardens through the influence of modern painting. In Brazil, Roberto Burle Marx's complicated intestinal patterns had their roots in the work of painters such as Miró. Thomas Church's famous kidney-shaped pool at El Novillero was unmistakably the product of the modern movement in art, just like the organically shaped sculpture that rose from its surface.

Sometimes the love of curves has been extended over the entire garden. Nurseryman Alan Bloom's influential garden at Bressingham in Norfolk was an amalgam of curving, tear-drop flower beds that defined a river of emerald grass running between them, with a rustic summerhouse to one side. If the whole thing were to be up-scaled to many acres, with trees instead of flowers, it could aspire to be a landscape park; such is the tradition from which it came, the curve, refined far beyond the natural, but still suggesting the natural.

In Britain, designer John Brookes introduced modern garden design to popular post-war culture in the same way that Church had done in America. If the straight line made sense in the outdoor living areas immediately around a house, the outer parts of his garden made full use of sinuously curving spaces, too wide to be a path, too narrow to be called a lawn or open space, where even if the planting to the sides was irregular and varied, an imaginary central line curved comfortably along and made the garden flow.

Great sweeps of planting, often on a large scale, were a central feature of James van Sweden's work. In a reaction to the standard American model of manicured neat lawn with borders, his designs evoked the prairies and featured bold swirls of massed planting of tough, often native perennials. He used the same principles of dramatic planting even in small spaces. As he said, 'you have to think big'.

Edna Walling's sketch plan for a garden at 'Willaroo', Coleraine, Australia.

LANCELOT 'CAPABILITY' BROWN

Ideal landscapes on a grand scale

1716–1783

LANCELOT BROWN, known universally as 'Capability' Brown, is arguably the world's most influential gardener, with André Le Nôtre (p. 84) a close second. His work has been copied throughout the world and his style remains much imitated today.

Still, it would be no denigration of Brown's skills to say that he was in the right place at the right time. The English aristocracy and families rich from international trade were keen to invest in their country estates and to demonstrate their importance by turning those estates into works of art – with their houses, and of course themselves, at the centre. The landscape spoke of the man.

Fashion, too, played a great part in the success of Brown's career; one should never underestimate people's ability to be bored by tradition. Until the early 18th century the great gardens of Britain had been formal and geometric, with a strong floral element, based on the monastic tradition and the influence of Italian and French gardens; rectilinear geometry reigned supreme. Major changes then began to emerge in the early 18th century with the 'landscape movement' under designers such as Charles Bridgeman and William Kent (p. 28), whose projects, on a large scale and scarcely using flowers, began to dissolve the distinction between a garden and its surrounding landscape. But

ABOVE Coloured engraving of Burghley House, near Stamford, Lincolnshire (1819), one of Brown's longest commissions. A natural idyll – or is it about control, power, and the people in the carriage who wield it? OPPOSITE Engraving of a portrait of Brown by Nathaniel Dance-Holland. The heavy, creased clothes tell of a life spent on the road.

still these early landscape gardens involved bold rectilinear strokes. They were also landscapes of allusion, with an intellectual and sometimes political subtext which the owners and their guests could enjoy unravelling. Not surprisingly, architectural ornament was a major element.

If Brown was the product of those early landscapers, what his best work had to offer was something completely new, in as much as it focused on the simplest elements of nature – grass, trees, landform and water. It appeared supremely uncomplicated, even if it did allow some architectural ornament. It was also timeless, despite being a vigorously fashionable reaction against the rectilinear manner. This is why its appeal has been so extraordinarily widespread and lasting (though not without its critics).

Also never to be underestimated is man's desire to avoid undertaking or paying for repetitive chores. For all their charms, the 17th-century rectilinear flower gardens

Parkland at Chatsworth, Derbyshire, with clumps of trees and a woodland belt on the horizon. A Brownian park was an economic landscape of forestry and grazing, as well as an aesthetic statement.

were unambiguously expensive in terms of labour, whereas Brown's green landscapes, with expanses of grass and planted woods, immediately had an economic value for their owners as a source of grazing and ultimately timber. Formal flower gardening did not entirely disappear, but what remained of it was tucked out of sight, often in walled gardens.

Brown was born of humble origins in deep rural Northumberland in northern England, where he spent seven years as an apprentice gardener. So bright and ambitious was he, and also lucky, that by 1740 he was working in Lord Cobham's kitchen garden at Stowe in Buckinghamshire, one of the most important gardens of the day, heavily emblematic of the political concerns of that time and widely visited by garden lovers. Very quickly Brown was out of the kitchen garden and working in the landscape begun by Bridgeman and then being softened by Kent, with whom

Brown was to work for six years. The Grecian Valley at Stowe is thought to be entirely Brown's work.

His skills as a watercolourist and ability to draw plans saw Brown, surely with Lord Cobham's approval and influence, working for other clients beyond his responsibilities at Stowe. When Lord Cobham died in 1749, Brown was able to move with his family to Hammersmith, a few miles outside London, and in 1751 set himself up independently as a maker of gardens. He called himself 'a place maker' (the term 'landscape gardener' was coined by his successor Humphry Repton).

Such was Brown's popularity in rich, fashionable circles that, only six years later, this smart country boy was appointed by the King to be Royal Surveyor of Gardens at Hampton Court Palace. Yet still Brown was busy travelling all over the country on private contracts for clients from both ends of the political spectrum, and he prospered. His son was schooled at Eton and by 1766 Brown was able to buy himself a not inexpensive country estate (£13,000) at Fenstanton in Huntingdonshire. Four years later he was appointed High Sheriff of the county.

Brown's career was not without its detractors. He found an enemy (and rival for clients) in Sir William Chambers, an early promoter of all things Chinese, including gardens. Chambers railed in print at Brown, not only as a destroyer of older gardens (which he regularly was), but also as a peasant from the melon-ground, 'a cabbage planter', risen beyond his station.

But Brown's popularity in cultured circles and the indelible mark his clients had invited him to make on their estates maintained his status despite his detract- ors' words. He was working with the society architect (and his son-in-law) Henry Holland now, and even designing perfectly good country houses himself. To help with his workload in private practice and for the King, he employed several foremen and loyal assistants, including Samuel Lapidge and Michael Milliken.

Brown worked on somewhere between 150 and 250 gardens, too varied and numerous to itemize here. Let it suffice to say that he was employed by the most influential men of the day: for kings George II and III of course; at Blenheim for the nation's military hero, the Duke of Marlborough, where the work cost a princely £30,000; at Chatsworth for the Duke of Devonshire; at Holkham for the Countess of Leicester; at Burghley for the Earl of Exeter; at Croome Park for the Earl of Coventry; at Alnwick and Syon House for the Duke of Northumberland; for St John's College, Cambridge; for Robert Drummond on a tiny 7-ha (17-acre) land- scape at Cadland. The list of his gardens goes on and on.

Great men accustomed to managing great estates could trust Brown's skills as a manager himself, and consequently his employment on the creation and refinement

Blenheim Palace, Oxfordshire, is one of Brown's greatest achievements. For all the perceived 'Englishness' of Brown's parks, he was keen to use new trees, including conifers, which were then being discovered in the New World.

of a particular garden or landscape would sometimes last for many years – 25 in the case of Croome Park. Respected as an able architect, he was no less admired for his technical skills in large-scale earth-moving, redirecting and damming rivers to create great lakes (often crossed by bridges), land drainage and forestry practice, and also for his adventurousness in using some of the new species of tree at that time being introduced from America.

The tragedy for us is that Brown did not write. He left no treatise large or small on his ideas for landscape gardens, how he thought about the solid volumes of woodland, the vacuities of grassy parkland, the accommodation of different curves, the flatness of water and depth of its reflections; only an account book and a small number of his plans, bills and letters remain. Brown was a doer, not a theorizer.

He was also a sound businessman and charged properly for his work, so that in time he became a wealthy man. He never handed the execution of his plans over to others but contracted the work in his own name, thereafter employing a favoured subcontractor to see it through. He would be away from home for several weeks at a time, traversing the country on horseback and covering many hundreds of miles in a single trip.

Almost more remarkable than his energy was his close relationship with his clients. He was known as a cool but thoroughly affable man who, despite his humble origins, could safely be invited to stay at the great house while he was surveying the estate and subsequently proffering his designs. Brown's work was there to stay, it represented the client's face on the world and it had to be something the client was thoroughly able to endorse. It made sense to know Mr Brown well enough to trust him in this intimate relationship, however fashionable his train of previous employers. That Mr Brown was also discreet is made plain by his employment by differing political factions of the day. It was William Pitt, Lord Chatham, who wrote 'you cannot take any other advice so intelligent.… I know him … to be an honest man, and of sentiments much above his birth.' It says a great deal that after his death his clients put up monuments to honour his name, at Croome Park and Wrest Park, something rarely accorded even to great architects.

If Brown's gardens swept away and overlaid the gardens of previous generations of great designers – George London and Henry Wise, Bridgeman, Kent and many others – still he was happy to retain elements where they served his purpose: a straight avenue or terrace here, a formal garden there. It is the inevitable fate of all gardens that they must change with the vagaries of fashion and the life of plants, and so not surprisingly most of Brown's gardens in turn have been altered since his death.

What was Brown's achievement? Some say he destroyed traditional geometric gardens and the early 18th-century emblematic landscapes of idea. But, like formal flower gardening, emblematic gardening was a style as likely to pall as any other, perhaps the more so since once an intellectual agenda is understood it can only repeat itself. It has also been said of Brown that he was a control freak playing God all the way to the horizon and trying to create a truly 'natural' landscape. In fact, Brown's idealized, serpentine landscapes are far from the hurly-burly scruffiness of real nature. They are a highly stylized form of curvilinear geometry, a type of minimalism on a monumental scale. It is their very simplicity that made Brown's gardens such an object of admiration and desire, and it is their simplicity that meant future designers could enjoy overlaying them with the new plants which the following 200 years of botanical exploration would bring. Brown regarded place-making as a practical expression of simple aesthetic principles and very little to do with fashion, 'for [fashion] is a word that in my opinion disgraces science wherever it is found.…'

J. M. W. Turner's painting, Petworth, Sussex, the Seat of the Earl of Egremont: Dewy Morning *(exhibited 1810). As Brown's trees matured and the protecting fences could be removed, the raised canopy caused by browsing animals began to introduce shadow-play and lighten the scene.*

Another verdict is that Brown merely laid down a template of his usual garden wherever he went and made the landform and water bend to it. There is some truth in this, but then all creative artists have their preoccupations which they develop over time in various versions. And it has to be remembered that what Brown was doing was radical; he was honing his style as he went along.

Brown never worked abroad. There was a French consultation and the Duke of Leinster offered him £1,000 to go to Ireland and look at his estate's 'capabilities'. Brown declined on the grounds that he had 'not finished England yet'. His death came from a heart attack, aged 67, on his daughter's doorstep.

HUMPHRY REPTON

Scenic alterations and pictorial inclinations

1752–1818

1752
The British Empire adopts the Gregorian Calendar.
Benjamin Franklin establishes that lightning is electricity.
Canaletto paints Warwick castle.
Birth of British architect John Nash.

1818
Frankenstein is published anonymously by Mary Shelley.
Jane Austen publishes *Northanger Abbey*.
John Ross sets off in search of the Northwest Passage.
Beethoven completes his Piano Sonata No. 29.

HUMPHRY REPTON, who followed in the footsteps of 'Capability' Brown, is a pivotal figure in the history of garden-making. It could be said that he ran with the baton offered by Brown, that he developed the Brownian landscape garden in new directions; or it could be said that this obsequious flatterer punctured the pure Brownian vision with the pin of utility. There is truth in both.

When Repton was born in Bury St Edmunds in Suffolk, Brown was already 36, and it took Repton another 30 years to decide that he himself should become, to use the expression he coined, a 'landscape gardener'. Unlike Brown, Repton was born to privilege. His father was an excise officer and his mother a minor heiress, so life was comfortable for him and his brother and sister, even if, as was common enough then, eight other siblings died in infancy.

The Reptons had ambitions for their children, and Humphry, having been taught by his mother, went to grammar school at ten before being sent to Holland, in order to learn Dutch, the language of trade. Thereafter he was tutored in Rotterdam in a well-connected family friendly with the Reptons; here he mastered the social sophistications that were to be the mainstay of his life far more than business. He read, went to the theatre, learned to sing and to play the flute and, above all else, he learned to draw and paint, a talent that was to become the basis of his career as a landscape designer. At 16 his father put him as an apprentice into the textile business in Norwich for five years.

Portrait frontispiece from Repton's memoirs (artist unknown). Theodolite, string and paint brushes set out Repton's stall as a landscaper and artist. To his left, in youth, he proposes pretty flowers in an urn, to his right a wild and wind-blown landscape.

ÆT:45.

ÆT.21.

Æt.63.

H. REPTON.

Repton surveying with a theodolite. Notice the join in the paper left of the lake, which will fold back to show 'before and after' views of his scheme.

With new-found freedom and sufficient money, Repton lived and dressed well. After only two years he fell in love with his future bride, and when he turned 21 in 1773 they married, his parents giving him the funds to set up on his own as a merchant. The first of their many children appeared two years later: John Adey Repton, who was to become an architect and work with his father.

But Repton's heart was in the arts, not trade, and his business lost money. When his parents died he sold up and with his legacy moved into a 17th-century brick manor house, Old Hall, with a modest estate. He had become, as he thought, a country gentleman farmer, and in this fine condition he made a garden, had more children and explored the world of the theatre until he ran into debt. But Repton was ever cheerful in the face of trouble. In the expectation of making money he took work as a civil servant in Ireland, hoping it would be a new opportunity to explore the artistic life, but in the end it was not a lucrative solution to his problems and he had to give up Old Hall.

With so much wealth cheerfully frittered away, Repton found himself a roadside cottage at Hare Street in Essex, which was to be his home for the rest of his life. Various schemes for making money followed and foundered; he even tried his hand at playwriting and literary criticism, though without success. And then he saw the light. He might not have a fortune himself, but he had made excellent connections in moneyed, artistic society. He would be a Landscape Gardener. Yet even now he was wonderfully casual about it; he would merely 'render my leisure profittable'. Without irony, he declared: 'Good taste can only be acquired by leisure and observation; it is not therefore to be expected in men whose time is fully employed in the more important acquirement of wealth or fame.' Or to put it another way, he and his rich clients needed each other.

Brown was by now dead, and his legacy was written in great landscapes the length and breadth of England. But Repton had two skills in which he far superseded

Before and after views from Repton's cottage at Hare Street. In his new scheme are flower beds, climbers and fruit trees; gone are the noisy geese and impenetrable fence, hidden the butcher's shop and rowdy carriage. Here are work and its rewards: a watering can and a chair.

Brown: he could paint easily and attractively, and he could write. (Brown left virtually nothing in writing.)

Gradually, Repton's business took off. His working method was to visit his client's house for a day or two, a cheerful and talkative house-guest well versed in the arts. He would walk the estate, taking levels and measurements, then go home to make one of his trademark Red Books – delightful leather-bound volumes (many survive) setting out his proposals in beautiful copper-plate writing and lavishly flattering his clients. The great trick of his Red Books was to illustrate his ideas by means of before-and-after watercolour views, demonstrated by the use of fold-over flaps. They were simple, ingenious and effortlessly alluring to the client, although even Repton knew they were only a partial representation of the changes he would make: 'I can show the effect of a new house instead of an old one, but I cannot describe those numberless beauties which may be brought before the eye in succession by the windings of a road, or the contrast of ascending and descending thro' a deep ravine of rich hanging woods.' Even so, they gave clients the perfect way of boasting to their friends about how they had improved their estates. For all the care that went into these presentations, Repton did not charge nearly enough for his services, and with a better business head could have ended his days a far wealthier man.

Often he advised on the architecture of the house as well as the garden, working closely with his son John Adey Repton (profoundly deaf since infancy, but nonetheless a successful architect) and with the Prince Regent's favourite architect, John Nash. To Repton's dismay, it was Nash's design that was used for the oriental fantasy that is now Brighton Pavilion, rather than his own.

Repton worked throughout England, although his projects were weighted towards his native East Anglia. He even designed gardens for Russell Square and Cadogan Square in London. His clients ranged from old aristocracy to new money, from the staggeringly grand Holkham in Norfolk to an ambitious *ferme ornée* at Endsleigh in Devon. Frequently he was asked to provide proposals to alter the work of his predecessors Bridgeman and Brown. How did his work differ from theirs? What was it in the formality of Bridgeman and the sweeping landscapes of Brown that needed improving? Without denigrating Repton's brilliant skill as a landscape designer, it can be summarized in two words: convenience and prettiness.

Unlike Brown's great parkland lawns which swept right up to the house, Repton offered a civilized formal terrace with gravel paths and neat flower gardens, a place of social comfort to separate house from park. How much more practical and useful this would be in winter. He himself sums it up nicely: 'Let [this garden] rather appear to be the rich frame of the landscape than a part of the Picture.'

Aquatint of Repton's design for the Prince Regent's Pavilion at Brighton, 1808. Repton, lover of social connections, was bitterly disappointed not to get the royal pavilion contract, which went instead to John Nash, the Prince's favoured architect.

Repton's parks were also more individually tailored to the quirks and complications of the existing landscape, requiring fewer transformations than Brown's majestic impositions, and Repton's watercourses were smaller and often full of movement, unlike Brown's serene, serpentine lakes. Where Brown's grand carriage drives would approach the house indirectly, offering flattering views of the house and greater estate along the way, Repton insisted that the best approach to the house was the most direct and that a meandering carriage drive was not necessary; an attractive circuit walk full of variety and surprise was every bit as enjoyable. Repton (in line with developing technology) was also required to include glass conservatories in his designs. His garden buildings were often rustic, sometimes draped in plants, and he made bold use of rose-clad treillage structures.

It was this domestication of the landscape garden that led Repton into fierce dispute with two Herefordshire landowners, Richard Payne Knight and Uvedale Price, who publicly attacked both Brown and Repton, proclaiming that any landscape garden worth its salt should be wilder, craggier, more like a painting by Claude or Poussin – 'Picturesque', in fact. With his usual affability, Repton refused to rise to the bait and declared that a garden need not look like a painting to be good and that what was needed was 'the happy medium betwixt the wildness of nature and the stiffness of art'. There was no need for a landscape to offer 'irritation' to the viewer in order to be satisfying. If his response seems lukewarm, it should be remembered that Payne Knight and Price were country squires living in houses in an already rugged landscape and could afford to be ardent theorists, unlike Repton, who was a busy professional designer with a reputation to protect, and sufficiently well known to be mentioned as a fashionable figure in Jane Austen's novel *Mansfield Park*. He was in the business of pleasing many more people than himself and his general good humour, too, made his response to the public spat conciliatory. (It was for just these winning qualities that Repton was engaged over the years to help with electoral campaigns, when friends needed hearts to be brought on side.)

Repton approached the issue of whether a garden should look like a painting with a scientific eye also. He took an interest in the science of optics and gave considerable space to it in his writings, showing how it affects our sense of scale and the way a garden is seen. He pointed out that in fact a canvas by Claude or a Poussin regularly represents a view of 20°, whereas in life – in a garden – we can see nearer to 180° and that therefore the opportunities to develop a real landscape are far greater.

In 1811, at the age of 59, Repton was in a carriage accident which left him crippled and confined to a wheelchair. Still he managed to work, and it was after this

View from the cottage at Endsleigh, Devon. Repton's scheme (bottom) has humanized the landscape, with a conservatory, properly level terrace, purposeful gravel walk, open space on the wooded promontory and a wisp of smoke.

The Vinery, from Fragments on the Theory and Practice of Landscape Gardening *by Repton and John Adey Repton, 1816. Utility is here made sufficiently beautiful for the lady of the house to be brought in to inspect the fruit.*

accident that perhaps his most famous and best-known landscape, at Sheringham Park in Norfolk, was begun. He felt he was at his finest here, that this was how he would like to be remembered. He died of a heart attack in 1818, having completed his last book, *Fragments on the Theory and Practice of Landscape Gardening*.

Like his predecessors' gardens, much of Repton's work has been regularly overlaid by new designs since his death, but his writings remain an invaluable source of information on the landscaper's mind. His work exists principally in three volumes, *Sketches and Hints on Landscape Gardening* (1795), *Observations on the Theory and Practice of Landscape Gardening* (1803) and *Fragments*, but there was also a considerable body of plays, light poetry and criticism. Then there are his wonderful Red Books, some now in libraries across the world, others still in the loving hands of the families on whose gardens Repton once worked.

FREDERICK LAW OLMSTED

Designing for urban life and public enjoyment

1822–1903

1822
Last major outbreak of yellow fever in New York.
Brazil declares independence from Portugal.
Egyptian hieroglyphs first deciphered via the Rosetta
    Stone.
Charles Babbage publishes his proposal for a 'difference
    machine', forerunner of the computer.

1903
Cuba leases Guantanamo Bay to the USA in perpetuity.
A Chicago dentist becomes the first owner of a Ford
    Model A automobile.
Death of frontierswoman and scout Calamity Jane.
First east–west transatlantic radio transmission.

ENTRAL PARK in New York is the most used and most famous urban park in the world. Designed in 1857 by Frederick Law Olmsted, the USA's first major landscape architect, it set standards for public parks that continue to be respected today, to the point that even now Olmsted's Central Park is what people think a public park should be. The miracle is that Central Park was Olmsted's first real foray into landscape design. Over the next forty years he went on to become the country's premier landscape architect, working on public parks, residential communities, hospitals, cemeteries, railway stations, university campuses and national parks. He was also an author, journalist, editor and significant social reformer. But it is for Central Park that the world knows Olmsted.

Olmsted lived through a period of huge change in America, as it developed from a rural economy through massive urbanization to industrialization and immigration (New York's population quadrupled between 1821 and 1855). Slavery reforms and the Civil War were taking place while the Park was being built, followed by a period of national reconstruction. It was a chance to build cities as people wanted them to be, rather than just being the result of a haphazard accumulation of developments over the centuries, as was generally the case in Europe.

Born of wealthy parents in Hartford, Connecticut, Olmsted began life as a farmer, fascinated, like Thomas Jefferson (p. 47) before him, by the scientific possibilities of modern efficient agriculture. At 26 he bought a farm on Staten Island, and fast became part of the New York social and literary scene. Family wealth allowed him to travel to Europe, where he was astonished by the new public city parks in Britain, in particular J. C. Loudon's Derby Arboretum and Joseph Paxton's Birkenhead Park, which were made all the more valuable because of the surrounding

Portrait of Olmsted by John Singer Sargent (1895), landscape architect and champion of the plants and natural beauties of the American wilderness.

poverty and crime that sudden urbanization brought in its wake. On his return to America Olmsted published an account of his travels, *Walks and Talks of an American Farmer in England*, and lectured widely on his experiences. The *New York Times* commissioned him to make similar tours of the southern USA, which led in turn to three further books. He became part-owner and editor of *Putnam's Monthly Magazine*, and so was able to commission writing on many aspects of social, scientific and political matters of the day.

In 1857 New York held a competition to design a new park to cater for its growing population, an idea originally proposed by landscape architect Andrew Jackson Downing. Olmsted, who had been appointed park superintendent, entered a proposal in collaboration with his future business partner, the British-born architect Calvert Vaux, and won. The 'Greensward Plan', as they named their proposal, was a long rectangle of 315 ha (778 acres), soon to be 342 ha (843 acres), of rough, hillocky, poor land in central Manhattan, where the city was fast growing outwards and upwards. The park took fully ten years to complete. Before work could begin, 1,600 Irish immigrants and freed American slaves were moved from shanties on the site. The location was rocky, with only a little poor soil, so the landscape could only be transformed with vast quantities of topsoil imported from New Jersey, together

Plan of Central Park, 1870. Olmsted's design owed much to his admiration for the innovative Birkenhead Park in Britain.

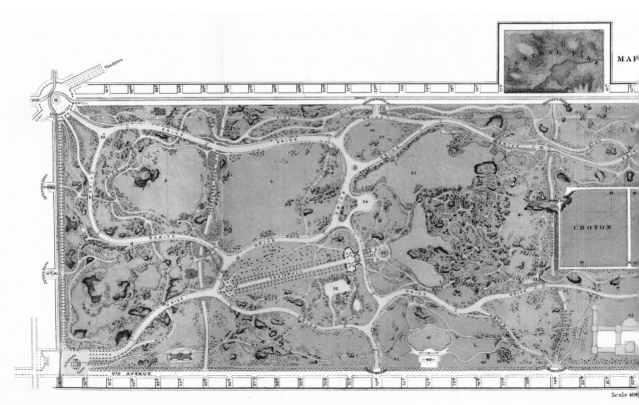

ABOVE Central Park was built as a recreational facility for the labouring classes of an expanding city. Today it is the city's green lung, surrounded by the houses of the rich.

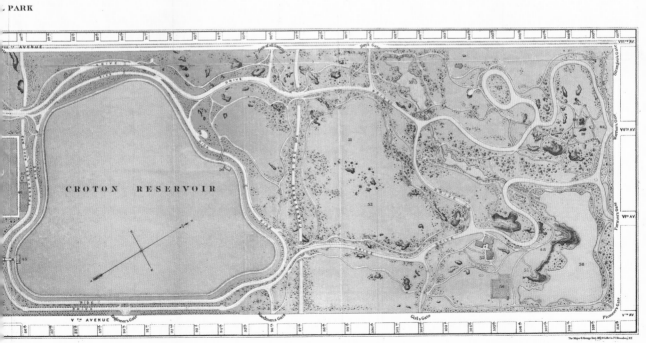

PARK

CROTON RESERVOIR

with the use of more gunpowder than was expended at the Battle of Gettysburg, machinery that could move mature trees and the labour of thousands.

Olmsted's plan drew directly on his British experiences. As a social reformer, his idea was to make a naturalistic park for everyone to enjoy, somewhere people could go and forget they were in the city. Circulation was key. Underlying the plan would be a grid of three sunken east–west roadways hidden by planting to allow vehicles to pass through the inevitable blockage that such an enormous greenspace created in the life of the city. In the opposite direction there would be three winding north–south carriage drives, made practical by Calvert Vaux's 36 bridges. Water was installed for practical and leisure purposes in a vast reservoir to serve the city, and in various smaller ornamental lakes.

As for the recreational virtues of the park, there were places for sport and winter skating, a picturesque pasture for sheep (which were retained until 1934) and a woodland ramble where people could leave behind the sights and sounds of the city in wild ravines, with walks along meandering paths through parkland with outcropping rock and thousands of new trees. The Bethesda Terrace, with formal garden and fountain, was the park's one concession to formality and symmetry, to which the wealthier citizens could be driven to admire the flowers.

The greater part of Olmsted and Vaux's park survives to this day. It resisted architect Richard Morris Hunt's 1863 attempts to formalize some parts in line with the grandeur of the surrounding developments, and the vicissitudes of neglect during the 1930s Depression. It has also successfully emerged from a dark period in the late 20th century when it became a crime-ridden no-go area.

But there was more to Olmsted's life than Central Park. During the Civil War he was Executive Secretary of what was to become the American Red Cross, taking care of the wellbeing of the armed forces. He then moved west to be superintendent of the Mariposa Mining Estate in California, where he improved miners' welfare and industrial planning. Thus were Olmsted's democratic and utopian ideas formed.

Aware of the importance of Yosemite and the ancient redwoods, he succeeded in setting up the USA's first publicly owned national park, securing its preservation and sustainable access. Later he achieved the same to save Niagara Falls from industrial development. Meanwhile, he was called on to design landscapes throughout America – Prospect Park in Brooklyn, important parks in Boston, Chicago, Detroit, Louisville, Rochester and Montreal, campuses for Stanford and Berkeley universities, the Vanderbilt's Biltmore Estate at Asheville, North Carolina, the Chicago World's Fair, suburbs such as Riverside, Illinois, and dozens more. Olmsted never tired until breakdown forced him to spend his last five years in a mental institution.

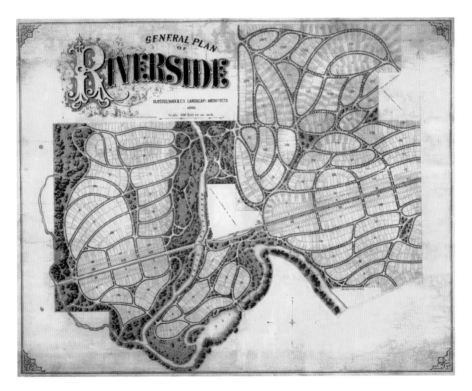

TOP *Prospect Park, Brooklyn, in a photograph taken in 1873 by George Bradford Brainerd.* ABOVE *Plan of Riverside, Olmsted's new suburban village in Illinois. Latterly he became a town planner as much as a landscape architect; it fitted well with his ideas about social responsibility.*

EDNA WALLING

An Arts and Crafts gardener in Australia

1895–1973

1895	1973
The National Trust is founded in England.	End of the Vietnam War.
The diesel engine is patented in Germany.	Giorgios Papadopoulos is ousted in a military coup in Greece.
Wilhelm Röntgen discovers X-rays.	The Sears Tower is completed in Chicago.
Oscar Wilde is sentenced to two years' hard labour for acts of gross indecency.	Death of Pablo Picasso in France.

FOR MORE THAN two hundred years the rich and wealthy across the world have copied and adapted the 18th-century English landscape park, and the opulently planted English domestic gardens of the 20th century are still an inspiration for gardeners everywhere. Gardening has been one of Britain's most conspicuous exports.

Sometimes these mirroring gardens have been created by the owners themselves in their own countries, and at other times by established English designers working abroad, perhaps on the French Riviera or in Tuscan villas. In Australia, Edna Walling was somewhere between the two. Born in England, she took the English Arts and Crafts style with her to Australia, but then as time went on she developed a planting palette and manner better suited to her new country. She was a Christian Scientist, classical music lover, skilled photographer, a red-headed practical gardener never without her broad-brimmed hat to keep the sun off, and happiest in a shirt and pair of jodhpurs; a tomboy in fact, charming, but challengingly selfish and confident in her abilities. She became the very un-*grande dame* of Australian garden design and the country took her to its heart. She remains one of its most lauded and best-known designers.

Walling was born in Yorkshire, England, and brought up in Bickleigh in Devon, where her father enjoyed teaching his convent-schooled daughter the skills of woodworking and how to admire and evaluate the qualities of the natural landscape on their long country rambles. Fire destroyed the uninsured store in which her father was a clerk, and in 1912 the family emigrated to New Zealand. Here Walling took work as a cook and cleaner before training as a nurse in Christchurch. Her father meanwhile found a job as a warehouse director in Melbourne, Australia, and a couple

Walling's enigmatic self-portrait, more interested in the job in hand than herself. She was a skilled photographer and used her own photographs to illustrate her books and articles.

of years later the family moved to join him. In 1916 Walling studied for a certificate in horticulture at Burnley Horticultural College, Melbourne, and then set up on her own as a jobbing gardener, an occupation she soon hated for its repetitiveness. The idea of *building* gardens, on the other hand, appealed to her practical instincts enormously and she began to find work, as so many beginner designers do, through recommendation from a friendly architect. She called herself not a landscape architect but a landscape designer.

Her career prospered and her style displayed the European tradition, with bold architectural features such as walls, pergolas, pools and colonnades, all dressed with generous but softly coloured planting; but there were always wilder, more sweeping and natural areas which included Australian native plants. She found herself working for the Australian diva, Dame Nellie Melba, and for Mrs Keith Murdoch (later Dame Elisabeth, mother of Rupert Murdoch). Commissions could cover several acres and have a large budget if not a large fee; they took her from Hobart to Perth to Queensland, and she began to write for the magazine *Australian Home Beautiful* (1926–46), answering letters and providing readers with watercolour garden plans. Helpers gathered around her small business – a book-keeper, a propagator and contractors such as Ellis Stones and Eric Hammond who would go on to be major influences in Australian design.

By the late 1920s success had allowed her to buy 45 ha (18 acres) of bush land at Mooroolbark east of Melbourne, where she built herself a small, primitively equipped but (to her) very satisfactory cottage. Naming it Sonning after the village on the Thames in Berkshire, she began to plant a garden rich in birches and her trademark liquidambar (sweet gum) trees. She then carefully divided the rest of the site into sixteen housing plots, which she sold off on condition that both the rustic cottage and its garden on each plot were to be designed by her, the cottage nestling into its garden like the ones she so fondly remembered in England. She called the development Bickleigh Vale, and it remains a charming period piece today. Repeating the

BELOW Photograph by Walling of her home, the Barn, at Bickleigh Vale, one of her own rustic suburbs. OPPOSITE Plan for a rose garden for Mrs Keith Murdoch, mother of Rupert Murdoch.

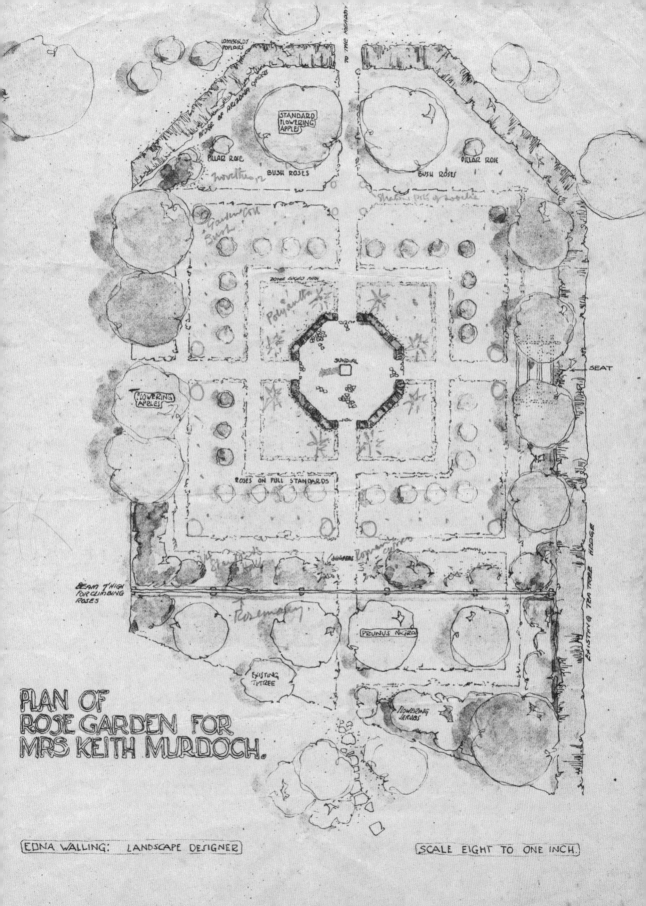

PLAN OF
ROSE GARDEN FOR
MRS KEITH MURDOCH.

EDNA WALLING: LANDSCAPE DESIGNER

SCALE EIGHT TO ONE INCH.

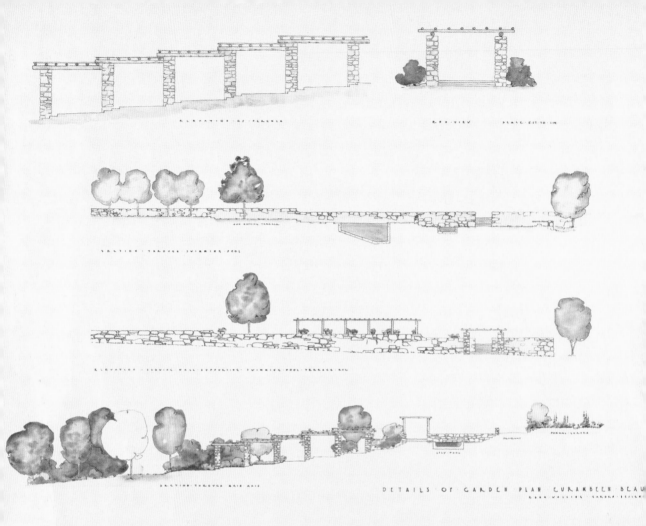

Walling's coloured drawing of details for a garden at Eurambeen, Beaufort, in Victoria, around 1937, with elevations of a pergola, a swimming pool and the main axis.

family's fiery history, Sonning burnt down in 1936, but undeterred, Walling built herself an even more basic dwelling known as the Cabin, measuring just 4.6 by 4 m (15 x 13 ft), which was in turn replaced by Sonning II. Nothing was ever grand.

She now began to write books that would help people make their own gardens. *Gardens in Australia – Their Design and Care* (1943) was illustrated with her own photographs and sketches and had run to four editions by 1950. *Cottage and Garden in Australia* (1947) even went so far as to recommend the cottager's choice of china. *A Gardener's Log* of 1948 was a collection of her journalism.

Pleased with the idea of the Bickleigh development, in 1948 she bought another 40 ha (16 acres) at Lorne, Victoria, near the coast, to be another 'village', and built herself a further cottage there, but this too was lost to fire. She was by

Colour photograph by Walling. Her gardens had a rural, relaxed English manner, usually belied by an un-English, ranch-style architecture.

now totally at home gardening in the Australian climate (climates might be more accurate) and her work began to use ever more native plants rather than the 'purple-leaved wonders' of the international nursery trade. Her book on her passion for conserving the native flora, *The Australian Roadside*, followed in 1952. 'The thought of any journey to a place where the trees and natural ground cover are still unspoilt is thrilling to me', she wrote.

Walling's final move was to the warmer climate of Buderim, Queensland, where she planned to make a village in a more Italian style. This and other similar developments were still incomplete at the time of her death.

THOMAS CHURCH

A modernist maker of gardens for people

1902–1978

1902	1978
Cuba gains independence from the USA.	China lifts the ban on the works of Aristotle, Shakespeare and Dickens.
The Electric Theatre, the first movie theatre in the USA, opens in Los Angeles.	President Carter postpones development of the neutron bomb.
The first Aswan dam on the Nile is completed.	Birth of Louise Brown, the world's first test-tube baby.
Birth of Ansel Adams, American photographer.	Start of the ongoing Afghan civil war.

SINCE PAINTERS like Miró, architects such as Le Corbusier and composers such as Stravinsky were working in Europe at the start of the 20th century, it seems obvious, now, that Modernism ought to have found its way into European garden design. Instead, it hopped the Atlantic to America, while the efficient elegance of Edwardian Arts and Crafts gardening lingered in Europe for another hundred years. In America, Modernism quickly emerged in the suburban West Coast gardens of Thomas Dolliver Church. He also pioneered the need for gardens to be functional places – to be designed so that people could live and play outdoors in the California sunshine. Church's gardens were for *being in*, whereas in his view European gardens were for *looking at*. For him, low maintenance and simple massed evergreen planting in tight-edged beds was more important than complex flower gardening.

His 1955 book *Gardens Are For People* could be the manual for many new suburban British or Dutch gardens today, so similar are they in concept and layout, although British gardens retain their complex gardening to be *looked at* and closely maintained. Church's gardens, therefore, can seem bald to Old World eyes. Like most small domestic gardens, few survive unchanged, and perhaps, on the principle that gardens are for the occupants' immediate use, he would not have objected.

Church was born in Boston, but grew up with his mother and sister in the Ojai Valley, southern California, where he absorbed the visual idiom of ranches, outdoor living, orange trees and the Spanish architectural styles. After a BA in Landscape Gardening and Floriculture at the University of California, Berkeley,

Thomas Church, around 1977 (not long before he died), dapper and affable, if not in his regular khaki garden-inspecting outfit and carrying a well-worn bag of tools.

DONNELL.
BATH-HOUSE

A drawing of poolside structures for the Donnell Garden, Sonoma County, and a magazine cover featuring the famous pool. Even in this sketch of the garden, it is plain that 'gardens are for people', to quote the title of Church's first book. The House Beautiful cover has become an iconic image of optimistic, post-war America, a home for heroes. Photographers are still drawn to the garden today, now with far richer colour reproduction techniques at their disposal.

he took a Masters in Landscape Architecture at Harvard. A Sheldon travel scholarship allowed him to tour round Europe for nine months, looking at the garden traditions there and producing as his thesis *A Study of Mediterranean Gardens and their Adaptability to California Conditions*. The idea of living indoors and outdoors had made as much sense in Renaissance Italy as it did in modern-day California.

Teaching posts followed at Ohio State University and Berkeley, before he turned full time to private practice, which would occupy the rest of his life. His commissions were mostly domestic, but with a few civic or commercial ones alongside. His office never employed more than four people.

'Tommy' Church was a winning and affable character, always casually dressed in khakis and carrying a briefcase plastered in airline stickers and containing tape measure, sketch pad, secateurs and hand saw. His first questions to a client were aimed at discovering precisely their needs from a garden – itself a flattering approach – and, with a budget in mind, a shopping list would emerge: a view, a swimming pool, well-fenced privacy, eating and drinking space, lighting, plenty of parking,

The beachside Martin Garden, Aptos, California: Church liked his zigzags, while the deck and curving planting beds receding into the landscape are a foretaste of the work of his fellow-American James van Sweden (p. 200).

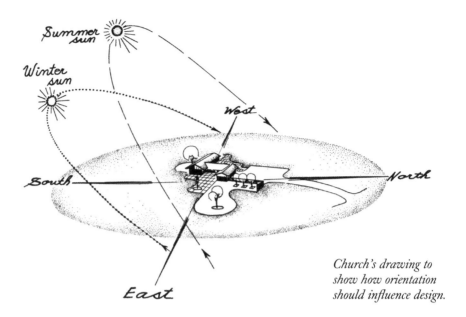

Church's drawing to show how orientation should influence design.

shade, some well-irrigated green lawn, and, if the owner was a keen gardener, spaces for some flowers, vegetables and composting. It was then a world where wives stayed at home with the children and husbands went out to work.

Those early gardens of the 1930s owed a great deal to the symmetrical, European, Beaux Arts style and employed ornate box parterres from the French tradition that would appear in all his gardens, even alongside striking Modernism. Following a further European trip in 1937 for the Paris World Expo, and the chance to look at the work of architects such as Alvar Aalto, the 1940s and 1950s saw his greatest experiments in the modern manner – the use of bold amorphous shapes often contrasting with rectilinear zigzags. In his later life he returned to a simpler, symmetrical, more classical manner, working on over 2,000 gardens overall.

Church's success was facilitated by his partnerships with contemporary architects, especially William Wurster, and his association with magazines such as *Sunset* ('the Magazine of Western Living') and *House Beautiful*, which showcased his work to a potential client base, just as *Country Life* had showcased Lutyens's work in England (p. 96), and gave him space to write about his ideas. Also like Lutyens, Church made gardens and offices for his editors. Exhibitions of his plans, notably at Cargoes store in San Francisco (where his wife Betsy was employed), put his work into the fashionable domain and made it a status symbol.

It was *House Beautiful* magazine that gave Church his place in history by running a feature on his garden at El Novillero (the Donnell garden) in Sonoma County, California, showing on its cover the kidney-shaped blue swimming pool with an abstract sculpture at its centre, flanked by mature oaks and overlooking the plain beyond. It was the American dream itself, an image of the enviable good life, simple, sunny and modern. It was also the beginning of the triumph of modern colour photography in the field of gardens, creating an icon that would last forever, a beautiful image showing not every single element of the composition, but a careful photogenic selection – the pool, the view, the trees.

In Church's later years he produced a second book, *Your Private World* (1969), derived from his journalism in the *San Francisco Chronicle* and featuring his work and ideas. Like *Gardens Are for People*, it was a thoughtful manual for the home-owner, not a technical treatise for professional landscape architects. His commercial projects and consultancies, at Longwood Gardens, Stanford University and the offices of *Sunset*, were few, yet he was respected across the profession; prestigious awards came his way from the American Institute of Architects, the American Society of Landscape Architects and the American Horticultural Society. For Church, Modernism was not an artistic obsession but a means of providing his clients with a serene, easily maintained environment of the kind they now desired to live in. As he wrote in *Gardens Are for People*, 'modernism is not a goal but a broad highway'.

White Memorial Plaza, Stanford University, one of Church's few commercial projects. It is interesting to compare Lutyens's Viceroy's Garden at New Delhi (p. 102).

ALAN BLOOM

Developer of island beds and popular plants

1906–2005

1906
The San Francisco earthquake destroys 80 per cent of
    the city.
The BCG immunization against tuberculosis begins
    development.
Deaths of Henrik Ibsen and Paul Cézanne.
Births of Dimitri Shostakovitch and John Betjeman.

2005
London terrorist bombings; 52 people die.
An earthquake in Kashmir kills 80,000 people.
YouTube founded.
Hurricane Katrina devastates New Orleans.

P LANT NURSERIES have always produced plantsmen who go on to be a major influence on gardens. James Russell, for example, started out at Sunningdale Nurseries and went on to plant the Rose Garden and Ray Wood arboretum at Castle Howard in Yorkshire; Graham Stuart Thomas (p. 244), who worked at Sunningdale Nurseries, later became Chief Gardens Adviser to the National Trust. Roy Lancaster, starting out at Hillier's Nursery in Hampshire, developed into a plant collector and editor of the hugely important *Hillier's Manual of Hardy Trees and Shrubs*.

Alan Bloom created his own nursery at Bressingham, in Norfolk, which became internationally famous for its wide range of hardy perennials. But Bloom also created his own 2-ha (5-acre) garden. Although mainly a demonstration garden, for trade and latterly retail customers, it was created according to Bloom's own ideas and principles when he was at the peak of his experience as a plantsman; its influence on its times was enormous. Bloom's own appearance may not have matched everyone's expectations of an influential nurseryman. Visitors to Bressingham would identify him easily, later in life, by his tall, wiry frame, his shabby jacket, long, flowing white hair and gold earrings, perhaps standing aboard one of his beloved steam engines. There was an attractive touch of the rebel about him.

Having left school at 15, Bloom first served as apprentice in several famous nurseries, including Wallace's of Tunbridge Wells, Kent, and R. V. Roger of Pickering, Yorkshire, and then began work in his father's cut-flower business at Oakington in Cambridgeshire. Young Bloom, ever the entrepreneur, decided market gardening was not a sound proposition and was determined to move into hardy plants – perennials and alpines. By 1931 he was running the business at Oakington and doing

Alan Bloom on one of his steam engines, at first used to clear land for the nursery and later as a tourist attraction, running beside and even through the garden.

just that, but after exhibiting for one last time at the Chelsea Flower Show in 1934 he gave up retail sales and concentrated on the wholesale trade. By 1939, his was the largest nursery of its kind in Britain, delivering mostly by rail.

Then the war came, ruining the nursery trade and forcing him to plough in his stock and grow food. His marriage foundered, leaving him with three young children to bring up. But he was an optimist, and revitalized the nursery after the war, mechanizing where possible and finding labour among demobbed soldiers and prisoners of war. For £11,000 he bought Bressingham Hall and around 90 ha (220 acres) of farmland in 1946. Bressingham is a chunky, 1740s block of a house, and as for the land, much of it was waterlogged fen abandoned to trees and supposedly ideal 'for sporting purposes'. Thus began decades of improvement, battling against the ill-draining waters of the Waveney valley, sometimes so boggy that a steam traction engine had to be brought in to help clear the trees.

These were personally hard times. Days were long and family life absent or neglected. Work stopped when it got dark and evenings of writing followed – sometimes a novel, sometimes a gardening book. It was a lonely, driven life, and if it was a success it took its toll on Bloom until, in 1948, he set up his farm and nursery as a Limited Company and escaped the pressure of his responsibilities by moving, with his children, to Canada to try a new life. Here he spent the next twenty months logging on Vancouver Island, trying his hand at farming in Ontario and even sometimes taking work as a casual labourer. None of it was a success, and when in 1950 he was told by his bank manager in England that he ought to come back quickly if his business was not to founder, he was happy to return to the challenge of the nursery trade he knew and loved. It had been the break he needed, if a rather dramatic one.

With the nursery turned around, Bloom launched a serious catalogue with which he intended to match the Dutch nurserymen in offering a fully comprehensive

BELOW Bressingham Hall and island beds, 1962. This tree-top view belies the sense of enclosure that Bloom's meandering beds produced on the ground. OPPOSITE Kniphofia 'Percy's Pride', still an international favourite.

list of perennials and alpines. The early post-war years had seen amateur gardeners focusing on labour-saving shrubs, but more complicated perennial plantings were coming back at last, and Bloom was ready to meet the demand. With the help of one of his hands, Percy Piper, he began to breed new and remarkably successful varieties, and to launch plants into the trade for other breeders. It is a rare garden or catalogue today that does not contain a few of his 170 introductions, including *Kniphofia* 'Percy's Pride' and *Crocosmia* 'Lucifer'.

Bloom was a self-confessed collector. 'The need for a compromise between what I ought to grow for profit and what I wanted to grow for love was with me already and would probably stay', he wrote in *The Bressingham Story*. Keen to see perennials better respected, he helped to found the Hardy Plant Society in 1957, and his desire to conserve old varieties prefigured the setting up of what is now known as Plant Heritage in 1978.

By 1957 Bloom had remarried, his sons were growing up and, with more help in the management of the farm and nursery, he began at last to make a garden. Already he had created a few scroll-shaped beds in front of the house, but now he had in mind something altogether larger, a cross between nursery stock beds, from which plants could be propagated, and a demonstration garden for his customers. Over the next few years it grew rapidly. Plants were brought in from the nursery and also arrived through a developing relationship with botanic gardens and important amateur gardeners, until the garden, known as The Dell, contained an extraordinary 4,000 different kinds. Much of the digging and building was done by Bloom himself or his existing staff, with a little extra help from student gardeners lodged in the Hall.

Bloom's desire was to demonstrate what could be done with perennials set free from the restrictions of traditional rectilinear herbaceous borders, and to select varieties that were stockier and more floriferous and so suitable for smaller suburban gardens. But his main object was to grow plants that did not need staking. This he achieved by creating his novel 'island beds', set not against a wall at the edge of a space, but out in the open lawn where wind and light from all sides would encourage sturdy and self-supporting growth. It worked, and it was a far cry from the straight-sided, formal borders of Nancy Lancaster, Rosemary Verey and Christopher Lloyd.

The Dell can be summed up as an informal arrangement of curvilinear banks, beds and pools, planted almost exclusively with alpines and perennials (a very few conifers and heathers found their way in) and secluded by mature tall trees. The island beds float in an undulating lawn which runs between them, sometimes a wide green 'valley', sometimes just a path. Ornament and focus are provided by the pools, a summerhouse and a bridge, which Bloom himself built.

It quickly became clear that here was something the gardening public wanted to see, not just buyers from the trade. Bressingham became a place of pilgrimage for amateur gardeners, by car and by coach, privately or in groups. The name of Bressingham and its famous wholesale catalogue grew, until in 1965 commercial logic demanded that the nursery should produce a retail catalogue also. Bloom retired in 1972 to concentrate on his garden, the Steam Museum he had set up and writing (over his lifetime he produced 30 books including self-published novels and countless articles). The Royal Horticultural Society awarded him both the Victoria Medal of Honour and the Veitch Memorial Medal. In 1997 he received an MBE.

Island beds in the Dell, then and now. Diverging formal curves offer a discreet but compelling proposal to walk around the beds and explore the all-important planting.

The importance of Bloom's island beds is that they were a triumph of the curvilinear approach to garden design. Were they natural? Not really, any more than the pattern of a Paisley fabric is natural. Their curvilinear shape was preceded in a more symmetrical manner by French parterres, by the patterns of small swirling flower beds cut into 19th-century British suburban lawns (which the writer Shirley Hibberd described as 'eels in ecstasy'), and by the relict Victorian fashion for winding paths and kidney-shaped beds to be found in ambitious public parks of the mid-20th century. Renaissance French and Italian gardeners had used small-scale scrollwork between straight lines, and many a British Victorian parterre echoed them. Bloom merely domesticated and simplified what they had begun, using a richer palette of plants and doing away with symmetry in the name of naturalism.

In the Dell's curvilinear wake came the 1970s fashion for heather and conifer gardens pioneered by Bloom's son Adrian, Rosemary Weisse's work in Westpark, Munich, in 1983 (although here filled with a wilder-looking and more ecologically correct planting), and work at Trentham, Staffordshire, by the Dutch designer Piet Oudolf (p. 280) in 2006, whose emphasis on grasses as part of the New Perennials Movement was already to be seen in the Dell. It is a seminal garden.

ROBERTO BURLE MARX

Graphic forms and native flora in Brazil

1909–1994

1909
Nicaragua executes 500 revolutionaries.
First tour of Diaghilev's Ballets Russes to Paris.
Foundation of Tel Aviv.
Louis Blériot becomes the first man to cross the English
    Channel in a heavier-than-air craft.

1994
Russia and China, and Russia and the USA, agree to de-
    target nuclear weapons against each other.
Rwandan genocide.
The Church of England ordains the first female priests.
Nelson Mandela becomes the first black president of
    South Africa.

ROBERTO BURLE MARX must surely be South America's most celebrated garden and landscape designer, showered with international awards and with commissions across the world, from South Africa to Vienna to the USA, but especially in South America and his native Brazil. Rio de Janeiro is a living gallery of his works in the same way that Barcelona is a gallery of the works of the architect Antoni Gaudí.

Perhaps Burle Marx has been celebrated particularly in the Anglophone garden world – Britain, the USA, Australia – precisely because his work is so different from anything found there, so much freer, more vigorous, vivacious, curvaceous, with a carnival spirit that appeals hugely to gardeners used to a more sober northern style firmly rooted in the rectilinear symmetry of the French and Italian traditions. If his work had any direct relationship to European precedents, it was to the 19th-century Gardenesque, with its brightly coloured flower beds wriggling around in suburban lawns, a style which lingered into the 20th century only in public parks and which, by the late 20th century, was on the whole considered unfashionable. And yet here was a flamboyant Brazilian reinventing the style with all the colour and vibrancy of its 19th-century predecessors and plainly revelling in it. He had found a freedom to which Europeans dared not aspire.

Burle Marx was also a champion of landscape and plant conservation in the wild, alarmed by the widespread destruction of forests for agriculture in Brazil; this too increasingly struck a chord with European sympathies. As if this were not enough, Burle Marx was also a very considerable painter, which further added to his international fame. He was in fact a genuine polymath. Born in São Paulo to a

Burle Marx at work in his studio surrounded by designs, 1955.

ABOVE The roof garden of the Ministry of Education and Health, Rio de Janeiro, designed in 1938. OPPOSITE Pedro do Rio, Residencia Cavanellas. The painter's curvilinear patterns in bright tropical colours contrast with that very European element – flat grass, the lawn.

German-Jewish leather manufacturer and an aristocratic Brazilian mother whose salon included artists such as Pablo Casals, the boy showed talent from the start and it was initially proposed that he should become a singer. But despite his poor eyesight, fine art and a love of plants prevailed. The family spent eighteen months in Weimar Berlin, where Burle Marx studied painting and was thrilled by the work of Picasso, Klee and Matisse, by opera conducted by Toscanini and Bruno Walter, by Diaghilev's ballet company, by formal and landscape gardens, and by the botanic gardens, where he first encountered native Brazilian plants under glass. He also found illumination in Karl Foerster's magazine, *Gartenschoenheit*.

After he returned to conservative Rio he was persuaded not to take up architecture at the National Academy of Fine Art, but enrolled instead to study painting under Leo Putz and Candido Portinari. But it was Lucio Costa, who taught architecture there, who recognized his talents and became his mentor and benefactor. He saw Burle Marx's efforts in gardening and gave him his first opportunities. Thus began Burle Marx's life of working with innovative young architects. He designed a garden for the Ministry of Education and Health in Rio de Janeiro, a project led by the architect Le Corbusier, followed by the city's Santos Dumont airport, where his love of water in landscaping quickly became apparent. Very soon he was able to set up in business on his own, both as a designer and as a supplier in usefully large quantities of the Brazilian plants he was advising his clients to use.

The Sítio Roberto Burle Marx was the designer's home. He was passionate about the ornamental use of native (and often dramatic) Brazilian plants, and was also a serious and active conservationist.

Despite being a poor businessman and living in politically turbulent times when working on civic projects involved treading carefully, Burle Marx built a highly successful career as a garden and landscape designer, alongside his conservation work, plant collecting and introduction of threatened plants into commercial horticulture (over fifty plants are named after him). He painted to the end of his life and received regular retrospective exhibitions in Europe. Lecturing about his work took him around the world, and he was also in demand as a designer of jewellery and society flower decorator. Unmarried, his artistic energies never flagged. Even in his later years he was taking on as many as twenty new projects a year. Undoubtedly his most famous and conspicuous project was the Avenida Atlântica, stretching along Rio's Copacabana beach. Here he wove together a long landscape of cars, cafés and social green spaces along a spine of black-and-white sinuously patterned paving. But equally important are his projects at various ministries in the new capital Brasília and at the Sítio Roberto Burle Marx, his long-time home, landscape garden and nursery; he managed to secure its future as a public foundation before his death.

It should be remembered that Burle Marx had no formal training as a landscape architect, and like many of the great 18th-century English landscape designers he employed draughtsmen to turn his very detailed drawings into work on the ground. He was an artist, keen to translate his experience and vision in other arts into the world of landscape and especially public landscape, which he felt was more important: thus Cubism and Expressionism and Abstract art all found their way into his garden designs. His work was the product of what the writer and thinker Arthur Koestler called the 'bisociation' of ideas, which he said underlay all creativity. It should be remembered, too, that Burle Marx's style, like that of many great artists, was a reaction against what preceded him, the gardening based around symmetry and the use of European or internationally sourced plants that were as widely employed in Brazil as in every other ex-colonial country. Burle Marx's achievement was to include in his designs Brazilian plants better suited to the climate, in a fresh and painterly way with an exuberant use of colour and foliage, and to have settled on a curvilinear style that worked so well with the contrasting clean lines of rectilinear modern architecture.

Promenade, Copacabana beach, Rio de Janeiro, well-known throughout the world, although many people may never have heard of the designer's name.

JOHN BROOKES

The room outside

BORN 1933

1933
Berthold Lubetkin's Modernist Round House built for
    gorillas in London Zoo.
Construction of Battersea Power Station commences.
Birth of Richard Rogers, architect of the new World
    Trade Center, Tower Three.
The Bauhaus school in Berlin closed by the Nazis.

IT HAS BEEN said that Modernism in the arts began in Russia and Germany in the early 20th century, but that in garden design especially it leap-frogged Britain and landed in America, appearing there in the work of men such as Thomas Church in the 1940s. John Brookes's great achievement in the 1960s was to bring Modernism back from America to Britain, where it is still replacing the classic, Edwardian and singularly effective Lutyens-and-Jekyll manner.

Brookes was born in the city of Durham, in the north of England, and educated there. Military service followed, after which he trained in commercial horticulture at County Durham's School of Horticulture. A three-year apprenticeship followed in Nottingham Corporation's parks department. But for all this practical horticultural beginning, it was design that appealed more, and Brookes managed to find work as an assistant to Brenda Colvin, one of the most forward-thinking landscape architects of the day. This confirmed his choice of career and he took a diploma in Landscape Design at University College, London, leading him to five years' work as assistant to Sylvia Crowe, that other lauded female landscape architect of the day. A broad interest in thinking across all the arts then took him to work as an editorial assistant on the magazine *Architectural Design*, after which, in 1964, considering himself suitably trained, he set up in private practice as a garden designer.

Brookes acknowledges his great influence was Thomas Church, whose guiding principle was that gardens were for people, to live in and to use, not merely to look at and maintain; gardens were in effect part of the house. No surprise then that in 1969 Brookes, now 36, published *Room Outside*, which established similar ideas for gardens in Britain, where the climate is so different from Church's California and there was so much of a pre-existing tradition of garden-making to be accommodated or modified.

The book was both fresh and a great surprise for British gardeners and designers, still recovering from the wartime doldrums, and its influence was – and still is – huge. Brookes has gone on to publish 24 books over his lifetime, mostly practical, explanatory books for enthusiasts, about how to design small domestic gardens, country and natural gardens, even indoor gardens, and all of them written in an approachable though still rigorous style, and often translated for the international market. Yet it is *Room Outside* that has become the seminal text.

Like Church before him, Brookes has a quiet, no-nonsense way of writing and drawing that speaks directly to the reader, dealing with design issues for beginners without making them sound daunting and yet never dumbing down. Brookes became the name synonymous with established, modern, practical design. Television has often used him as the wise voice of authority on garden design issues, especially in the BBC's *Small Town Gardens* of 2003. In 2004 he received the MBE for garden design and services to horticulture, and the Award of Distinction from the American Association of Professional Landscape Designers.

Brookes taught design in person as well as through his books. He directed the Inchbald School of Garden Design, a highly respected private college, and in 1978 he

Denmans, with the famous oil jar; plants appear unregimented and free to advance and retreat as the season demands.

Curving lawns and paths pay tribute to Thomas Church, a source of inspiration for Brookes, although Brookes's planting is far richer.

set up the Inchbald School of Interior Design in Tehran. To him, the idea of designing interiors is not so far removed from designing gardens; both require the same sense of liveable space. But the venture also appealed to his feeling that design has fewer boundaries than people suppose, and that good garden designers actually ought to have an education and an ongoing interest in fields such as painting and sculpture, as artists go through the same processes of understanding proportion and movement, space and colour as do garden designers. He finds an awareness of these sister arts troublingly lacking in many aspiring young garden designers.

In 1980 Brookes founded his Clock House School of Garden Design at his own home and 1.6-ha (4-acre) garden, Denmans, at Fontwell in Sussex. The Clock House is a set of converted outbuildings and walled garden once belonging to the great house, which now sits separated on the other side of a busy road. It had a garden already when Brookes came to it, belonging to Joyce Robinson, but Brookes has gone on to make it his own, and famously so.

Denmans nicely captures the Brookes style. Nothing is grand. Cars sit tucked into trees quietly out of the way, but close to hand. French doors connect the indoor living space with a generous terrace outside; but this is not a showcase for cool min-imalist paving, it is very much a gardener's space, full of plants standing on or arching over it. In the selection of plants, Denmans is very much a traditional English garden; no surprise that many of Brookes's commissions abroad have been for 'English' gardens, whether in Japan or Chicago.

And yet Denmans is also unmistakably modern. A circuit of the garden rarely passes through a narrow space, but rather through a series of sinuous, gently advan-cing spaces. Some are of grass, others of gravel. Best known is a long, snaking path of gravel flanked by quiet architectural planting. It could be said to be a winding path except that really it is the planting that winds, bulging out into the gravelled space. And these plantings fall gently to the gravel, not as muscular mixed borders but in a quiet, open-textured descent. In the centre of the path the eye is temporarily halted by a tall oil jar surrounded by plants as if self-sown there. It has been photographed by half the world, amateur and professional, an iconic image that surely must have been in Beth Chatto's eye when she made the Dry Garden in Essex (p. 272), with its same ebbing and flowing of plants on to its gravel core.

One of the garden's larger open spaces, an irregular oval of grass, has its entire centre, but for a couple of yards of path around the perimeter, filled with longer grass where small spring bulbs grow. It gives the space a *raison d'être* through the simplest of strokes. And it says a lot about Brookes's designs: this is neither the long grass of traditional English gardens, where it would have been kept to the wilder edges of the garden, nor is it an affair with the contemporary fashion for wildflower meadows. It is just a simple Brookesian means of making a space work harder, a cool designer's eye applied to an area which also happens to be surrounded by busy English, plant-rich gardening.

Brookes's teaching career has taken him all over the world, not least to Harvard, Kew, New York, Toronto, Johannesburg, Australia and New Zealand. He has run garden schools in Chile and Argentina, as well as at home in England. For three years he was Chairman of the Society of Garden Designers, an organization set up to bring together and promote the work of talented designers. Brookes himself has always found commissions mostly by word of mouth. As with Church before him, he likes to talk to his clients about their needs and desires for the garden before he sets to work. Brookes the man creates a relationship to underlie the project and in doing so is easy company, serious about his ideas, but a magnificent giggler when provoked.

Since the 1980s garden design in Britain has got into gear behind Brookes's push to Modernism, but he finds plenty of what is done now to be more about style and the desire to be different than about usefulness for the client. Installation gardening

A recent project in Patagonia, with an 'S' of steps and landings leading quietly down to the water and with a magnificent view of mountains as a backdrop.

he finds interesting, but that is all. Conversely, some young designers perhaps find Brookes's work old hat – he has been designing for 50 years and has not leapt into the arms of computer-aided design (which he finds produces clinical results); but this is perhaps to confuse fashionability with desirability. Brookes feels that, far from being out of date, he and his work are still fighting the model of boring lawn with a few plants around the outside, and that, in fact, too little has moved on since the mid-20th century.

Commissions over the years have included hotels, city squares, department store roof gardens and even airport lounges, among those from private clients. But today it is country gardens that hold his interest, whether at home or abroad, even Patagonia, because of the opportunity to make gardens in a rural but not nostalgic way. So often his client asks for yet another old-fashioned English garden, and he has to persuade people that there is more on offer and that English does not mean old-fashioned, that any good design will grow out of what is in and around the garden already. Brookes loves to look down from an aeroplane at the field systems of a new country and consider what that says about the way the landscape is used, and to let that localness inform the way he designs a garden. And he is still very active and still flying and working around the world – Moscow, and now St Petersburg – designing gardens that suit the particular landscape.

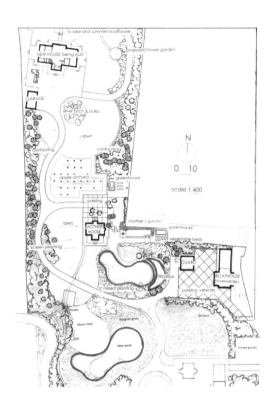

*John Brookes, now in his 80s,
still travels worldwide and
works on all continents: here
a project outside St Petersburg
– the American, domestic, post-
war style which originated with
Thomas Church is desirable in
Russia today.*

JAMES VAN SWEDEN

Modern, naturalistic gardens

1935–2013

1935
Amelia Earhart flies solo from Hawaii to California.
President Roosevelt's second New Deal helps combat the
    effects of the Great Depression.
Frank Lloyd Wright designs the house Fallingwater, in
    Pennsylvania
Birth of Elvis Presley.

2013
Edward Snowden discloses US surveillance operations.
North Korea conducts a third underground nuclear test.
President Morsi of Egypt deposed in a military coup.
Election of Francis, the first Jesuit pope, from Argentina.

THERE'S A DISTINCT exuberance about the gardens of James van Sweden, or, more accurately, the gardens of James van Sweden and German émigré Wolfgang Oehme. Large and small, public and private, they were mostly created around Washington, DC, and the 'New American Garden' style brought a fresh look to gardens. In place of stolid evergreens, high-maintenance lawns and splashes of annual colour, came a great wave of massed perennials in meadows, even prairies of them, providing movement and easily maintained year-long interest. In the tradition of Thomas Church, van Sweden and Oehme also believed that gardens were for using, for living in.

Van Sweden himself was an exuberant, outgoing character, in contrast to the more taciturn Oehme, and enjoyed business and promoting his work, unusual in the reticent world of gardens. He was born into the Dutch community of Grand Rapids, Michigan. It was an earnestly religious family, his father a building developer and his great-grandfather an architect. The young van Sweden was fascinated by the natural world and loved walking in the dunes around Lake Michigan, in the meadows and woods growing beside railroad tracks and in the warmer landscapes and opulent 1920s gardens around Fort Myers in Florida, where the family spent the winters.

Having trained for five years as an architect at the University of Michigan, and, admiring what was happening in the landscape design programme there, he applied to study landscape architecture at the University of Delft in the Netherlands; his wife found work as an architect. It was a chance to see Europe, and in their old VW they drove around Italy, France, Yugoslavia, Greece and Egypt. Van Sweden was captivated by Vermeer's paintings of Dutch interiors, with their beautifully designed spaces and paving.

Oehme and van Sweden in their early days in the 1970s, running a garden design and planting business from van Sweden's house in Georgetown, Washington, DC.

Returning home in 1963, he was hired by urban planners Marcou, O'Leary and Associates and remained with them for thirteen years, soon becoming a partner. When the firm was bought out by Westinghouse in 1973, his windfall allowed van Sweden to consider setting up his own business. In 1971 he bought a townhouse in Georgetown, Washington, DC, and asked the Baltimore landscape architect Wolfgang Oehme to design the garden. He had met Oehme in 1964 and been hugely impressed by his dramatic, generous planting, which in a small garden seemed all the more striking. Van Sweden's busy social life brought the garden to public attention and it was so admired that he gave up urban design, because it was 'political' rather than 'productive', and in 1975 went into partnership with Oehme to create gardens. His clients were ready and waiting.

The firm first operated from a spare bedroom in the Georgetown house, and the pair spent their time making simple sketches, filling a car with pots and going off to plant gardens. Van Sweden could not believe he was being paid to have such

Ferry Cove, Sherwood, van Sweden's weekend house; he enjoyed the contrast between rectilinear modern architecture and motile, grass-rich planting.

fun. As time went by his architectural skills came to the fore again as he specialized in designing the bones of the gardens and landscapes they made, with a small office staff to help. A commission for work at the Federal Reserve Building in 1977 saw them established as brave new players in the landscape world.

By 1990 van Sweden was starting to write books and to teach and lecture. His and Oehme's *Bold Romantic Gardens* of 1990 was in effect a manifesto of how he thought gardens should be made, but it also showcased and thereby publicized their work, in the same way that *Gardens Are for People* had popularized the work of Thomas Church in California 35 years previously.

For all the lushness of planting in a van Sweden and Oehme garden, geometry was certainly not absent, especially around buildings, but it was made romantic by its dressing of soft, enveloping herbaceous planting. Domestic lawns that ran uninterrupted to the street were given a screening of loose shrubs, behind which the whole lawn could be transformed into a wave of perennials. Van Sweden wanted planting that could be read from a passing car as well as by someone on foot; there was never anything spotty about the gardens. A small garden was given instant drama by large plants and large leaves. In a bigger or civic garden, plants would be used in the hundreds, in great sweeping swathes. What mattered most was that the plants were tough in heat and drought, flowered for six to eight weeks, and retained a good winter presence; the manipulation of colour was less important than texture.

Favourite plants included such architectural stalwarts as sedums, perennial cone-flowers and Joe Pye weed. Grasses were a hugely dominant feature, not least for their ability to move in the wind and respond to the changing light; they brought the romance of natural landscapes and a composed wildness into urban settings.

Van Sweden employed a generous scale in his use of water, too. Pools were not decorative and incidental, but a structural element of the design. Visits to Japanese gardens impressed on him the need for the precise control of scale and the impact of a borrowed landscape. It is no surprise that he was an admirer of the brightly col-oured landscapes of Roberto Burle Marx (p. 188) and even of the great, green-only landforms of 'Capability' Brown (p. 148).

At Ferry Cove, van Sweden made the transition from house to natural landscape with the kind of plantings that appeared broadly natural but in fact contained great numbers of closely managed and selected plants. Grasses played a large part.

The projects of which van Sweden was proudest include the Rockefeller Park in New York and his work at the Chicago Botanic Garden (although he undertook many significant civic projects including the National World War II Memorial, the US National Arboretum and the Treasury Building and National Gallery of Art). He was forever fond of his Georgetown house, so influential for his career, and of the Rosenberg garden (1983), which he felt showed best what he could do. When it came to the manipulation of the underlying landform he wished merely to create an unobtrusive terrain; it was the bold planting of open space in a garden that mattered to him most – the sheer expanse of it.

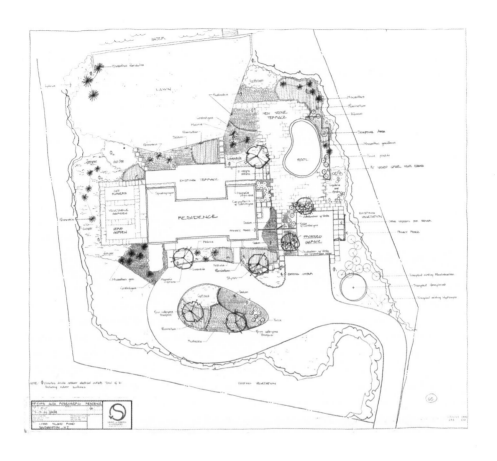

GARDENS OF PLANTSMANSHIP

THE CHINESE TALK about 'building' gardens, not 'planting' them. It's a telling statement, for the classic Chinese gardens are about the creation of symbolic landforms and structures, with (by European standards) a modest number of symbolic plants bringing life to the scene. European gardens come from a different tradition, one in which new plants were avidly collected from all corners of the globe and accommodated in gardens or under glass.

Garden designers and landscape architects, whose primary job is to design spaces, often despair of the European gardener's obsession with plants. Surely it's the structure of a garden that should come first – the spaces, the landform, the relationship to the surroundings? And isn't the planting that follows only a form of decoration? The argument will run forever, and the answer will always be that great gardeners are a happy blend of space-maker and plantsman. Occasionally – very occasionally – a person comes along who has both skills, or at least by trial and error in their own garden has managed to create somewhere that successfully combines the two factors.

But let's be clear: if planting must follow space-making, it is no less a skill in its different way, and decorators – plantsmen – have made some of the most exciting gardens of the past 150 years. Visitors to such gardens, who may not themselves be gardeners, have been thrilled and inspired to learn for themselves about growing plants and making a garden; for most visitors it will be the process rather than the result that matters most. We should be grateful, as this serves a purpose in the modern urbanized world to encourage more people to connect with the living environment and to value it.

There are many different kinds of plantsmen gardeners. Some are colourists, people for whom the greatest pleasure is in placing flowers to create sophisticated, attractive effects. The results may be loud or subtle, and both are hard to do really well. Subtle may be fashionable in one decade and loud in the next, but that does not belittle either style if the work is ambitious.

In his garden at Giverny, the French Impressionist painter Claude Monet was brilliant at harmonizing the kind of bright colours that came to life in sunshine. At Great Dixter in England (designed by Lutyens), the gardener and writer Christopher Lloyd was a master of rich, hot colours; his 1990s Exotic Garden was a melting pot of vibrant hues and subtropical architectural foliage. It was outrageous fun and the pleasure was in the game of getting it right every year, of making everything flower and well, with no gaps, of keeping all the plates spinning in the air together. In a much subtler way, the watercolourist and *grand dame* of Edwardian gardening Gertrude Jekyll was a wonder at making colours flow sympathetically through the spectrum. Later in the century, the Dutch designer Mien Ruys would go on to produce results that were softer and greener still.

Plantsmen have always been champions of natural planting and the patron saint of wild gardening was the Irish gardener, writer and publisher William Robinson. Through his writings his influence is as strong today as it was in the 19th century. We should never have had the work of Beth Chatto, nor her garden in Essex, if it were not for Robinson and his ideas about growing plants only in conditions that properly suit them. Chatto's garden was laid out using great loops of hose-pipe arranged on the ground, and it belongs to the curvilinear school of design, but her habitat-controlled plant association has inspired two generations of gardeners. Dutchman Piet Oudolf has made a hit in New York with his more modern, grass-rich palette of plants, a fashionable *rus in urbe*. At Ninfa in Italy, Lelia Caetani persuaded highly bred shrubs and climbers to look at home over the ruins of a medieval town. In scorching Arizona, Steve Martino has raised the desert flora to complete respectability, banished resource-hungry exotics, and decades ago invented sustainable gardening.

Some plantsmen's fascination has been the juxtaposition of plants not just for colour, but to dress a whole scene with close contrasts of tone and foliage and sheer romance; this was what Vita Sackville-West and Rosemary Verey set out to do. Others have been collectors, like Graham Stuart Thomas, making gardens that manage to accommodate large numbers of only one kind of plant and still look good – no easy task. All of them have had a passion for plants – they are gardening's brilliant decorators.

Planting plan by Piet Oudolf for a project in Germany.

WILLIAM ROBINSON

Father of naturalistic flower gardening

1838–1935

1838
The Coronation of Queen Victoria in Westminster Abbey.
The People's Charter drawn up in UK, demanding
    universal suffrage.
Britain leads Indian Army into first Anglo-Afghan war.
Birth of John Wilkes Booth, actor and assassin of
    Abraham Lincoln.

1935
The board game Monopoly begins to be marketed by
    Parker Brothers.
Aeroplanes banned from flying over the White House,
    Washington, DC.
Stalin opens the Moscow Metro.

PEOPLE WILL ARGUE forever about whether William Robinson was a great gardener. Certainly he was a great pundit, with many books and periodicals to his name. He was a single-minded, lifelong and vociferous campaigner against the geometric bedding schemes that had helped define Victorian gardens, favouring instead a more naturalistic style of planting. His own and only garden, Gravetye Manor, in Sussex, was in fact less pioneering than might be expected given that he had been trumpeting his ideas literally for decades before he began it.

More than anything, Robinson was a prophet – of the age of truly naturalistic gardening. It is possible to trace his influence quite clearly in the wildflower meadows being planted by Daisy Lloyd, mother of Christopher (p. 264) at Great Dixter during Robinson's lifetime, through the late 20th-century garden of Beth Chatto (p. 272), where every plant had to grow in conditions to which it was ideally suited by nature and with appropriate companions, to the 21st-century love affair with annual 'meadows' and prairie planting in public spaces, as seen at London's Olympic Park of 2012. Robinson's words in his influential book, *The Wild Garden*, are as useful to gardeners today as they were in 1870 when it was first published, and if it was *The English Flower Garden* of 1883 that went into so many editions and brought him the title 'Father of English Flower Gardening', it is *The Wild Garden* that is his greater memorial.

Robinson was born in Ireland and began working as a gardener while still a boy. His skills brought him to the attention of David Moore, curator of the Botanic

Portrait of William Robinson, gardener, author, publisher, who rose from rags to respectability and riches by sheer force of personality and, some might say, bloody-mindedness.

Gardens at Glasnevin, and, with letters of introduction from him, Robinson left Ireland aged 23 to begin a remarkable and lucrative career in England.

Despite his humble origins, Robinson was socially impressive and seems to have possessed both an appealing intellectual curiosity and the gift of the gab, a combination that won over people who shared his passion for plants and gardens. Sometimes an intellectual from a very ordinary background will transform himself into a member of an entirely different social milieu, but Robinson seems never to have quite got away from his garden-boy origins; there was always a sense of us-and-them in his writing, of servant and master. If so, Robinson was ever the servant who liked to know far better than his masters. Buying Gravetye Manor estate and making its garden must have felt to him an extraordinary achievement.

Moore's introductions landed Robinson a job as foreman of the herbaceous and British native collection at the Royal Botanic Society's garden in Regent's Park under curator Robert Marnock. Once again, Robinson's confidence won him personal study tours of public and private botanic gardens throughout Britain, during which he made ever more professional contacts. He began to contribute to the *Gardeners' Chronicle*, a serious horticultural journal, and in 1866 he was elected to the Linnaean Society under the sponsorship of Charles Darwin. It was now time for him to strike out alone.

Robinson left the Royal Botanic Society, took a crash course in French and spent a year effectively as a journalist in Paris, reporting for *The Field*, *The Times* and the *Gardeners' Chronicle* on horticultural aspects of the year-long Universal Exhibition of 1867. France was a revelation to him. If the rigid formality of Versailles made him apoplectic with anger, he marvelled at the unexpectedly high quality of skilled French horticulture and plantsmanship, town planning and cemeteries; so he quickly wrote a couple of books on the subject. The following year saw him off to the Swiss Alps, which gave him material for *Alpine Flowers for English Gardens*, part encyclopedia and part tirade against unnatural rock gardens, and based on his French experiences he published *Mushroom Culture*.

His fifth book, *The Wild Garden*, appeared in 1870. This was a plea for gardens large and small to do away with neurotic, artificial, bedded-out gardens in favour of naturalism, and – here's the important part – to introduce tough garden plants into the outer parts of a garden or estate, where they could settle down and look every bit as attractive as natives. Cheaply, too, adds Robinson's inner garden-boy. The first edition was unadorned, but by the 1881 edition it was lavishly illustrated by the artist Alfred Parsons, who was to work with Robinson through the rest of his literary career; his picturesque, cottagey style set the tone for people longing for

The Thames at Shiplake by Alfred Parsons, a painter fascinated by gardens and Robinson's long-time collaborator on books and magazines. He also provided illustrations for short stories by Thomas Hardy. OVERLEAF *Painting by Beatrice Parsons of the borders on the main terrace at Gravetye Manor.*

cosy domestic architecture that was at one with nature. No wonder Robinson was admired by Arts and Crafts prophet John Ruskin.

In 1870 Robinson toured America, coast to coast, discovering ever more plants, conifers especially, that he might use in British gardens. Now, with seven books under his belt, he added magazines to the mix, and *The Garden* appeared in 1871. He was to edit it until 1899, at which time he handed the helm to his deputy E. T. Cook, with Gertrude Jekyll in joint control. Robinson's connections allowed him to attract all the most highly respected contributors from international horticulture, including Ruskin himself. It became Robinson's platform for his ongoing war against formal 'architects' gardens'.

After publishing a short-lived magazine in French, Robinson launched his other great and highly profitable title, *Gardening Illustrated* (at first called just *Gardening*), in 1879. This was a publication more for the amateur, with regular advice columns, while at the same time he turned out yet further books – on asparagus, French cemeteries and more.

Robinson's *The English Flower Garden* of 1883 was his all-in-one opus, on how one ought to make a garden in correct (Robinsonian) taste, and the plants with

which to do so. He was now becoming rich and was far too busy for a wife. A house was another matter. In 1885 he bought the Gravetye Manor estate in Sussex. The house, originally built in 1598, underwent major refurbishment, with obsessive attention paid to wood fires and fire-proofing (stubborn Robinson refused to insure).

Here at last Robinson had his own garden, and the chance to put into practice

all the ideals he had been so loudly proclaiming for the last 30 years. It was pure romance, with the comfortable, old stone house set in rolling, wooded countryside, and yet it was not nature run amok as might have been predicted, but rather a perfectly common-sensical approach to making a garden in countryside, based on principles that are still in use today. Since the land dropped away before the house, there was formal terracing; Robinson saw nothing unnatural in that since it was practical. His rectangular terrace, subdivided into a pattern of geometric beds, was acceptable to him so long as the planting was not gaudy and blocky in High Victorian style. Below the terraces he made his meadow of wild and cultivated flowers leading to a pond, and around the whole estate he found scope for picturesque planting of non-native trees on a vast scale. It was the kind of garden that would lead to the typical Arts and Crafts gardens of Edwin Lutyens, who used simple, bold and necessary garden architecture, dressed (in his case by Gertrude Jekyll) in a romantic and relatively natural manner. Topiary would, of course, have been a step too far for Robinson.

From this comfortable base, the ageing Robinson became ever more aggressive in print against architects' gardens designed on paper (he always 'designed' on the hoof). When Reginald Blomfield's *The Formal Garden in England* appeared in 1892, Robinson launched himself against this scholarly defence of formality and

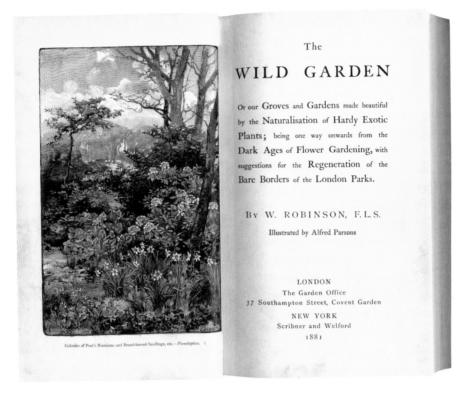

The

WILD GARDEN

Or our Groves and Gardens made beautiful by the Naturalisation of Hardy Exotic Plants; being one way onwards from the Dark Ages of Flower Gardening, with suggestions for the Regeneration of the Bare Borders of the London Parks.

By W. ROBINSON, F.L.S.

Illustrated by Alfred Parsons

LONDON
The Garden Office
37 Southampton Street, Covent Garden
NEW YORK
Scribner and Welford
1881

Colonies of Poet's Narcissus and Broad-leaved Saxifrage, etc.—*Frontispiece.*

Illustration and title page from an edition of The Wild Garden. *Robinson's great passion was for the use of garden plants in country settings or rougher parts of the garden, where they would 'look' wild.*

structure with his own book, *Garden Design and Architects' Gardens*. A major public spat ensued, with neither party emerging victorious. For Robinson, it was fame at last, his life's mission in the headlines. It also gave him the chance to talk about the work he had done for other gardens (only a small amount), notably replanting the garden at Shrubland Park in Suffolk, laid out by the architect Sir Charles Barry.

Robinson initially continued to manage his publishing enterprise from Gravetye, going up to London on the train every morning, although for the last 25 years of his life this energetic man was confined to a wheelchair, possibly as a result of a long-term syphilitic infection. But from Gravetye, cared for by a faithful nurse, he published still more books on domestic management. He died in 1935, leaving his estate for forestry purposes; it rapidly went downhill, until the house was reprieved decades later by being made into a hotel. If only the bones of his garden remain, Robinson's ideas still grow from strength to strength in gardens elsewhere.

CLAUDE MONET

Painting with plants

1840–1926

1840
Birth of Auguste Rodin, Émile Zola and Thomas Hardy.
New Zealand declared a British colony.
Charles Wilkes's United States Exploring Expedition
    proves Antarctica is a continent
The Penny Black, the world's first postage stamp, is
    introduced in Britain.

1926
British General Strike, Martial Law declared.
Birth of Queen Elizabeth II and Fidel Castro.
John Logie Baird demonstrates a mechanical television
    system.
The League of Nations abolishes all types of slavery.

THE WORLD KNOWS Claude Monet primarily as a great Impressionist painter, but much less as a gardener, and yet gardens were an important part of his life, especially his garden at Giverny, 75 km (45 miles) west of Paris, which he developed and gardened with his own hands until success as a painter allowed him to employ others. What kind of garden is Giverny? It is effectively two gardens, separated stylistically by half the world and physically by a busy road: one is the formal setting for his house, the Clos Normand, the other his naturalistic pool garden where he grew water lilies.

For all Monet's position in the avant garde of painting, the first garden in design terms was perfectly traditional, with fruit and vegetables, long straight borders of popular French flowers – irises, roses, sunflowers, nasturtiums, geraniums – and a path leading direct from the road to the front door. What made it special was the intensity with which it was gardened, the number of borders and the vitality of the carefully contrived colour schemes. In garden-speak today, 'carefully contrived' usually means 'subtle', and yet Monet's colour schemes were far from quiet; they revelled in the same bright splashes and contradictions that gave life to his paintings. And he painted the garden, again and again, because as he said the light changes every half hour.

ABOVE Photograph of Monet painting in his studio in 1920. OPPOSITE The Artist's Garden in Giverny *(detail), by Monet, 1900. Narrow side paths weave among massed plantings of his favourite flowers, here irises, which he regularly painted.*

Autochrome of Monet in his garden at Giverny, 1921. His style of gardening was in some places wildly romantic, but determinedly formal in others. In design terms, he was no innovator.

There was no restraint about Monet's Clos Normand, nothing calmly natural except the plants themselves. Farmhouses like his were in fact more likely to have animals close by, and the odd row of flowers, with the vegetables in the corner of a field. Monet's garden in its busy-ness was more like a little 19th-century public garden. In no sense was it a secret and subtle demesne. Indeed the central path that ran from the front door – his *grande allée* – finished at the road, which was then also a railway track. Even if the population was far smaller in his day, riding past Monsieur Monet's garden must have been a memorable sight for any traveller passing by. And that is how Monet first found the house himself – riding by on the train.

Monet was a grocer's son, born in Paris but spending his childhood at Le Havre on the Normandy coast, where he loved to sketch. He was encouraged by the painter Eugène Boudin to paint in the open air – *en plein air* – which was to become the Impressionists' preference. As young men often did, he joined the army at 21, but, after a bout of typhoid, got out and studied art in Paris. Here he met the greats of his time – Renoir, Sisley and so many more – and began to paint seriously. His regular model was Camille Doncieux, whom he married after the birth of their son Jean in 1870. It was the year of the Franco-Prussian war and the family escaped the troubles to England, where Monet studied paintings by Turner and Constable. Finding their way back to France via the Netherlands a year later, the couple settled at Argenteuil on the Seine, poor, but with Monet already keen to garden. He collected Delft jardinières and enjoyed the striped, ribbon borders of vibrantly coloured bedding plants that were the fashion of the period.

In 1874 Monet exhibited his *Impression: Sunrise* in Paris, alongside works by other non-establishment painters such as Degas, Cézanne, Pissarro and Renoir, and thus was the term Impressionist born. But before his career could take off, Camille was diagnosed with tuberculosis. The Monets were taken in by Ernest Hoschedé and his wife, Alice, at their country home at Vétheuil, until Camille died in 1879. Ernest Hoschedé, store-owner and patron of the arts, was shortly afterwards declared bankrupt and fled to Belgium, while Alice looked after the two Monet boys along with her own six children. Then in 1883 Monet saw that farmhouse set in its orchards from the train, and the entire ménage moved to Giverny, with Monet marrying Alice on Ernest Hoschedé's death nine years later.

The house, the barn (his studio) and its surrounding land were rented. With a little help, Monet removed the fiddly box-edged potager by the house and the lines of spruces flanking the front path. By 1890 Monet's work was selling well; he bought the property for 22,000 francs and began, now as proud owner, to renovate and develop the garden. His famous blue-green shutters appeared, as well as the *grande allée*'s broad iron pergola covered with roses. In symmetrical beds to either side, irises flanked lesser borders and plants were allowed to naturalize – poppies, verbenas and nasturtiums. Colour schemes enhanced the natural effects of light: blue in the shade, yellow and orange in the sun. Standard roses and clematis on tall pyramids emerged from lower plantings. Flowering cherries and apricots blossomed, and beneath the trees were baskets of plants growing as if they had been picked and arranged there. Monet could afford gardeners now, seven of them, issued with daily written instructions from the master. A greenhouse for orchids appeared and a second studio.

In expansionist mood, in 1893 Monet bought land the other side of the road to make a water garden, and having negotiated the practicalities and local politics of diverting the river, he succeeded. The door in the wall at the bottom of his *grande allée* was now the portal to a completely different kind of garden, and if not strictly Japanese (he became a great collector of Hokusai prints) it was Japanese in the simplicity of its conception: sinuous ponds ringed by trees, shrubs and bamboo were

ABOVE Monet in his water garden, around *1922.* Smartly kept curving paths encircle the pool. Pendent wisteria flowers on the bridge will be reflected, like the willow, in the water. The scene is all about reflection. *RIGHT* The Japanese Footbridge, *1899.* The bridge and its reflection create a formal frame for the more abstract composition of the lilies in the water.

Giverny today, the central path leading up to the front door from the road and water garden. Monet painted this vista time and time again, in spring, in high summer, and in autumn when sprawling nasturtiums almost covered the path.

spanned by a green bridge smothered in wisteria, and covered in groups of luscious, luminous water lilies bought from the great French nurseryman Latour-Marliac who was then breaking new ground as a breeder of this plant. Painting the lilies, finally on huge canvases in an abstract manner, became Monet's *idée fixe* for the last years of his life.

Giverny became a focus for painters, often American, as well as for the contemporary art world of France. Monet swapped plants with his near neighbour, the painter Gustave Caillebotte, whose quiet images of smarter, simpler gardens of the period clearly demonstrate just how extravagant Monet's garden really was. It inevitably faded after his death until in the 1980s a Foundation was established to give it a brilliant new lease of life.

GERTRUDE JEKYLL

Arranging colours in a harmonious whole

1843–1932

<table>
<tr><td>

1843

A thousand pioneers set out in the first major wagon train on the Oregon Trail to the American Northwest.

The *Economist* is first published in London.

Birth of Henry James, novelist.

</td><td>

1932

The Nazi Party becomes the largest in the Reichstag; 6 million German unemployed.

In England, James Chadwick discovers the neutron.

Opening of the Sydney Harbour Bridge.

The Great Depression hits financial rock bottom in America.

</td></tr>
</table>

A S THE 19th century drew to a close, the more imaginative and ambitious gardens were increasingly not those of the great aristocratic estates, but were to be found on a smaller scale – elegant, domestic, even family gardens, measured in acres rather than tens of acres. And the most revered creator of these was Miss Gertrude Jekyll, self-taught gardener, plantswoman and garden-maker. Would we know of her today, were it not for her collaborations with the great architect and garden designer, Edwin Lutyens (p. 96)? Certainly, for her own garden at Munstead Wood in Surrey was the prototype for the most interesting gardens of the period, and her 15 books and thousands of magazine and newspaper articles were classics not only of her own time, but also invaluable manuals for the plant-rich, domestic gardening that followed during the rest of the 20th century and are still revered today. This large, rather plain, blue-stocking spinster made a far greater mark than ever she imagined possible.

She was born in the 1840s, the close contemporary of Claude Monet and Thomas Hardy, when Queen Victoria was newly crowned. By the time she was designing her last planting schemes in the 1930s, Modernism had arrived and Hitler was coming to power. However, whereas Modernism established itself firmly in the fine arts of Europe, it was never really taken up in European gardens. At her peak, between 1890 and 1914, Jekyll's work might be described as contemporary nostalgia.

How should one pronounce Jekyll? Her preference was Jeekyll ('rhymes with treacle', as gardeners say). She was born in London, just north of Piccadilly, into a wealthy though not aristocratic household, and lived there for the first five years

Photograph of Jekyll, around 1879, independent and tough. Spectacles tell of her problematically poor eyesight.

of her life. The family then moved to Bramley House in the leafy and at that time thoroughly rural lanes of west Surrey, where, as in the Wessex of Hardy's novels, the traditional crafts of the countryside and agricultural life still prevailed; it was a comfortable life for Jekyll and her four brothers. She grew up a solitary, bright, quick-witted girl, and if not a tomboy then convinced of her own rightness in most things. She learned to sing (her mother was a friend of Mendelssohn) and to ride, and to identify the wild plants of the countryside and understand the traditional crafts practised in the working people's cottages. Not that she was a rebel against the class system; she grew up in a house full of servants and later was always firm in her dealings with her household and large staff of gardeners.

As was usual then for young ladies, part of her education was to learn to draw and paint in watercolours, which she did with great accomplishment. A brief spell at the new Cheltenham Ladies' College did not suit this self-contained girl, more interested in what she could do with her hands than with deport-ment and the prospect of married life. By eighteen she was happily established at the South Kensington School of Art in London, beginning to develop her artistic ambitions. She became enthusi-astic about the theories of the art critic and writer John Ruskin, whose influential *Modern Painters* had first been published in 1843, the year of her birth (she later knew both Ruskin and William Morris, two founding fathers of the Arts and Crafts movement). She learned about colour har-monies and became familiar with the intricately formal Kensington garden of the Horticultural Society (later the Royal Horticultural Society), designed by William Nesfield (p. 90) in a style she was later to call cold and soulless. She also began to travel around the Mediterranean countries with her artistic friends, painting land-scapes and flowers and learning new local crafts.

A painting by Jekyll from her travels in Algeria. She was as familiar with exotic vegetation and hard light as she was with the softer effects of the English climate.

Aged 25, Jekyll moved with her family to Wargrave Hill in Berkshire, still unmarried and highly accomplished in many skills: gold, silver, leather, rush and lace work, flower arranging and photography, and riding and singing. Her paintings were exhibited in London and friends began to ask her for designs to decorate the interiors of their houses. She met her future friend William Robinson (p. 208), who had published *The Wild Garden* in 1870 and would later employ her to write for his various horticultural magazines and contribute on the subject of colour to his book *The English Flower Garden* of 1883. She also began to advise on and make designs for gardens and planting. Following the death of her father in 1876, she and her old mother moved back to Surrey. Jekyll experienced a feeling of relief and pleasure at returning to her beloved leafy landscape. A house at Munstead was built for them, and she developed a garden for it, with a parterre, a 48-m (160-ft) flower border, pergola, rock garden and nut walk.

The house and garden at Munstead Wood, built for Jekyll (and very much with her) by Lutyens. It has no grand façades, but sits quietly among its trees.

Photograph by Jekyll of the Michaelmas daisy border at Munstead Wood. Poor eyesight led her to the bigger picture, to appreciate how one colour, or one shade of a colour, led to the next. It was a subject she often wrote about.

But independence beckoned, and Jekyll, now 40 and with sufficient means, bought an adjoining 6-ha (15-acre) triangle of rough woodland where she could make a house and garden for herself alone. With the garden six years planted (part formal, part wild) and coming along nicely, Jekyll considered who might be her architect for the house and happened to meet an up-and-coming architect named Edwin Lutyens, then only 20. The result was a lifelong friendship, but more immediately and after intense collaboration, the building of a head gardener's cottage, a temporary wooden house for Jekyll, and later the main house itself, Munstead Wood, in its long-allocated place within her now semi-mature garden.

Jekyll and Lutyens went on to make over a hundred gardens together during the period 1890 to 1914 – a quarter of the 400 or so commissions she undertook. 'A Lutyens and Jekyll garden' would become a byword for an Edwardian blend of high-quality architecture and quietly sophisticated planting. Many of her commissions were only for planting plans or parts of gardens rather than whole gardens, and she worked with several other influential architects such as Robert Lorimer, Herbert Baker and M. H. Baillie Scott. But it was her work with Lutyens, fostered initially by her family connections and then, as he became established, by Lutyens's own, that established her reputation and popularity in artistic, affluent society.

The Lutyens-Jekyll method was to visit the site together (sometimes it had no existing house) and discuss its architectural and horticultural capabilities, each helping the other to see its opportunities and limitations; Lutyens would then work on a design and Jekyll would draw up the planting. Contrary to the popular conception that Jekyll's planting was deliciously smothering, she planted with a light touch, which allowed Lutyens's intricate architecture and water works to be shown to best advantage; only in her great flower borders and woodland gardens was her planting more extravagant. In fact much of the simple planting employed in courtyards and around houses was so light and unromantic that were it not for the accompanying Arts and Crafts architecture, it might be taken for work of the 1940s and 1950s.

Photograph by Jekyll of borders at Munstead Wood. Such large borders were possible then because garden labour was so much cheaper.

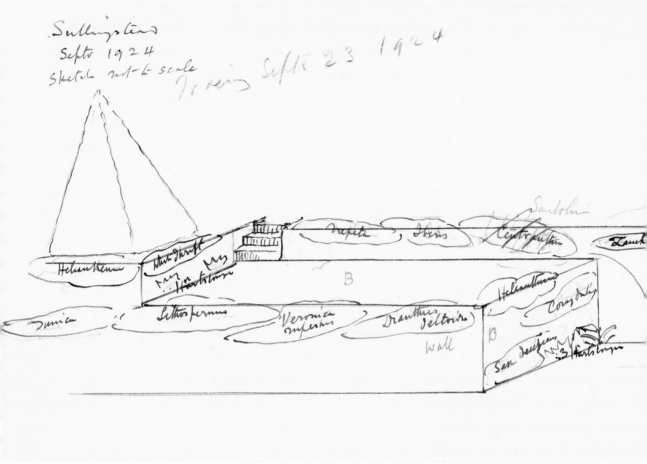

The pair made three gardens for Edward Hudson, proprietor of *Country Life* magazine, for which Jekyll began to write and which championed their work: the Deanery, at Sonning in Berkshire, Lindisfarne Castle, Northumberland, and Plumpton Place, Sussex. Sometimes the gardens were heavily patterned, as at Hestercombe, Somerset, and Marsh Court, Hampshire; sometimes one would lead to a magnificent rural view, as at Orchards, Surrey, and sometimes one was enclosed, as at the Deanery. But always there was that generosity and substance of planting that marked out Jekyll's work. She had experience and knowledge of a massive range of plants, including breeding many herself, and she valued the importance of foliage itself in a way that was then entirely fresh.

Although Lutyens remained a firm friend of 'Bumps' Jekyll, after 1914 they worked less and less together as his career as an architect expanded internationally. But still she was busy with her planting designs, now mostly done by correspondence since her already poor eyesight had so deteriorated; for the last 25 years of her life she preferred to remain in the vicinity of Munstead Wood.

Her books are as highly regarded now as they were in her day, in particular *Wood and Garden* (1899) and *Colour in the Flower Garden* (1908). Their guidance on

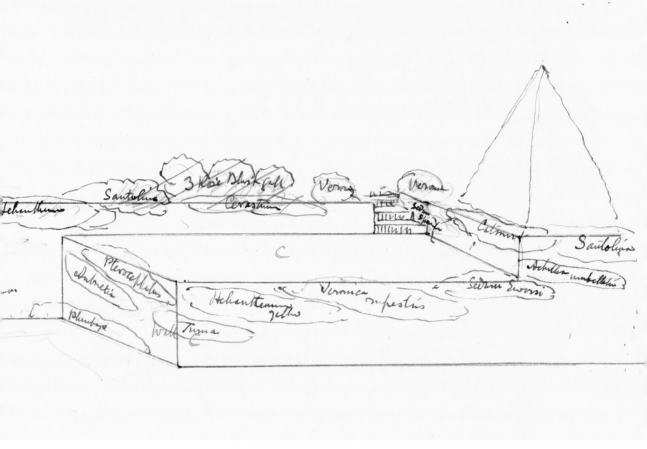

An unusual 3D drawing by Jekyll for planting at Sullingstead (1924), showing trailing plants in particular. It was common for Jekyll herself to supply many of the plants used in her designs, sometimes accompanying them and supervising the planting herself.

complex planting and plant association is still of value to all ambitious gardeners. Some fashion-conscious gardeners today dismiss Jekyll's style as one which has lingered too long and been slavishly copied for a hundred years at the expense of developing true Modernism in British garden design. And the New Perennials school of design, which focuses on the massing of grasses and perennials, finds Jekyll's Arts and Crafts manner old-fashioned. In fact both are forms of romance – Jekyll's for simplicity and lost craftsmanship in an industrializing age, and the New Perennialists for nature's complexity and a lost agricultural idyll in a now industrialized age.

After Jekyll's death, the garden at Munstead Wood quickly faded, as did most of her commissioned gardens, although several, especially some of the Lutyens collaborations, have been restored and given statutory protection. Jekyll's papers were dispersed, but a major part was bought by the garden designer Beatrix Farrand and lodged at the University of California, Berkeley.

VITA SACKVILLE-WEST

Formality of design and informality of planting

1892–1962

1892

Ellis Island accommodates its first immigrants to America.

The first performance of Tchaikovsky's *Nutcracker* in St Petersburg.

Thomas Edison patents his two-way telegraph.

Birth of J. R. R. Tolkien, author of *The Lord of the Rings*.

1962

Nelson Mandela arrested and later put on trial.

Death of Marilyn Monroe.

Edward Albee's *Who's Afraid of Virginia Woolf?* opens on Broadway.

Rachel Carson publishes *The Silent Spring*.

VITA SACKVILLE-WEST'S garden at Sissinghurst Castle, near Cranbrook in Kent, receives more visitors a year than any other garden in Britain. People come from all over the world to see it – so many that timed tickets are often necessary. Never was a garden so popular, but why? Its planting is romantic, its plan simple and classical; it is divided into compartments of modest size, which people can imagine themselves copying at home. But more than this, Sissinghurst is buoyed up by the remarkable story of its makers, Vita Sackville-West and her husband, Harold Nicolson.

The 'castle' where they lived consists of several separate buildings set at some distance apart within the garden. Visitors can enter some of them, including the tall Elizabethan Tower where Sackville-West herself slept and worked, and could enjoy views of the garden and her beloved county of Kent beyond. In short, Sissinghurst was both domestic and bohemian, and irresistibly romantic. No wonder people like it.

Vita was born Victoria Mary Sackville-West, only child of the 3rd Baron Sackville and grand-daughter of a Spanish dancer, at Knole, in Kent, an Elizabethan mansion whose combined wings cover an extraordinary 1.6 ha (4 acres). It was her childhood domain and as a writer she loved its history, tracing her family and the artworks the house contained back to the 16th century. It was one of the crowning disappointments of her life that she could not inherit Knole; instead ownership followed the title and Knole passed to her male cousin. Sissinghurst was in a sense her

Harold Nicolson and Vita Sackville-West sitting on the steps at Sissinghurst, 1960. Broadly speaking, he was the spatial designer and she the plantswoman who dressed the layout. It was an open but successful marriage.

Knole, Kent, in an illustration of 1880. Vita Sackville-West was born in this sprawling Elizabethan mansion set in its rolling deer park and loved it intimately, giving tours of it even as a child. She was deeply disappointed not to inherit it.

compensation for the loss of Knole; it was her means of attachment to the landscape and its history (Sissinghurst had once been owned by the Sackvilles).

Like all girls of her class in that period, Vita came out into aristocratic society, at eighteen, and as she progressed from ball to ball in town and country she was courted by some of the richest young men in the land. Travel then took her round much of Europe. Surprisingly, despite her strong homosexual attachments elsewhere, in 1913 she married Harold Nicolson, a lively, high-flying young diplomat five years her senior and son of a diplomat, Sir Arthur Nicolson. It was a true marriage of minds.

Living at first in Constantinople where Harold was posted, the Nicolsons then bought a house, Long Barn, close to Knole; here they had two little boys and made their first garden. Although Vita had not married into great wealth, Long Barn was expanded during those years of the First World War to become a substantial house, well supplied with servants in a manner to which she was accustomed. The architect and garden designer Edwin Lutyens (p. 96), a good friend of her mother, was called in to help, and Vita began to learn about plants with a true amateur's passion. But still she considered herself principally a writer, a poet and a novelist, a romantic ambition she would pursue with vigour and considerable success to the end of her life. As a mother, however, she was decidedly cool.

Life at Long Barn was not smooth. Vita fell desperately in love with Violet Trefusis, daughter of Alice Keppel, mistress of the Prince of Wales, and the pair eloped to Paris, where Vita dressed as a man, causing a scandal in England. It was a tortuous affair, and Harold and Violet's husband, Denys, played a loyal role in alleviating its progress and eventual demise. While Vita was glad to return to the 'sunny harbour' of Harold and her family, it set the pattern for the future of their marriage, both of them pursuing homosexual affairs but always coming back to the security of each other's comfortable love. For Vita, her uncertain sexuality was both a pleasure and an agony, but it also suited her romantic view of life (her mother had also had a discreetly open marriage). Today, better known than Vita's affair with Violet Trefusis is her more platonic relationship with the Bloomsbury novelist Virginia Woolf, ten years her senior, whom she met in 1922 and was close to until Woolf's suicide in 1941.

As the 1920s progressed, Harold abandoned the diplomatic life to write (journalism, biographies, novels), spending much of the week in their London home and

The garden at Sissinghurst seen from the Tower. The Cottage was one of several separate buildings that the family used in tandem to serve as a house. The garden compartments varied: one circular, one linear, one simple lawn, one of complex planting.

ABOVE The Nuttery in spring – an idealized woodland floor, to be seen from paths running down either side. OPPOSITE *The White Garden, with the Tower rising beyond. Old brick walls and hedges of all sizes formed the bones of the garden, making its skeleton attractive even in winter. Vita's desk was high in the Tower.*

weekending with Vita at Long Barn. But when nearby chicken farming threatened to spoil the attractions and peace of Long Barn they began to look for a new home. They considered that most romantic of moated Sussex castles, Bodiam, before settling in 1930 on a collection of derelict and uninhabitable farm buildings wrapped around by an ancient moat and orchards at the centre of a small agricultural estate – the remains of Sissinghurst manor. It was a project that would occupy the rest of their lives.

The Tower became Vita's private sanctuary, where she slept and wrote. Quarters for Harold were created in the South Cottage, while the boys, Nigel and Benedict, had the Priest's Cottage. One vast living room was made for them all in a long, Knole-like range of buildings at the entrance. Daily life meant crossing courtyards at any time of day and night.

Vita wrote busily. Her epic poem *The Land* won the Hawthornden Prize for 1927 and was admired by William Robinson (p. 208). Meanwhile the garden took shape: in age-old fashion, Harold, now a Member of Parliament, designed the classical layout of the spaces and Vita planted them. Whose is the greater contribution? Probably, like their marriage, it is a successful blend of opposites.

There were simple green spaces owing a debt to Knole, as well as geometrically divided cottage gardens where Vita could play with subtle colour schemes, a long nuttery carpeted with primulas that Gertrude Jekyll would have admired, a rose garden filled with the many old varieties that Vita loved and in which she was fast becoming a recognized expert, a lime walk (Harold's 'Unter den Linden') underplanted with early spring bulbs, an orchard, and of course hedges of yew. The White Garden, famous for its statue of a Vestal Virgin by Tomas Rosandic sheltered by a weeping silver pear tree, was especially wonderful by moonlight.

During the war years Harold was busy in London, and their sons served in the army. The garden was cared for by children and landgirls; hay was cut from the lawns, but always the great yew hedges were properly maintained. Indoors, Vita was at work on another epic poem, *The Garden* (published in 1946), a romantic exploration of advice, taste and memories and a far cry from the modern manners of poets such as Auden and Eliot. Even so, it won the Heinemann Prize and Vita spent her entire winnings on azaleas.

The garden had been open to visitors under the National Gardens Scheme since 1938 (Vita called them the 'shillingses' as that was the entrance fee) and its popularity began to grow. In 1946 she was given a column on the *Observer* newspaper, which she wrote for fourteen years, almost until her death; its intimacy was welcomed by her readers, and visitors to Sissinghurst felt they knew her. Vita gardened herself alongside her professional help, while firmly maintaining Edwardian ideas about her superior position as an amateur with good taste. She took time to travel the country, inspecting and staying at all the great country houses as inspiration for her writing, and she served on the National Trust's Gardens Committee. The Royal Horticultural Society gave her its Victoria Medal of Honour and she was created a Companion of Honour for her services to poetry.

Vita's book In Your Garden *is one of four collections of her pieces written for the* Observer. *The tone was chatty, in a rather grand manner.*

How did Sissinghurst look in its prime? It was more messy than it is today in the care of the National Trust; Vita's style was always artfully and purposefully untidy, never too pristine – a fault she observed in 'professional gardeners'. She herself set on the (joint) lady head gardeners, Pamela Schwerdt and Sibylle Kreutzberger, who continued to look after the garden when it was transferred to the National Trust by her son Nigel in 1967 in lieu of death duties. Vita always swore that it would never fall into the Trust's hand while she was still alive, however much she valued the institution.

During the last five years of her life, she and Harold went on six-week winter cruises to Japan, South America and the Caribbean, looking at the beauties of nature; as a result they spent longer together at a stretch than ever they had in the course of their marriage. She was troubled with arthritis now and even fell down the Tower stairs on one occasion. Tired, she settled back to gardening only and gave up her column in 1960. Illnesses followed and she was diagnosed with cancer, dying in 1962. Harold followed her in 1968.

The White Garden, best seen on a moonlit night, was the inspiration for thousands of others around the world. Its appeal is that it is simple in so many ways, although still richly planted: the best of both worlds.

MIEN RUYS

Experimenter with new materials and plants

1904–1999

1904
The USA begins work on the Panama Canal.
Birth of Chinese leader Deng Xiaoping.
Premiere of Puccini's *Madama Butterfly* at the Teatro alla
    Scala in Milan.
The first New York Subway underground line opens.

1999
Vladimir Putin becomes acting President of Russia.
Thabo Mbeki elected President of South Africa.
Bill Gates becomes the richest man in the world.
The Melissa virus attacks the internet.

SOMETIMES AN ARTIST comes along who never achieves popular recognition, but still, in a quiet way, commands the greatest respect from fellow artists. A musician's musician, an architect's architect, or, like Mien Ruys (Wilhelmina Jacoba Moussault-Ruys), a gardener's gardener. Designers today will tell you that Ruys was one of the most important gardeners of the late 20th century; one of those artists, perhaps, who bridges two styles, not outrageously novel, but without whose influence the next generation might not have emerged. Ruys does indeed form such a link, between traditional mid-20th-century gardening and the more thoroughgoing New Perennials movement as seen in the work of designers such as Piet Oudolf (p. 280).

Ruys's father, Bonne Ruys, had founded the Royal Moerheim Nursery aged 22, in 1888. He was a seedsman and later a breeder of delphiniums and phlox at Dedemsvaart in the east of the Netherlands, close to the Dedemsvaart canal which led to the river Vechte and the coastal trade routes. The company grew fast, exhibited at London flower shows and became one of the largest suppliers of perennials in Europe, with its own narrow-gauge rail track running around the nursery for moving plants that prefigured the rolling bench systems used today in hi-tech Dutch flower production under glass. The nursery received its Royal Warrant in 1904, and by 1909 it was even advertising to the USA. Its name has gone on to appear on plants well-known across the world, such as the blue spruce *Picea pungens* 'Moerheimii' and most famously the sneezeweed (once used for making snuff) *Helenium* 'Moerheim Beauty'; *Phlox* 'Mien Ruys' is a short white variety.

Aged nineteen Ruys started work in her father's business, not on the plant production side but as a designer on the landscaping side, which her father had

Photograph of Mien Ruys at work designing.

been developing in response to the diminishing trade in perennials during the First World War. 'Today is the first day of my career', she wrote in her diary. Her skills very soon became apparent and her responsibilities grew until she was in charge of the department. She had begun to make a garden at her parents' house, with two straight paths crossing each other at a small square pond set under orchard trees, edged with a soft planting of woodland perennials intended to look after themselves. It was a disaster – the conditions were entirely wrong for the plants she had chosen. It made her appreciate the necessity of learning about which plants would grow well together attractively. And so in 1924 she began to make a series of gardens on the nursery, to experiment to see what would thrive together and to serve as a demonstration of plants for the nursery's clients. In the end, her gardens covered 6.5 ha (16 acres).

Among the first to be made was the Wild Garden (1924), a more successful version of the one she had created for her parents, where the way in which plants spread and thrived when left largely to their own devices could be observed. The Old Experimental Garden (1927) was a more colourful affair in full sun, a long border

Rosa Spier house, Laren: the use of railway sleepers became one of Ruys's trademarks, and her generous use of grasses prefigured the New Perennials movement.

in the Jekyllean tradition facing a long shrubbery across a lawn, and designed to demonstrate how a border could look good over an extended season.

Where did her inspiration come from? At that time there was all too little written about creative plant association, although she did follow and respect the work of Karl Foerster, a Potsdam nurseryman and founding father of the use of perennials in civic planting in Europe. She visited England, where she met Gertrude Jekyll (p. 222) at her home, Munstead Wood; she spent time at Wallace and Co. at Tunbridge Wells, Kent, one of the leading British nurseries of the day; there was also a semester at the newly formed school of garden and landscape design at the Berlin-Dahlem Botanic Garden.

Realizing she needed to learn about construction as well as planting if she wanted to make gardens successfully, she studied architecture at Delft in 1931–32, a traditional course, but one that enabled her to meet forward-looking architects, landscape architects and urban planners. It was through these contacts that she was asked to undertake a joint project with the architect Gerrit Rietveld, from Utrecht. Rietveld had exhibited at the Bauhaus and was a member of the De Stijl group; in the 1920s he had begun to take an interest in social housing and prefabrication using concrete. With Ruys he went on to build a new factory for the weaving firm de Ploeg, established in 1923 as a cooperative; around the factory, at Bergeijk, Ruys made a park. In the years before the Second World War the bulk of her work was for private clients who wanted her 'English look', with soft flowing borders; but still she continued to add to the experimental gardens at Moerheim, which acted as a showcase for her work.

Her knowledge of plants had now grown enough for her to be able to put her own words into print with the encouragement of her husband, Theo Moussault, publisher of the weekly paper, *De Groene Amsterdammer* (green because of the colour of the ink). Ruys's book on creating and maintaining borders appeared in 1939, ran to six editions and was later translated into German and Swedish; one on ponds in the garden followed in 1941. In the years after the war fewer commissions came from private clients and her work moved more towards civic and communal projects. Further writing followed, too. Her book on perennials (*Het vaste plantenboek*)

For KNSM, a shipping company which had its own island in the central waters of Amsterdam, Ruys made a small park in 1956. Intended for the emigrants and their relatives when departing for the Caribbean or Surinam, it was also used by the staff.

of 1950, was written with her biologist brother Dr Dan Ruys. Unusually for its day, it covered the history of perennials and how to use them in various situations, from cottage gardens to roof gardens, with serious detail given on where to grow them, what soils they preferred and how to care for them. In 1955 Ruys and her husband founded the quarterly magazine *Onze eigen tuin*, whose title translates as *Our Own Garden*, which thrives to this day. This was a chance for her to popularize her ideas about perennials and modern garden design generally.

And the modernity of her designs? In those post-war years she became known in the trade as 'Oblique Mien' for her use of diagonal and oblique lines instead of the four-square tradition, a mechanism that helped to make small spaces look larger and irregular spaces less awkward. The concept could be observed in her latest Moerheim demonstration gardens.

The Sunken Garden of 1960 brought her a new nickname, 'Sleeper Mien', because in it she promoted for the first time the use of wooden railway sleepers – railroad ties – as a means of making steps and raised beds. Twenty years later this

Two of Ruys's demonstration gardens, one naturalistic, one formal, showing how both lush naturalistic planting and planting that relies on simple blocks of one species work happily alongside modern architecture. Note the Modernist's love of square rather than rectangular units of paving.

would become the height of fashion in popular British domestic gardens. More Moerheim gardens followed through the 1970s and 1980s – a Square Garden of primary colours in the geometric manner of a Mondrian painting; a lawn-less Flower Terrace; the Yellow Circle Garden, where a circular larch hedge enclosed a circular yellow border, itself surrounding a circular lawn with a paved edge. In the Marsh Garden stepping-stone squares floated in lines over the surface of the water. The Grasses Garden of 1993 demonstrated her love of grasses, set among gravel.

The Mien Ruys Tuin (Gardens) still exist in Dedemsvaart as a foundation, having gained independence from the nursery in 2008, and three of the gardens – the Wild Garden, the Old Experimental Garden and the Water Garden – have been declared National Monuments by the Dutch government. As a sequence they represent the changes in garden design during Ruys's lifetime and demonstrate what made her style so admired by her fellow-designers and the press: the simple, purposeful and undecorated use of geometry, created with modern materials such as concrete, wood and plastic, and softened by a contemporary mixture of perennials and grasses, boldly used in a domestic setting. She may not be familiar to amateur gardeners, but across Europe they copy her ideas without realizing it.

GRAHAM STUART THOMAS

Conserver of old plants and gardens

1909–2003

I N ADDITION TO his many other talents, Graham Stuart Thomas was a specialized kind of gardener, for he was at the forefront of garden restoration during the third quarter of the 20th century. As such, he was in the vanguard of the movement that was to play such an important role in international tourism in Britain and abroad. But those other talents were also impressive. He was a successful nurseryman, a collector and historian of roses, a highly skilled artist in botanical drawing and watercolours, a prolific author, enthusiastic singer of madrigals and, in his reserved, gentlemanly way, quite the dandy. A waistcoat and a flower in his buttonhole were part of his regular attire.

Thomas was born in Cambridge, where his father worked for the university. He was one of those quiet children who become interested in plants at a preternaturally early age. By six he was growing fuchsias, and soon after he was collecting alpines bought with his pocket money. At eight he announced that he would be a gardener. By fifteen he had already begun his lifelong work of collecting roses. At seventeen he became at trainee at the Cambridge University Botanic Garden, which allowed him to sit in on university lectures in botany, and he worked on the development of the rose garden there.

By 21 he was working at the Six Hills nursery, Stevenage, under the famous alpine expert Clarence Elliott. While there he met Peter Beales, who went on to become one of the world's greatest growers of old rose varieties. He quickly moved on to be Foreman at Hillings nursery in Surrey, where after some years he became a director. Knowing Gertrude Jekyll's writings, he wrote to her (now aged 88) and she asked him to tea and thereafter made him (rather in the way she had made Lutyens)

Graham Stuart Thomas with the rose 'Graham Thomas', introduced in 1983 by his friend, the breeder David Austin. Offered a new rose in his name, this was the one Thomas chose; it was voted the world's most popular rose in 2000 by the World Federation of Rose Societies.

one of her little projects. Thomas would cycle over to Munstead Wood to discuss colour with her and how making a garden is a form of fine art. Meanwhile his fascination with roses grew, especially the old varieties, many of which only flowered once a year but had a charm and beauty far beyond the modern Hybrid Teas and Floribundas that were pruned hard and often to turn them into flower-production machines. The roses he liked were respectable shrubs, of size and character, and climbers too.

He got to know the keenest rose enthusiasts of the day, including the Messel family at Nymans and Constance Spry, but at the same time watched rose nurseries with outstanding collections fail and their plants lost or dispersed. He became friends with James Russell, plantsman and Old Etonian, who had bought Sunningdale

Nursery and specialized in woodland shrubs and rhododendrons as well as old roses, and designed schemes for grand old schoolfriend clients with great success. Thomas, eleven years Russell's senior, was employed as nursery manager and money man (he later became a director). The nursery became famous as an ornament in itself, a fine place to go to see roses and rhododendrons, with planting schemes as skilled in the use of foliage as of flowers.

When in 1948 the National Trust took on its first garden, Hidcote Manor, it was not surprising that Thomas was invited to advise on the project, and in 1955 he

Thomas's roses at Mottisfont Abbey, which opened in 1974. His preferred palette consisted of soft colours in the Jekyllean style, perfectly accommodating his old rose varieties. Fashions in colour would change dramatically with the arrival of Christopher Lloyd's exuberant, polychrome Exotic Garden in 1993.

was made their official Gardens Adviser, a job he held for 20 years, when he was awarded an OBE for his services. His responsibilities included 110 gardens spread across England, Wales and Northern Ireland. Thomas worked for the National Trust at a time of great opportunity. There was a realization that a good garden around a mansion was a great attraction to people to visit the house, which always cost far more to maintain. But the Trust's gardens were then in poor condition and often drearily planted. Thomas's achievement across his 110 gardens was to give them life again. Hidcote, fresh from the care of its owner Lawrence Johnston, needed to be revived. At Sissinghurst, Vita Sackville-West's rather romantic and often muddled way of gardening was put into better order with the help of its two brilliant head gardeners. At Mount Stewart in Northern Ireland, Thomas was able to indulge his interest in unusual plants, and at Stourhead in Wiltshire he saved Henry Hoare's landscape masterpiece from being smothered by rhododendrons to let the lake and vistas speak again.

As a recognized expert, Thomas wrote a manual on roses for Sunningdale, the precursor of perhaps his three most important books, *The Old Shrub Roses* (1955, with a foreword by Vita Sackville-West), *Shrub Roses of Today* (1962) and *Climbing*

Watercolour by Thomas of two hellebores, 'Bowles's Yellow' and Helleborus atrorubens, *used on the dust jacket of his* Perennial Garden Plants *of 1976. The book became a gardener's bible and is still invaluable today, although some superior modern varieties have appeared since.*

Mottisfont Abbey: the majority of old rose varieties flower only once a year, whereas most modern varieties flower all season and are more vigorous, so Thomas had to work hard to create planting schemes and vistas that would continue to be of interest while his old roses were not in flower.

Roses Old and New (1965). In these he talked about the wild species and how they had been cross-bred to produce the different kinds of hybrid roses – Noisette, Tea, Wichuriana, Multiflora, Hybrid Perpetual, China, Scots, Rugosa, Bourbon, Gallica, Damask, Centifolia, Alba, Portland and Musk. Then he described the named varieties, some of them hundreds of years old, with romantic names such as 'Ispahan' and 'Cuisse de Nymphe'. One of his greatest favourites was 'Madame Hardy' (1832), a pure white Damask rose.

Thomas sold his interest in Sunningdale in 1971 and had therefore to find a new home for his rose collection. For a while it was housed none too glamorously at the Royal National Rose Society's garden, but Thomas wanted better for it. It happened that at one of the National Trust's properties, Mottisfont Abbey in

Hampshire, a house created from an Augustinian priory, the tenancy agreement on the walled kitchen garden has just run out. It was the perfect opportunity to make a new garden incorporating the collection. Opening in 1974, it was to become his greatest feat of garden-making, where, naturally, his work was inspired by Jekyll. He continued to take a great interest in it even after his retirement from the National Trust, at which point he became a consultant to the Trust rather than its full-time chief adviser.

Mottisfont was divided into quadrants, each centred on a lawn and revelling in a luscious, foliage-strong mixture of roses and perennials, while across the centre of the whole garden, wall to distant wall, ran a pair of parallel herbaceous borders of which Jekyll herself would have been proud. Structure came in the form of low box hedges, tall dolmens of clipped yew and some trellis work. It was not modern, but it was supremely well done – a form of educational nostalgia. People still love it. It is his memorial, alongside the yellow honeysuckle *Lonicera* 'Graham Thomas', and the yellow rose 'Graham Thomas' bred by his dear friend the rosarian David Austin.

Thomas's own small cottage was a base where he wrote his books by hand, sang in his living room with its two pianos and wrote long letters. Books continued to appear through the 1970s. *Plants for Ground Cover* explored a popular preoccupation of the day and one that was mightily useful to Thomas as he tried to take neglected large gardens under control and needed to keep maintenance to a minimum. *Perennial Garden Plants, or the Modern Florilegium* followed (1976), and has remained one of the great books of all time on perennials. Today some of the names have changed due to taxonomic revisions and new varieties have superseded some of Thomas's, but as a guide to growing it remains as useful as ever. These two books, together with those by him on roses, are his greatest authorial achievement, perhaps with the addition of *Colour in the Winter Garden* and *The Rock Garden and Its Plants*.

The dust jacket of *Perennial Garden Plants* featured a watercolour portrait of a greenish and a maroon hellebore painted by Thomas himself, and the book was well served with more of his delicate line drawings. He later devoted a whole book to his plant portraits and received a Gold Medal for them from the Royal Horticultural Society, for whom he worked alongside Christopher Lloyd on expert plant evaluation committees. The two men were a great contrast to each other – Lloyd outspoken and uncompromising, Thomas fastidious and precise.

In the years following Thomas's work for the National Trust, garden restoration became a regular aspect of both the private and public sector. The Garden History Society had been formed in 1966 and was now used by government as

As Chief Gardens Adviser to the National Trust, Thomas worked on the rejuvenation of Ham House, London. The approach to restoration then was to give a garden a revival in affordable and broadly period style rather than to pursue a historically accurate restoration.

an advisory body with legal powers. Garden archaeology became an accepted scientific discipline. The whole attitude to restoration changed. If Thomas's approach had been to revitalize a garden and if necessary give it a dressing of new planting or gardening that suited the period of the house, the new fashion was for strictly accurate restoration, taking the garden back to a well-documented and significant moment in its history. Thomas's intention was to give pleasure and increase the property's income, whereas now the aim was to be correct and to do nothing rather than something that was not a recreation based on hard evidence. Only history will tell whether this latter approach will be regarded as sensitive conservation or a lack of nerve to make changes to gardens in the manner which, historically, their owners had always enjoyed.

LELIA CAETANI

A profusion of plants among the ruins

1913–1977

<table>
<tr><td>

1913

The Ford Motor Company introduces the first moving assembly line.

Construction of the new federal capital of Australia at Canberra.

Stainless steel is invented in Sheffield.

Premiere of Stravinsky's *Rite of Spring*, in Paris.

</td><td>

1977

Spain holds its first democratic elections for 41 years.

Optical fibre is first used for telephones.

Death of Elvis Presley.

British Airways starts regular supersonic Concorde flights to New York.

</td></tr>
</table>

ITALY IS WELL SUPPLIED with gardens made by ex-patriate English and Americans wanting to create something in a grand Renaissance style – Iris Origo at La Foce, Lord Lambton at Villa Cetinale, Harold Acton at La Pietra – but it is less common to find a garden made in the wilder, more naturalistic tradition of William Robinson and Gertrude Jekyll. Ninfa is such a garden and Lelia Caetani was the person who gave it its greatest incarnation. The word is appropriate because Ninfa is a garden with an ancient history, but it was Lelia Caetani who polished it until it could be described as 'the most romantic garden in the world'. She herself was half Latin and half Anglo-Saxon, and so is the garden.

A life of Lelia Caetani must begin with the life of Ninfa itself, the ruined town among whose remains she gardened. The walled settlement of Ninfa sits under the rocky scarp of the Lepini hills south of Rome, on the edge of the Pontine marshes. When the town was last populated, in 1381, it was well supplied with spring water to power mills and had nine churches to minister to its people, but it was sacked, burnt and its citizens put to the sword; gardening here still brings up plenty of bones. The cause was feuding between the local aristocracy, and Ninfa's lords, the Caetani, never rebuilt it. The best stone was stripped to construct their hilltop castle at Sermoneta, and Ninfa became a green ruin, admired in the 19th century, like many a ruined abbey, for its picturesque beauty. Such was its first incarnation.

Five centuries after the sack, the fourteenth Duke of Sermoneta (the Caetani title) married a high-society if not aristocratic Englishwoman, Ada Bootle-Wilbraham. Ada was a lover of the countryside, and together husband and wife made a great house at Fogliano with a Victorian garden full of palms and seasonal bedding. Ninfa, with its crystal-clear springs, was a beautiful place for a picnic.

The garden at Ninfa was planted among and on the ruins of the town, which was sacked in the 14th century. Water comes from the high hills behind, to form the backbone, the soul of the garden.

In 1917 Ninfa passed to their son, Gelasio, who began its second incarnation. With an archaeologist's eye and with labour from Austrian prisoners of war from the First World War, he cleared trees and stabilized the ruins and river banks, repaired the tower and the town hall, and planted pines, cypresses and ilex to give shelter, shade and privacy. It was a garden of sorts, with a thatched summerhouse and a new wooden bridge, which, together with Ninfa's ancient stone bridge, created circuit walks to a new peach orchard. Ada, now a widow, planted roses. With Mussolini's good will, Gelasio managed to have the mosquito-ridden marshes drained, at which point Il Duce confiscated the drained land. Gelasio died childless in 1934, leaving Ninfa to his nephew Camillo (Lelia's brother), but to be administered by the boy's father, Gelasio's brother, Roffredo.

Here begins Ninfa's third incarnation. The young Camillo was killed in the Second World War and it was in effect Roffredo and his American heiress wife,

One of Lelia's paintings, looking back to Ninfa – with its signature tall cypresses and flat-topped pines – from the marshes beyond, now an important nature reserve. Access to garden and reserve are strictly limited.

Lelia was a moderately successful painter, exhibiting in Paris and America, and her skill with colour helped form her approach to planting. She was familiar with the ideas of Jekyll on the use of colour and was an admirer of William Robinson.

Marguerite Gilbert Chapin, having moved to live at Ninfa from their home in Paris, who began to develop the garden. Roffredo made pools and streams while Marguerite got her hands dirty planting flowering cherry trees, weeping willows, magnolias, irises and great scrambling roses to clad the ruins.

Ninfa's fourth incarnation, under Lelia, came into being as Marguerite relinquished control of the garden to her daughter. Lelia had been born in Paris and developed into a slim, stately young woman, blue eyed and dark haired, who preferred the company of her artist's easel to busy socializing. 'Painter and Gardener', says her memorial, and for Lelia painting was a major part of her life (her work was exhibited in Paris and America) and helped shape her ideas about colour in the garden. At Ninfa she worked in the garden alongside Marguerite as, gradually through the 1940s, it became more the daughter's garden than the mother's. Marguerite was at heart more interested in her literary endeavours; she founded two literary magazines, *Commerce* and *Botteghe oscure*, the latter edited by Giorgio Bassani, who wrote much of *The Garden of the Finzi-Continis* (1962) there in the garden at Ninfa. Contributors to her magazines ranged from Dylan Thomas

The art in gardening at Ninfa has been never to let the plants smother the ruined stonework, but still to maintain the feeling that they are in control. Of course they are not; there is constant pruning and discreet architectural repair.

to Truman Capote, and lunch at Ninfa might include Evelyn Waugh, Gore Vidal or The Queen Mother.

Lelia was married in 1951 to Hubert Howard, son of the diplomat Sir Esme Howard, Baron Penrith; Hubert had arrived in Italy with the Allies during the liberation and went on to work in military intelligence in Rome. Both Hubert and Lelia were devout Catholics. Through him she got to know and love English gardens and landscapes, and to admire the works of William Robinson, Gertrude Jekyll and Vita Sackville-West. In England she also discovered the famous Hillier and Sons nursery, and bought from them lavishly from 1949 onwards.

In due course Herbert began to run the estate at Ninfa while Lelia developed the garden. Only a couple of years after their marriage she underwent surgery for cancer, leading to further operations in the 1960s, and no children came along. Instead Ninfa became their absorbing occupation. For Hubert the conservation of Ninfa as a haven for nature became paramount and he managed to set up legal protection for it, including the adjacent marshes.

Ninfa is a garden principally of water, grass and flowering trees and shrubs, set among the old walls and towering conifers, and at its most colourful in spring.

There is just one area of flower gardening for summer, growing on banks of rubble. Its manner is wild and yet it is clearly planted; it is horticulturally unsophisticated, but outrageously romantic.

Lelia extended the boundaries of the garden across the river and cut down her mother's weeping willows to allow for more detailed planting of smaller trees and shrubs, constantly experimenting to see what would grow in this landscape of fallen stone and old lime mortar: camellias, yes; rhododendrons, no. And so a palette of soft colours developed – pale roses, cherries, magnolias, bamboos, endless ferns, wisteria, lavender – always planted to dress the ruins, whether it was the second storey of a church or a stub wall only knee-high. In its spring profusion, the rockery was Lelia's greatest delight and a reminder of the English Lake District and the Alps. She wanted the garden to seem always on the verge of abandon, with Nature about to reclaim it, and yet full of beauty, each plant lightly managed to show its true character. She made Ninfa a place of respect – respect for plants and respect for the lives of those who in death lay silent beneath the rubble. The romance of it all is almost tangible even today.

After Lelia died in 1977, Hubert continued to look after the garden until his own death ten years later. Ninfa and the marshes are now exquisitely cared for by their protégé Lauro Marchetti and the Fondazione Roffredo Caetani.

ROSEMARY VEREY

International yet domestic grandeur

1918–2001

1918
Germany signs an Armistice on 11 November, ending the First World War.
Bolsheviks execute Tsar Nicholas II and his family.
Spanish flu, first identified in Kansas, turns pandemic and kills 30 million in six months.
In the UK, women over 30 get the Vote.

2001
In the attacks on the World Trade Center, New York, 2,997 people die; the USA invades Afghanistan.
Same-sex marriage legalized in the Netherlands.
Decoding of the human genome published.
Start of foot-and-mouth outbreak in the UK; 10 million sheep and cattle slaughtered.

ROSEMARY VEREY, queen bee of English country house gardening, was best known for her garden at Barnsley House in the Cotswolds, Gloucestershire. In fact, it may have been more widely recognized than she herself was, because it was full of photogenic cameos at a time when high-quality colour photography and cheaper printing were just taking off. And its influence, thanks to Verey's tireless energy and popularizing enthusiasm, was enormous on both sides of the Atlantic. By the end of her life, Rosemary Verey's eighteen books had sold better in the USA than in Britain, and wherever she went she could charm the fruit off the trees.

Her beginnings were modest enough. Rosemary Sandilands was born into a military family and her mother was an actress. She was a resilient character from the start, and her childhood revolved around sport and horses. A bright child, she went to University College, London in 1937 to study economics and mathematics, while simultaneously taking her part in the London debutante scene. Here her life now changed. She met and in 1939 married David Verey of the Royal Fusiliers, five years her senior, trained as an architect at Trinity College, Cambridge, and an architectural historian. In the manner of the times she gave up her degree and together they moved into a flat in Hounslow, near today's Heathrow airport.

After war broke out David was away on active service and was not to see Rosemary again for three years, by which time she had learned to be a tough, independent mother of their first son. When peace came David began working with the

Jerry Harpur's influential picture of the laburnum walk underplanted with alliums; the design was by Rosemary and David Verey, with a little help from Russell Page. The same view was used on the cover of Verey's book The Englishwoman's Garden *published in 1980.*

Ministry of Housing in Gloucestershire, a post he would hold for twenty years, and they took a house there. Once more, Verey's life revolved around hunting, tennis, church and her (now four) children.

In 1951, when she was 33, her parents-in-law moved out of the family home, Barnsley House, near Cirencester, a fine stone rectory of 1697 with Victorian additions, and David and Rosemary moved in. Yet again, the practicalities of family life initially took precedence, and a good deal of the garden was removed to make way for a pool, a tennis court and grass for the children's ponies, while Rosemary herself tutored her two girls at home to begin with.

In the late 1950s with the children grown up or away, Rosemary now needed another occupation; gardening would fill the gap and became her passion. David introduced her to medieval and formal 17th-century gardens, and it was he who called in Percy Cane to design a garden, but Cane's garden was not to be. His ideas absorbed, Verey's own garden began to take shape. The garden was in fact a joint venture, despite the fame and publicity that surrounded Rosemary in later years. It was a loving marriage, and as in the case of Sissinghurst and Vita Sackville-West and her husband Harold Nicolson, it was David who planned the layout, the

The potager (OPPOSITE) and knot garden (ABOVE) at Barnsley were derived from Verey's passion for garden history. The knot garden sat like a rug outside French windows, while the potager was across a lane at the back – images of it inspired a whole fashion for potagers.

bones of the garden, its structures and vistas, and it was Rosemary who embellished these with her glorious planting.

Rosemary showed her true colours. She read furiously, including old herbals and classics of the garden repertoire such as Gertrude Jekyll and William Robinson, acquiring knowledge. And she made contacts in the garden world, meeting and charming and learning from important garden makers, seeing gardens like Hidcote, entering the Royal Horticultural Society's flower shows and buying plants from influential nurseries such as Nancy Lindsay's. David imported the much photographed old temple (from Fairford Park) and its circular pool and screen gates, and it was he who laid paths and created the lime *allée* and commissioned the first of their sculptures – a column – from Simon Verity. Rosemary's greatest contributions to the garden structure were the laburnum-and-allium walk, which was to feature on the cover of her first book and has been much photographed and imitated ever since, and the potager, an ornamental vegetable garden inspired by the recreated formal garden at Villandry in France. Based on her appreciation of garden history and her extensive library of historical gardening books, she designed this in an archaic, geometric style, as she did her knot garden of clipped box laid out under one wall of the house.

Her great skill was to draw from the features of historic gardens and adapt them to the smaller setting at Barnsley House, then embellish them with her own opulent, carefully contrived planting, of the kind not seen since before the war. Colour, scent, foliage and a sense of movement were all important. It was ebullient gardening again after years of drabness and austerity.

Verey also started to write now, articles at first and then books, in a steady stream, sometimes about gardening and sometimes beautifully photographed com-

pendiums of other people's gardens. *Classic Garden Design: How to Adapt and Recreate Garden Features of the Past* (1984) is considered by some to be her best book, along with *The Garden in Winter* (1988), although the popular influence of *The Englishwoman's Garden* (1980) and *The Englishman's Garden* (1982) cannot be overstated. She and David began to travel and lecture abroad – he on architecture, she on gardens. When he died in 1984 she was bereft.

Every year now saw her in the USA at least once, promoting her books and lecturing about gardens and Barnsley, attracting large and appreciative audiences. The garden was first opened to the public in 1970 and visitors flocked there. Verey was asked to make planting designs for the great and good, from Prince Charles, Elton John and Oscar de la Renta, to a Tokyo department store and the New York Botanical Garden. She was a great communicator and teacher, if sometimes intimidating, and was always networking, making contacts and encouraging others. She was awarded many honours on both sides of the Atlantic, including an OBE in 1996. Despite health problems, she was for most of the time her usual self, full of enthusiasm for gardening and keen to pass on her knowledge. She died in 2001, the *grande dame* of English gardening. After her death Barnsley was sold and today is a restaurant and hotel, with the garden maintained beside it and new features added, though it has lost its presiding spirit.

ABOVE Rosemary Verey greets Prince Charles. OPPOSITE Irish yews and sprawling helianthemums transformed the main path from the glazed back door of Barnsley into a picture as much as a path. It exemplified Verey's liking for small, romantic vistas.

CHRISTOPHER LLOYD

Adventurous and innovative gardener at Great Dixter

1921–2006

1921
The Red Army invades Georgia.
Irish War of Independence.
Russian famine: 5 million die.
Birth of Prince Philip, Duke of Edinburgh.

2006
The Space Shuttle *Discovery* is launched on a mission to the International Space Station.
Alexander Litvinenko dies from Polonium poisoning in London.
Google buys YouTube for $1.65 billion.

CHRISTOPHER LLOYD MAY well turn out to to be the most widely known flower gardener the world has ever seen, not just for the excellence of his abilities as a gardener at his home, Great Dixter in Sussex, but also because of the times in which he lived.

In the late 20th century people were better off than ever before. They had cars, which facilitated leisure tourism, and increasingly they had homes of their own and the aspirations to go with them. The media catered for their dreams for their gardens with a barrage of television and print; magazines and books improved by leaps and bounds in the wake of digital publication and the extraordinary improvements in colour printing. Lloyd could write brilliantly and was at the height of his powers in those last three decades of the century, making Dixter, if not the most visited (that accolade goes to Sissinghurst), then arguably the most photographed and published flower garden of the day.

What made Lloyd such an extraordinarily successful and supremely skilled gardener? It was his attention to detail and his brilliant memory for precisely when a plant flowered, as well its colour and cultural requirements; this was coupled with a ruthless streak, which led him to discard all plants except those he considered the best and to employ his legendary impatience in getting rid of lesser plants. Press and public lauded the way that even in old age he was open to innovation, to the point where they liked to suggest (mistakenly) that he welcomed change for change's sake. It was in fact a very rare breed of optimistic impatience that drove him.

In 1993, an impatient and mischievous Lloyd transformed Lutyens's perfectly pleasant, enclosed, Edwardian rose garden into a hotbed of exotic flower and foliage. Garden historians threw up their hands, but it was in fact a return to an older, 19th-century mode of planting.

Dixter as Lutyens left it, an old timbered hall house with sympathetic modern additions, sitting high on a massive brick plinth. The subsequent hiding of that plinth with billowing vegetation has given the house a whole new romance. It still dominates the garden, but genially so, like a grandfather.

Lloyd was one of six children born to Daisy and Nathaniel Lloyd, who, in 1910, employed the architect Edwin Lutyens to build them a new home at Great Dixter, through the amalgamation of two medieval timber-frame houses (one brought from elsewhere), held together with some contemporary but sympathetic additions of Lutyens's own design. It was a romantic triumph, set at the heart of a garden of which Lutyens drew up the bones – the walls and paths and open spaces – leaving the Lloyds the pleasure of decorating them through their detailed planting. Daisy was the plantswoman; Nathaniel, wealthy through early retirement from industry and now an amateur architect and thirteen years Daisy's senior, was the creator of Dixter's many yew hedges and topiary pieces. His *Garden Craftsmanship in Yew and Box* of 1925 remains an important and useful book.

Daisy Lloyd was a determined matriarch to whom family was everything (she was distantly related to Oliver Cromwell and not lacking in his single-mindedness). Motherhood was in fact so central to her self-worth that she clung with a ruthless hand to Christopher, her youngest, a rather fey and terribly shy little boy. When he was not much more than a toddler he was Daisy's garden companion, learning Latin names and how to spell them at her knee, and engaging in a daily gardening correspondence with her from school (Rugby) that would leave many a professional gardener feeling inadequate. Letter writing in a literary style was an obligatory part of Lloyd family life. Mother and son shared a passion for the garden. Daisy loved her grand Edwardian borders, but, new to the times, she was also keen to grow plants in grass, as recommended by William Robinson in *The Wild Garden* of 1870. The young Lloyd absorbed it all, continuing to develop these flower meadows set in formal situations throughout his life. His abilities as a field botanist were superb.

A lonely time studying Modern Languages at Cambridge and an even unhappier time in the army at the end of the Second World War left him back in England in 1946, feeling socially and professionally uncertain. His preferred option was to fall back on Dixter, the garden and Daisy, to open it to the public and set up a nursery.

Lloyd with his mother Daisy and the inevitable dachshund. He lived with his powerful mother until she died in 1972, when he, the house and the garden took on a new lease of life.

Where some might have had a neat mown lawn leading to the front door, the Lloyds had a flowering meadow, in the style of William Robinson. Lloyd was an expert on field botany and had a lifelong interest in meadows and wildflower gardening.

A degree in Decorative Horticulture from nearby Wye College was followed by a brief spell teaching there, but his innate Lloydian stubbornness led to upset and he resigned, thrown ever more back on Dixter.

By the 1950s Lloyd began to have articles published in horticultural journals and would lecture to amateur groups on a vast range of topics, using his own excellent photographs, for which he had inherited a considerable talent from his father. But his first great milestone as a writer was to be employed in 1962 as a weekly columnist in *Country Life* magazine, which continued without a break (even after major heart surgery) until 2005. The column became a British institution.

Books followed, in particular a monograph on *Clematis* (1965), and thereafter a trio that established him as a witty, observant and helpfully useful writer on plantsman's gardening – *The Well-Tempered Garden* (1970), *Foliage Plants* (1973) and *The Adventurous Gardener* (1983). The first of these is still one of the most enduring and best-loved classics of garden literature.

In the middle of all this Daisy died, leaving Lloyd alone at Dixter. With her possessive influence gone, a second half of his life began. He learned to cook, and Dixter became a place where people from every aspect of his range of interests would congregate for the weekend – gardeners, botanists, musicians, students. The opera season at Glyndebourne, which the Lloyds had attended since it was instituted in the 1930s, became ever more important. He developed friendships with the food writer Jane Grigson, leading to his book *Gardener Cook* (2001), and the nurserywoman and gardener Beth Chatto, with whom he would later collaborate on *Dear Friend and Gardener* (1998). Columns followed in the *Observer* and *Guardian* newspapers and he was awarded the OBE in 2000.

Through the 1970s and 1980s the garden was perhaps slightly eclipsed by Lloyd's new-found social life. Head gardeners came and went. Dixter was a little shabby when compared to Sissinghurst down the road, sparkling under National Trust care. Even so, Lloyd took trouble to encourage young gardeners and enjoyed visits from students at Wye College, keen to learn how a large garden and plant collection functioned.

Dixter's monumental Long Border was the garden's showpiece until the fashions for exotic gardens and meadow gardening (inspired not least by Lloyd) made it seem a little old-fashioned, however brilliant its planting.

In 1993 one such visit included a young man by the name of Fergus Garrett, who very quickly was appointed head gardener at Great Dixter and stayed there for the rest of Lloyd's life. With the boundlessly energetic Garrett in support, Christo, as he was affectionately known, could now achieve anything, and he began to undertake the series of re-dressings of the garden that made him famous, the more so since he was now lecturing about Dixter throughout the English-speaking world. In particular, Lutyens's rose garden was summarily emptied – to the horror of many – and replanted as an Exotic Garden, with tender, exotic, architectural and wildly colourful plants. This was a style of planting that appealed at a time when people were becoming aware of the likelihood of a warming climate. It was widely assumed that a warmer climate would mean that gardeners would need Lloyd's subtropical plants, an idea far from the truth and not least because the planting was so very water-hungry. In fact in Britain the climate looks set simply to be more variable and no more suited to subtropicals than ever it was. Still, aesthetically the style had great appeal. And meanwhile other parts of the garden were also transformed: the stock beds for the nursery became in effect bright flower borders, a prairie garden in long grass was tried, and the few pots that once stood by the front door became great theatrical arrangements all over the garden. It was dizzying and all superbly done.

Books continued to flow, three in particular of note, all of which owe a considerable debt to the efforts of Garrett, who assisted the physically failing man. *Colour for Adventurous Gardeners* (2001) summed up Lloyd's bold attitudes to colours, and which ones are compatible (note his dazzling knitwear), and led to some television exposure. *Meadows* (2004) set out most valuably his lifelong experience in the Robinsonian manner of wildflower gardening (even his father's immaculate topiary lawn had now turned into a meadow), while *Succession Planting for Adventurous Gardeners* (2005) explored his love of labour-intensive replanting during the season to ensure a continuous succession of colour.

Before he died, Lloyd set up a private charitable trust to look after Dixter, with Garrett firmly at the helm and licensed to continue gardening in the same adventurous manner. Garret has proved an able disciple and upholds Lloyd's dazzling standards of gardening while cultivating an ever greater profile for the garden.

Lloyd was once described by designer Andrew Wilson as a 'decorator', which, if it displeased him, was not unfair. Lloyd was no garden designer and he admitted it, but he was a consummate plantsman and gardener. One day his work may well provide the ultimate iconic images of 20th-century gardening.

Fergus Garrett, Lloyd's last, brilliant head gardener and companion, Malus floribunda *and Lloyd. Garrett still runs the garden, now a trust, with Lloydian panache.*

BETH CHATTO

The right plant in the right place

BORN 1923

1923
Mount Etna erupts, making 60,000 homeless.
Hyperinflation in Germany.
The first vaccine for diphtheria.
The Hollywood sign is inaugurated in California.

BETH CHATTO IS a heroine to all those gardeners of the late 20th century who fell in love with perennials after the post-war years of gardening austerity, when stolid, low-maintenance shrubs were *de rigeur*. Being a successful combination of garden-maker, nurserywoman, journalist and author during the great boom years of British gardening, Chatto has become familiar to gardeners across the world. In England, she is by the far the best known and affectionately regarded female garden-maker, even if there are bigger names in the world of celebrity garden journalism.

Her 2.5-ha (6-acre) garden at Elmstead Market in Essex is in some ways a curious creation – a compelling and cosy blend of domesticity and naturalism. People love it and they love the idea that she lives in it, in a simple modern house from the 1960s where they could imagine themselves living. There is nothing grand here (unless it's the few ancient oaks that punctuate the garden), nothing aristocratic, no straight lines, no sculptural focal points and almost no views beyond the garden; it is all about the plants and the ways of putting them together, which Chatto calls her 'tapestry gardening'.

She has always championed the idea that successful gardening demands that every plant should be grown in conditions similar to those in which it is found in the wild – 'right plant, right place' – rather than encouraging the gardener to indulge plants with unnaturally favourable conditions at the cost of more labour and resources. As a consequence, she is highly respected by practitioners of the New Perennials Movement (such as Piet Oudolf), even if they tend towards a more academically natural style, richer in grasses, and (since the movement sprang from civic beginnings in Germany 100 years ago) a less domestic manner more suited to public spaces.

Chatto with Christopher Lloyd, two of the greats of late 20th-century British flower gardening.

For all its popularity, Chatto's garden is not modern in the 21st-century sense, but rather the product of the 1960s to 1990s, with the great perennial revival. Yet her gravel garden of 1993 caught exactly the spirit of the coming times, focusing as it did on dry conditions just as the threat of global warming was becoming apparent. Even today, twenty years later, this part of her garden catches, if not quite the look, then certainly the spirit of the moment.

Garden designers, and especially those who prefer a greater degree of rectilinear formality, have less affinity with her garden. As she herself explains, she developed each area by understanding the growing conditions it offered, delineating the shapes of serpentine beds and lawns with hose-pipes, and then choosing a palette of plants that would thrive there. 'I've got this jig-saw of plants set out on the ground and I ask myself, how am I going to put them together?' The result is a garden that demonstrates planting for various different situations – a water garden, a dry garden, spring garden, woodland garden and so on. And although this is a highly rational principle, it created a garden where the presence of the creator is meant to

Beth Chatto laying out the shape of a bed with hose-pipe. But it was the planting within that mattered – clever, species-rich, modern, ecologically sensitive and practical.

be invisible; it is as if the plants were in control. How different this is from the auto-biographical and iconographic garden of Roy Strong or the work of a designer such as Christopher Bradley-Hole, for whom the rational principles of geometry and the Golden Section are intended to be enjoyed directly as part of the experience.

Chatto was born at Good Easter, near Chelmsford in Essex, an ordinary local girl, and she trained to be a teacher. During the Second World War she met Andrew Chatto, thirteen years her senior and a son of the Chatto publishing firm. They married in 1943 and lived for eighteen years in his mother's house, not so far from the land within which the garden now stands, and which had been bought for Andrew in the early 1930s to make a fruit farm.

In 1960, when Beth Chatto was 37, they moved to the farm and built the new house, next to a scrubby piece of (agriculturally speaking) wasteland. She had had no formal horticultural education but had gardened as a child, explored garden-related school projects during her teacher training, and grown vegetables during the war at the village school where she then taught. Her interest in wild plants was bolstered by Andrew Chatto's lifelong research into plant habitats; it became one of the founding and constantly cited principles of her way of gardening.

Early in her married life she met the painter Cedric Morris, who had set up his school of art at Benton End, at nearby Hadleigh. She became a regular visitor, learning about the use of colour and acquiring knowledge from his passion for species plants and bulbs and the hybridizing of irises and field poppies. It was a meeting place for artists and gardeners of all kinds, including Lucian Freud, Maggie Hambling and Vita Sackville-West.

In the 1950s Chatto had taken up flower arranging with the Chelmsford Flower Club, where she discovered that arrangers were struggling, both locally and nation-ally, to find interesting and unusual plants, for foliage especially. As she travelled around giving demon-strations, the idea came to her that there was room for a nursery offering just such plants. Thus in 1967 her business, Unusual Plants, was born. In 1975 she exhibited at one of the Royal Horticultural Society's Westminster shows and won a Silver Medal. Encouraged by this success, she then exhibited at the Chelsea Flower Show in 1977 and won a Gold Medal, as she did for ten consecutive years. Those first exhibits are remembered by a whole generation of gardeners as something entirely fresh and new.

In 1978 she published *The Dry Garden*, the first of her eight books, followed in 1982 by *The Damp Garden*, *Beth Chatto's Gravel Garden* in 2000 and *Beth Chatto's Woodland Garden* in 2002. By the 1980s she was lecturing throughout the world, sometimes in the company of her good friend Christopher Lloyd, and was awarded the OBE in 2002.

The garden itself grew in stages, each new area taking on a different charac-ter according to the position and conditions, starting with a wet ditch below the house which she turned into a series of ponds, and ending with a woodland garden,

ABOVE One of Chatto's award-winning displays at the Chelsea Flower Show. Her nursery, Unusual Plants, displayed plants naturally, an innovation at the time. OVERLEAF The springtime woodland garden is one of her last major ventures.

The water garden was the first area of Chatto's garden to be developed. As with every new part that followed, she wrote a book about it, in this case The Damp Garden, *which became required reading for plantsmen.*

principally for spring interest. But for all this strict accommodation of growing requirements, the garden still retains a domestic feel; it certainly does not come across as an institutional demonstration garden.

Always struggling with the near-drought conditions of the East Anglian climate, a gravel garden followed in 1993, just as her Sussex friend Christopher Lloyd was making his madly water-hungry Exotic Garden; the public loved both. The gravel garden was made on a strip of cruelly stony ground that was once a car park and its aim was to see whether, using only companionably drought-tolerant plants from all over the world, and after thorough preparation of the soil, the garden could survive without any watering. To all intents and purposes it did, and it has gone on to be the best-known part of her garden. It provides a wonderful lesson for anyone wanting to garden on hot stony ground.

Chatto's style of garden design has always remained the same, composed of sinuous estuaries of open space set out with a hose-pipe, be they grass or gravel, with curving beds of mixed, intensive planting, from small bulbs through perennials and shrubs to trees and climbers. Always she has in mind the Japanese principle of triangles learnt from flower arranging – a tall, aspiring shape, a rounded, weighty shape, and a weighty, tiered shape, the whole composition lifting the view upward, 'painting the sky', as she calls it. She uses interesting and unusual plants, but they are all tried and tested.

Now in her mid-90s, Chatto has never been one to willingly delegate responsibility, but at last her family looks set to take on the management, and the enterprise appears set fair to continue. The garden still gives great pleasure to large numbers of people every year and commands huge respect throughout the garden world. And if modern garden designers lament British design being stuck in an Edwardian time warp of Arts and Crafts gardening in the Lutyens and Hobhouse manner (strong built geometric structures softened with generous planting), then the Chatto style of abundant and intelligent planting around serpentine spaces with not a straight line in sight offers a possible alternative, and one that can point the way forwards.

The gravel garden showed what could be achieved on dauntingly dry, gravelly land by using the right plants. It struck a chord with gardeners beginning to be anxious about global warming, and it was new and heart-lifting, though squeezed between the drive and car park.

PIET OUDOLF

Pioneer of new perspectives in planting design

BORN 1944

1944
Soviet troops liberate Crimea and change Turkish place
    names to Russian.
D-Day landings: 155,000 Allied troops land in Normandy.
Last eruption of Mount Vesuvius.
The world's first undersea oil pipeline links England to
    France.

T O CALL THE DUTCHMAN Piet Oudolf a garden designer is to say both too much and too little, for his most dramatic design schemes have been made for civic and institutional clients, while his garden work has never been of the domestic, house-softening variety. He is above all else a brilliant planting designer.

Oudolf is a tall, blond bear of a man, whom you could take as easily for the captain of a tea clipper as a garden designer (the term must suffice). That his English is excellent should be no surprise, since his design work is best known in the English-speaking world of Britain and America, the latter now the location of 70 per cent of his commissions. He was born towards the end of the Second World War, his father a restaurateur and bar owner in the countryside near Haarlem. Mathematics was Oudolf's forté, but he went into the family business, married his wife Anja and they had two boys. By the time he was 25 he was looking for more stimulation, and after a series of unsatisfactory jobs went to work for a garden centre, where he discovered that plants were his passion. While working in a landscape design and contracting office he studied landscape contracting and thereafter set up his own business making gardens.

Through the 1970s he hungrily visited gardens across Europe, with his family in tow, making friends and contacts as he went. In 1981, aged 37, he bought a house with some land way out in the east of the Netherlands at Hummelo, where he could set up a nursery selling the plants he wanted to use in his own planting designs

OPPOSITE Young Piet and his wife Anja at Hummelo, both earnest, energetic plantspeople and keen to get out and see what was happening in other countries. The nursery and garden at Hummelo became a shrine for plantsman gardeners.

Hummelo, with its famous yew hedges clipped into waves. Oudolf's winter silhouettes succeed best in a cold continental climate as experienced in mainland Europe or America. They have as much interest and beauty as in their full summer glory.

but which were not then easy to find in commerce. For a few years he was in partnership with Romke van de Kaa, once head gardener to Christopher Lloyd, but they parted in 1985. Anja Oudolf came into the business to run the nursery, while Oudolf himself spent his time scouring specialist nurseries in Britain, Denmark, Sweden and Germany for the kinds of semi-wild plants, perennials in particular, that suited his planting style. These he then put into serious breeding programmes at Hummelo, resulting in many fine new varieties.

The nursery ran as a retail enterprise, not making much money but well known for its open days in August, which were attended by plantsmen from far and wide. Photographers from magazines came too, keen to compete for images of the new style of planting to be seen in Oudolf's garden. By the end of the 1980s, he was becoming better known and his design work began to take off at last.

Oudolf has always been pragmatic about the scope of his own skills and happy to work as a planting designer alongside landscape architects, whose expertise is in designing spaces and infrastructure. His attitude to writing is equally honest and most of his books have been collaborations with other authors. In 1990 he published his first book, later translated into English as *Planting the Natural Garden*, with Dutch garden designer Henk Gerritsen. When it was translated into Swedish Oudolf was asked to speak at a conference in that country. This became a starting point for the New Perennials movement with which Oudolf is so closely associated. Following on from the Perennial Perspectives conferences held at Kew, its aim was to promote the use of perennials in a low-maintenance way in civic planting, and thus to bring some joy to an otherwise sterile civic palette, with its heavy reliance on shrubs and evergreens. Oudolf helped set up Future Plants, a nursery collective for which he was charged with finding or breeding new plants, many to be licensed for sale under Plant Breeders' Rights. Ironically, given it was based in Europe, it was to Future Plants that he turned when he later needed large volumes of American plants for gardens in America.

Through the 1990s Oudolf's planting style began to evolve from clipped forms and blocks of perennials and grasses (his own garden was famous for its yew hedges

Seed heads and grasses in frost: Oudolf's skill is in planting naturalistically while including large-enough swathes of any one variety to make a strong effect. It is a sophisticated and romantic upgrade of nature.

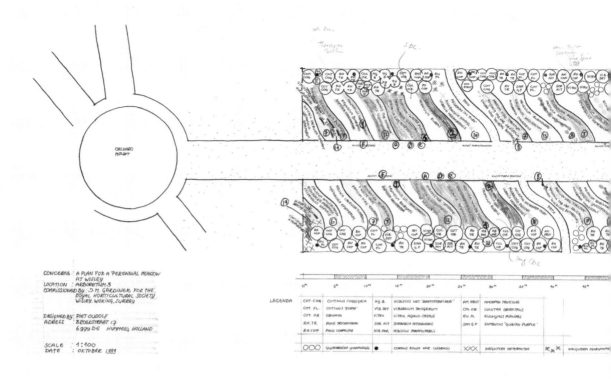

CONCERNS : A PLAN FOR A PERENNIAL MEADOW
AT WISLEY
LOCATION : ARBORETUM 3
COMMISSIONED BY : J.M. GARDINER, FOR THE
ROYAL HORTICULTURAL SOCIETY
WISLEY, WOKING, SURREY

DESIGNED BY : PIET OUDOLF
ADRESS : BROEKSTRAAT 17
6999 DE HUMMELO, HOLLAND

SCALE : 1 : 100
DATE : OKTOBER 1999

LEGENDA						
COT. COG	COTINUS COGGIGRIA	HY. B.	HIBISCUS HET 'BRATTISONIDEN'	AM. FRUT	AMORPHA FRUTICOSA
COT. FL.	COTINUS 'FLAME'	VIB. BET	VIBURNUM BETULGERUM	COL. OR.	COLUTEA ORIENTALIS
COT. OB.	OBOVATA	VITEX	VITEX AGNUS-CASTUS	EU. PL.	EUONYMUS PLANIPES
R.H. TR.	RHUS TRICHOCARPA	SOR. AIT	SORBARIA AITCHISONII	SAM. G.P.	SAMBUCUS 'GUINCHO PURPLE'
R.H. COP	RHUS COPALLINA	HIB. PAR.	HIBISCUS PARAHUTABILIS		
◯◯◯	GLYCORRHIZA YUNNANENSIS	●	CORNUS ROUGA VAR. CHINENSIS	✕✕✕	INDIGOFERA HETERANTHA	❋ ❋	INDIGOFERA AMBLYANTHA

clipped into waves) to a more mixed, looser style. The garden he made for John Coke at Bury Court, Hampshire, became his showcase in Britain, and when in 2000 Rosie Atkins, the editor of the magazine *Gardens Illustrated*, asked him to design the planting for a Chelsea Flower Show garden created by Arne Maynard (it received a Gold Medal and the Best in Show award), Oudolf became widely admired. Commissions came in for a great bank of waterside planting at Pensthorpe wildfowl reserve in Norfolk and for a huge walled garden at Scampston in Yorkshire. A pair of enormous double borders followed for the Royal Horticultural Society in its garden at Wisley. More collaborative books appeared.

By now his fame had spread to America, even if in his native Netherlands he was still principally known as a nurseryman. He won a competition to plant the Lurie Garden, a giant roof garden over an underground car park, for the city of Chicago, and in 2002 was asked to work on the Battery at the southern tip of Manhattan, for the Gardens of Remembrance. He was at work again in Manhattan in 2004 on his best-known project, the High Line. This 2.4-km (1½-mile) linear park

Oudolf's plan for the huge double borders at the Royal Horticultural Society's garden at Wisley. Typically, the borders have a shrubby screen behind and the various perennials run in diagonal washes that continue across the central grass path.

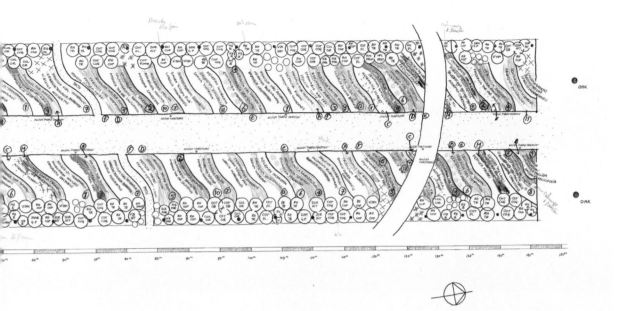

raised 10 m (33 ft) above the ground on a disused railway line winds its way through New York's lower west side. It was a dream project which he would gladly (as he says) have done without a fee. The planting, set on the landscape architect's framework, manages to look lush even in places where the soil is only 40 cm (16 in.) deep. Oudolf meticulously researched the native plants of the American prairies for both the Lurie Garden and the High Line, and this kind of *rus in urbe* manner gave his planting huge appeal to New Yorkers.

Cementing his position among America's favourite designers, 2007 saw him at work on an important domestic garden on Nantucket. In Britain, Oudolf was asked to make a garden at Trentham Hall in Staffordshire (alongside Tom Stuart-Smith), which combines serpentine grass paths and lawns with large beds of perennial planting in organic shapes; on the ground plan its bold curls and curlicues relate straight back to Alan Bloom's work in the 1970s or to Beth Chatto's gardens, but the planting is unequivocally Oudolf, with vigorous blocks of tall grasses and statuesque perennials, many of them well over head-high, effectively walling in some of the pools of lawn. In 2014 his garden at the Hauser & Wirth gallery in Somerset opened, using a similar combination of a grassy estuary separating banks of (more scattered) perennials, and it looks set to be the new object of desire for chasers of Oudolf's work.

The High Line, a hugely popular linear park made on a disused overhead railway line in downtown New York. Oudolf is principally a planting designer and was called in to dress the landscape architect's plan with his own colourful blend of romantic, rural naturalism. Native American perennials were carefully researched for suitability and incorporated into the scheme.

What is it that makes Oudolf's planting so special? Over the years it has moved on from drifts consisting of single-species planting to ones of mixed species, then to a more scattered planting punctuated by repeated taller accents, and most recently to a matrix planting of perennials overlaid with a sowing of annuals. He works on paper, drawing his designs with coloured pens, using tracing paper to add in his seasonal overlays.

None of his work has set out deliberately to recreate ecologically correct habitats in the manner of the German school, for sustainability's sake; rather, it has used a mixture of species and cultivated varieties from different parts of the world which coexist happily on minimal maintenance. Oudolf is quite clear: his schemes can be expected to last fifteen years, and only then with suitably skilled maintenance; he likes his gardens to remain faithful to his original planting plans. Modern or not, he admits to his planting being both romantic and nostalgic, a brave admission from someone at the peak of fashion's wave. Like a meadow, the planting is rich in swaying, transparent grasses, and contains overlapping layers of plants that provide both a long season of flower and also strong winter skeletons, as visually and emotionally compelling as at the peak of summer; it is his way of demonstrating the passage of time and life's transience.

Colour and colour association are not of as vital interest to Oudolf as they are to gardeners of the more traditional, Jekyllean school of gardening, but the naturalistic scatter patterns of his planting avoid any great clashes. For Oudolf, associations of texture are far more important, and a frosted winter scene of brown and ivory is just as attractive as the same scene in high summer. Oudolf makes the gift of both seasons to his audience, and in particular to his urban audience, capturing the spirit of the age through beauty and utility disguised as wildness.

The Lurie Garden, Chicago, might be seen as a huge, naturalistic parterre-cum-prairie, made of great swathes of perennials and grasses. Once again the space is enclosed on its two open sides by planting, here two great shoulders of hedging.

STEVE MARTINO

Naturalistic planting in desert gardens

BORN 1946

1946
Birth of Donald Trump, property magnate and
    presidential candidate.
Syria officially recognized as independent from France.
First underwater nuclear test, at Bikini Atoll.
Tupperware first sold in the USA.

MANY OF THE BEST garden designers – Lutyens, Christopher Bradley-Hole – were architects first, and so was Steve Martino; it's an excellent training. But Martino would take this further: he has suggested that architects should also be landscape architects, so close is the relationship between the two disciplines. And yet, for all his fascination with the built structure of gardens Martino is best known for his planting. Typically it consists of low-maintenance, native plants and more specifically desert plants – he

lives in Phoenix, Arizona. The Steve Martino look, with jagged cacti and wispy golden palo verde trees, startlingly coloured concrete walls, hard shadows and shining pools, was developed for reasons of commonsense sustainability thirty years ago, before most of the gardening world had even begun to think about such issues. Some say he invented it. Without changing anything he did, he moved from heretic to hero.

Martino was born just after the Second World War, and admits he was an urban delinquent who dropped out of school. He was a ranch wrangler at the Arizona Boys' Ranch, taking other teenagers out riding in the desert or visiting the simple cactus garden of an old 'hermit type' living in a trailer. Rides into the San Tan Mountain park got him hooked on the landscape of the desert.

ABOVE Steve Martino. OPPOSITE In any climate, moving expensive mature plants involves many technical challenges – top-heavy, spiny, easily scarred succulents may seem invincible, but they need thorough care to get them into place undamaged.

Plain, rendered walls in the Spanish tradition, often coloured, are a perfect opportunity for shadow-play and give protection from hard sunlight and hot winds. This oasis, like others everywhere, includes the sight and sound of formally managed, running water.

As plants seemed interesting, he got a job with a landscape architect. Because of his passion for the local flora, he was appalled by the way the industry constantly and thoughtlessly used the kind of plants that could be found in commercial landscaping all over the world. This was landscaping which, more to the point, was actually destructive of the natural environment. Why would anyone set out to erase the natural environment of the Sonoran Desert and replace it with something so artificial when it had so many attractions of its own, and ones that could easily be adapted for use in gardens and urban landscapes? 'Why not celebrate the desert rather than make apologies for it?' he asked.

After two years he decided to study art and architecture at Arizona State University, and quickly came to the conclusion that landscape architecture using suitable planting was a subject every architect should know about. The work in Texas of the Italian émigré architect Paolo Soleri, with its respect for the local landscape, was an inspiration. After two years in an architect's office and having worked on a few landscaping projects, he found by 1975 he had become almost by accident a landscape designer with his own practice.

Photographs cannot transmit exactly how heat feels. In the Sonoran Desert the annual rainfall is 13–18 cm (5–7 in.). The sunlight is blinding. In some years there can be between 30 and 40 days above 43°C (109°F). Plants that can survive this, even enjoy it, are not within the experience of most landscape architects, especially if they have been educated in kinder climates, but in the course of his career in the American Southwest, Martino has changed public and professional awareness so that most designers now know how to use native plants. It has become the norm.

The Sonoran Desert climate is as tough on people as it is on plants, which is why shade and shelter are such an important part of a garden there. The native flora does not include the shade-bearing broad-leaved trees typical of more temperate climates, and plants have adapted to the heat by sealing their moisture inside impermeable succulent bodies or by reducing their leaves to minimal proportions so that transpiration is reduced. Shade and shelter, therefore, must be provided by the creation of walls and buildings. Martino says his work is simply making a connection between architecture and nature, rather than putting plants around buildings, and that a good garden demands an emotional response. Like Thomas Church, Martino aims to make places where people want to live. His minimum requirement for a garden says it all: 'a tree, a wall and a chair with a little water'.

The cactus house in the Desert Botanical Garden in Arizona at sunrise. The desert flora has species in need of conservation and is close to Martino's heart and profession. The national collection of cacti here is second to none.

Martino's love of adobe-like concrete walls has arisen in part from looking at vernacular Mexican architecture, and he is happy to prove the ecological acceptability of using concrete when necessary. The rich colours he employs are vital in compensating for the way the glaring desert light washes out colours and shadows. He incorporates other modern or hi-tech materials, too, and as a great lover of borrowed landscape he often uses glass. His gardens are not without water, but he places it in formal geometric tanks and rills, in the way that the precious liquid was used in the hot-climate gardens of the Moors and Persians. Martino was astonished when he visited the Court of Lions at the Alhambra in Spain that there were no old plants. Only the structure was old, and it made him see that plants must always be

secondary to structure. A garden should work as a space before it is planted.

Obviously Martino does love to plant, and is fascinated by the way the glaucous desert flora stands out against richly coloured architecture. Early in his career he found it almost impossible to buy native plants to recreate the desert vernacular of his projects (today it would be easy), and so he collected seed and grew them himself. He also realized that desert birds rely for food on insects more than seeds, and so by satisfying that need, a garden would quickly develop its own entourage of pollinators and predators. This was his 'Weeds and Walls style'.

At the Desert Botanical Garden in Papago Park near Phoenix, Arizona, Martino designed the award-winning Sybil B. Harrington Cactus and Succulent Galleries, which opened in 2008. Steel mesh tunnels 8.5 m (28 ft) high are supported on terracotta-coloured concrete arches, providing a carefully managed outdoor environment for desert plants from all continents. Their positions were determined in part by some old specimen cacti too large to move, but Martino also arranged them to frame views outwards to the desert buttes. The object was to create somewhere with its own integrity and sense of place before the collections of smaller plants were installed beneath the tunnels.

Creating a roof of cactus pad 'tiles', not so very different perhaps from the green roofs made in temperate climates using sedums and houseleeks, which are also succulent.

One of his most visible projects is the Tree of Life, made in collaboration with the New York artist Jody Pinto, also in the Papago Park. The park, once home to the iconic saguaro cactus, *Carnegiea gigantea*, capable of growing up to 18 m (60 ft), has been grazed beyond regeneration by rabbits, and the Tree is a creation of stone pillars, rills and terraces, set to harvest the waters of a desert wash whose course was undone by adjacent road building. The terraces are now the site of a spectacular and self-sustaining regeneration of desert plants.

This same attention to the relationship between garden and desert is seen again in a domestic garden he made in the Tucson foothills. Around a modern house hunkered down into the landscape, paths lead out from every door, through the garden and into the surrounding desert. Formal pools close to the house soften the sun-baked prospect and also provide drinking places for the desert animals. Martino is never apologetic about using water imaginatively, but he also never fails to make it look like the civilized luxury it is in a desert climate. Coupled with desert planting, this is what makes a Martino garden so recognizable.

A garden in Tucson, where the brief was to link the garden with the landscape and provide walks straight out into the desert. The same plants grow in garden and desert, making the geometric lines of the house at home in the landscape.

FURTHER READING

GARDENS OF IDEAS
Wen Zhengming

Clunas, C., *Fruitful Sites: Garden Culture in Ming Dynasty China* (London: Reaktion; Durham: Duke University Press, 1996)

Clunas, C., *Elegant Debts: The Social Art of Wen Zhengming, 1470–1559* (London: Reaktion; Honolulu: University of Hawaii Press, 2004)

Keswick, M., *The Chinese Garden* (London: Frances Lincoln; Cambridge, Mass.: Harvard University Press, 2003)

Murck, A. and Fong, W., 'A Chinese Garden Court', *The Metropolitan Museum of Art Bulletin*, 38, 3 (1980–81)

Valder, P., *Gardens in China* (Portland: Timber Press, 2002)

Hachijo Toshihito and Hachijo Toshitada

Attlee, H., *The Gardens of Japan* (London: Frances Lincoln, 2010)

Goto, S., *The Japanese Garden, Gateway to the Human Spirit* (New York: Peter Lang, 2003)

Itoh, T., *Imperial Gardens of Japan* (New York: Weatherhill, 1972)

Kuck, L., *World of the Japanese Garden* (New York: Weatherhill, 1982)

Murasaki Shikibu, *The Tale of Genji* (London: Penguin Classics, 2003)

William Kent

Hunt, J. D., *William Kent, Landscape Garden Designer* (London: Zwemmer, 1987)

Jourdain, M., *The Work of William Kent: Artist, Painter, Designer and Landscape Gardener* (London: Country Life; New York: C. Scribner's, 1948)

Mowl, T., *William Kent, Architect, Designer, Opportunist* (London: Jonathan Cape, 2006)

Richardson, T., *The Arcadian Friends: Inventing the English Landscape Garden* (London: Bantam, 2007)

Weber, S. (ed.), *William Kent: Designing Georgian Britain* (London and New Haven: Yale University Press, 2013)

Wilson, M. I., *William Kent, Architect, Designer, Painter, Gardener* (Routledge & Kegan Paul, 1984)

Henry Hoare

A Description of the House and Gardens at Stourhead ... with a Catalogue of the Pictures (Salisbury: J. Easton, 1800)

Batey, M. and Lambert, D., *The English Garden Tour, a View into the Past* (London: John Murray, 1990)

Hunt, J. D. and Willis, P. (eds), *The Genius of the Place. The English Landscape Garden 1620-1820.* (London: Elek, 1975)

Hyams, E., *The English Garden* (London: Thames & Hudson; New York: Abrams, 1966)

Jacques, D., *Georgian Gardens, The Reign of Nature* (London: B. T. Batsford, 1983)

Woodbridge, K., *The Making of Stourhead, Henry Hoare's Paradise* (London: National Trust, 1965, repr. from the *Art Bulletin*, 47)

Friedrich Franz of Anhalt-Dessau

Der Vulkan im Wörlitzer Park (Berlin: Nicolai Verlag, 2005)

Exhibition catalogue: *For the Friends of Nature and Art. The Garden Kingdom of Franz von Anhalt-Dessau in the Age of Enlightenment* (Berlin: Hatje Cantz, 1997)

Günther, H., 'Franz, Prince of Anhalt-Dessau', in Taylor, P. (ed.), *The Oxford Companion to the Garden* (Oxford: Oxford University Press, 2006)

The Garden Kingdom of Dessau-Wörlitz, www.gartenreich.com/en/index.html

Thomas Jefferson

Ambrose, S. E., *Undaunted Courage: Meriwether Lewis, Thomas Jefferson and the Opening of the American West* (New York: Simon and Schuster, 1997)

Baron, R. C. (ed.), *The Garden and Farm Books of Thomas Jefferson* (Golden: Fulcrum, 1987)

Bernstein, R. B., *Thomas Jefferson* (Oxford and New York: Oxford University Press, 2003)

Betts, E. M. and Bolton Perkins, H., *Thomas Jefferson's Flower Garden at Monticello* (Charlottesville: Thomas Jefferson Memorial Foundation, 1986)

Hayes, K. J., *The Road to Monticello: The Life and Mind of Thomas Jefferson* (Oxford and New York: Oxford University Press, 2008)

Randall, H. S., *The Life of Thomas Jefferson* (New York: HarperPerennial, 2014 [1888])

Ian Hamilton Finlay

Abrioux, Y., *Ian Hamilton Finlay: A Visual Primer* (Edinburgh: Reaktion, 2004)

Finlay, A. (ed.), *Ian Hamilton Finlay, Selections* (Berkeley: University of California Press, 2012)

Hamilton Finlay, I., *The Dancers Inherit the Party* (Edinburgh: Polygon/Birlinn, 2004)

Hunt, J. D., *Nature Over Again: The Garden Art of Ian Hamilton Finlay* (London: Reaktion, 2008)

McIntosh, C., *Ian Hamilton Finlay, a Memoir* (Bremen: Vanadis Texts, 2014)

Sheeler, J., *Little Sparta: The Garden of Ian Hamilton Finlay* (London: Frances Lincoln, 2003)

www.littlesparta.org.uk

Sir Roy Strong

Strong, R., *Creating Small Gardens* (London: Conran Octopus 1986)

Strong, R., *The Roy Strong Diaries 1967–1987* (London: Weidenfeld & Nicolson, 1997)

Strong, R., *The Laskett: The Story of a Garden* (London: Bantam, 2003)

Strong, R., *Roy Strong: Self-Portrait as a Young Man* (Oxford: Bodleian Library, 2013)

Strong, R., *Remaking a Garden: The Laskett Transformed* (London: Frances Lincoln, 2014)

Charles Jencks

Jencks, C., *The Garden of Cosmic Speculation* (London: Frances Lincoln, 2003)

Jencks, C., *The Universe in the Landscape: Landforms by Charles Jencks* (London: Frances Lincoln, 2011)

www.jupiterartland.org

www.northumberlandia.com

www.crawickmultiverse.co.uk

www.charlesjencks.com

Alexander Reford

Beringer, H., *Chambres Vertes* (Québec: Jardins de Métis, 2000)

Reford, A., *Des Jardins Oubliés 1860-1960* (Québec: Publications du Québec, 1999)

Reford, A., *Reford Gardens* (Anjou, Québec: Fides, 2001)

www.refordgardens.com

GARDENS OF STRAIGHT LINES

André Le Nôtre

Baridon, M., *A History of the Gardens of Versailles* (Philadelphia: University of Pennsylvania Press, 2012)

Brix, M., *The Baroque Landscape: André Le Nôtre and Vaux-le-Vicomte* (New York: Rizzoli, 2004)

Hazlehurst, F. H., *Gardens of Illusion: The Genius of Andre Le Nostre* (Nashville: Vanderbilt University Press, 1980)

Mariage, T., *The World of André Le Nôtre* (Philadelphia: University of Pennsylvania Press, 2010)

Mukerji, C., *Territorial Ambitions and the Gardens of Versailles* (Cambridge and New York: Cambridge University Press, 2010)

Thompson, I., *The Sun King's Garden: Louis XIV, André Le Nôtre and the Creation of the Gardens of Versailles* (London: Bloomsbury, 2006)

William Nesfield

Blomfield, R., *The Formal Garden in England* (London: Macmillan, 1901)

Elliott, B., 'Master of the Geometric Art', *Journal of the Royal Horticultural Society*, 106 (1981), 488–91

Elliott, B., *Victorian Gardens* (London: B. T. Batsford, 1986)

Evans, S., *Nesfield's Monster Work: The Gardens of Witley Court* (Hereford: Peter Huxtable Designs, 1994)

Ridgway, C. (ed.), *William Andrews Nesfield, Victorian Landscape Architect: Papers from the 1994 Bicentenary Conference* (York: Institute of Advanced Architectural Studies, 1996)

Tooley, M. J., *Exhibition Guide*, William Andrews Nesfield Bicentenary Exhibition (University of Durham Library, 1994)

Sir Edwin Lutyens

Edwin Lutyens, Architectural Monographs 6 (London: Academy Editions, 1979)

Hussey, C., *The Life of Sir Edwin Lutyens* (Woodbridge: ACC, repr. 1984)

Irving, R. G., *Indian Summer: Lutyens, Baker and Imperial Delhi* (New Haven and London: Yale University Press, 1983)

Lutyens, M., *Edwin Lutyens by His Daughter* (London: Black Swan, 1991)

Ridley, J., *Edwin Lutyens: His Life, His Wife, His Work* (London: Chatto & Windus, 2002)

Stamp, G., *Edwin Lutyens: Country Houses: From the Archives of Country Life* (London: Aurum, 2001)

Weaver, L., *Houses and Gardens of E. L. Lutyens* (Woodbridge: ACC, 2001 [1913])

Lawrence Johnston

Hayward, A., *Norah Lindsay: The Life and Art of a Garden Designer* (London: Frances Lincoln, 2007)

Jones, L., *Serre de la Madone* (Arles: Actes Sud, 2003)

Lees-Milne, A., *Lawrence Johnston, Creator of Hidcote Garden* (London: National Trust, 1977)

Lord, T., *Best Borders* (London: Frances Lincoln, 1994)

Pearson, G. S., *Lawrence Johnston: The Creator of Hidcote* (Chipping Campden: Hidcote Books, 2010)

Pearson, G. S. and Pavord, A., *Hidcote: The Garden and Lawrence Johnston* (London: National Trust, 2007)

Whitsey, F., *The Garden at Hidcote* (London: Frances Lincoln, 2007)

Russell Page

Page, R., *The Education of a Gardener* (London: Collins, 1962)

Russell Page: Ritratti di Giardini Italiani (Milan: Electa, 1998)

Schinz, M. and Van Zuylen, G., *The Gardens of Russell Page* (New York: Stewart, Tabori & Chang, 1991; London: Frances Lincoln, 2008)

'The Archive of Russell Page', *Garden Museum Journal*, 31 (2015)

Turner, B., *Beacon for Change: How the 1951 Festival of Britain Shaped the Modern Age* (London: Aurum, 2011)

Nicole de Vésian

Jones, L., *Nicole de Vésian – Gardens. Modern Design in Provence* (Arles: Actes Sud, 2011)

Jones, L., *Mediterranean Landscape Design, Vernacular Contemporary* (London and New York: Thames & Hudson, 2012)

Jones, L., *New Gardens in Provence* (New York: Stewart, Tabori & Chang, 2006)

Jones, L., 'Nicole de Vésian Gardens', *Pacific Horticulture* (2011)

Penelope Hobhouse

Hobhouse, P., *The Country Gardener* (Oxford: Phaidon, 1976; Boston: Little Brown, 1989)

Hobhouse, P., *Plants in Garden History* (London: Pavilion, 1992)

Hobhouse, P., *On Gardening* (London: Frances Lincoln; New York: Macmillan, 1994)

Hobhouse, P., *Penelope Hobhouse's Garden Designs* (London: Frances Lincoln; New York: H. Holt, 1997)

Hobhouse, P., *Penelope Hobhouse's Natural Planting* (London: Pavilion, 1997)

Hobhouse, P., *Gardens of Persia* (London: Cassell, 2004)

Christopher Bradley-Hole

Bradley-Hole, C., *The Minimalist Garden* (London: Mitchell Beazley; New York: Monacelli Press, 1999)

Bradley-Hole, C., *Making the Modern Garden* (London: Mitchell Beazley; New York: Monacelli Press, 2007)

Compton, T., 'Christopher Bradley-Hole', in Taylor, P. (ed.), *The Oxford Companion to the Garden* (Oxford: Oxford University Press, 2006)

Richardson, T., *English Gardens in the Twentieth Century* (London: Aurum, 2005)

www.christopherbradley-hole.co.uk

Fernando Caruncho

Cooper, G. and Taylor, G., *Mirrors of Paradise: The Gardens of Fernando Caruncho* (New York: Monacelli Press, 2000)

Richardson, T., *Futurescapes* (London and New York: Thames & Hudson, 2011)

www.amastuola.eu/the-vineyard.php

www.fernandocaruncho.com

GARDENS OF CURVES
Lancelot 'Capability' Brown

Brown, J., *The Omnipotent Magician: Lancelot 'Capability' Brown, 1716–1743* (London: Chatto & Windus, 2011)

Hinde, T., *Capability Brown: The Story of a Master Gardener* (London: Hutchinson, 1986)

Mowl, T., *Gentlemen and Players: Gardeners of the English Landscape* (Stroud: History Press, 2010)

Robinson, J. M., *Temples of Delight: Stowe Landscape Gardens* (London: National Trust, 1994)

Stroud, D., *Capability Brown* (London: Faber, 1975)

Turner, R., *Capability Brown and the Eighteenth-Century Landscape* (Stroud: History Press, 2013)

www.capabilitybrown.org

Humphry Repton

Daniels, S., *Humphry Repton: Landscape Gardening and the Geography of Georgian England* (New Haven: Yale University Press, 1999)

Repton, H., *Sketches and Hints on Landscape Gardening* (London: W. Bulmer, 1795)

Repton, H., *Observations on the Theory and Practice of Landscape Gardening* (London: J. Taylor, 1803)

Repton, H. and Repton, J. A., *Fragments on the Theory and Practice of Landscape Gardening* (London: T. Bensley, 1816)

Repton, H., selected by Loudon, J. C., *The Landscape Gardening and Landscape Architecture of the Late Humphry Repton* (London: Forgotten Books, 2015)

Stroud, D., *Humphry Repton* (London: Country Life, 1962)

Frederick Law Olmsted

Beveridge, C. E., *Frederick Law Olmsted: Designing the American Landscape* (New York: Universe, 1998)

Beveridge, C. E. (ed.), *Frederick Law Olmsted: Plans and Views of Public Parks* (Baltimore: John Hopkins University Press, 2015)

Olmsted, F. L., *The Cotton Kingdom: A Traveller's Observations on Cotton and Slavery in the American Slave States, 1853-61* (New York: Da Capo, 1996)

Olmsted, F. L., *Yosemite and the Mariposa Grove: A Preliminary Report, 1865* (Yosemite Association, 1995)

Olmsted, F. L., *Walks and Talks of an American Farmer in England* (London: Forgotten Books, 2012)

Rosensweig, R. and Blackmar, E., *The Park and the People: A History of Central Park* (Ithaca: Cornell University Press, 1994)

Twombly, R. (ed.), *Frederick Law Olmsted: Essential Texts* (New York: W. W. Norton, 2010)

Edna Walling

Barrett, M. (ed.), *The Edna Walling Book of Australian Garden Design* (Richmond: O'Donovan, 1980)

Dixon, T. and Churchill, J., *The Vision of Edna Walling: Garden Plans 1920-51* (Hawthorn: Bloomings, 1998)

Hardy, S., *The Unusual Life of Edna Walling* (Sydney: Allen & Unwin, 2010)

Walling, E., *Gardens in Australia: Their Design and Care* (Melbourne: Oxford University Press, 1943)

Walling, E., *On the Trail of Australian Wildflowers* (Canberra: Mulini Press, 1984)

Walling, E., *Country Roads: The Australian Roadside* (Lilydale: Pioneer Design Studio, 1985)

Walling, E., *Letters to Garden Lovers, 1937–1948* (Frenchs Forest: New Holland, 2000)

Thomas Church

Church, T., *Gardens Are for People* (New York: Reinhold Publishing, 1955)

Church, T., *Your Private World: A Study of Intimate Gardens* (San Francisco: Chronicle Books, 1969)

Streatfield, D. C., *Calfornia Gardens: Creating a New Eden* (New York: Abbeville Press, 1994)

Treib, M. (ed.), *Thomas Church, Landscape Architect: Designing a Modern California Landscape* (San Francisco: William Stout, 2003)

Alan Bloom

Bloom, A., *Hardy Perennials* (London: Faber, 1957)

Bloom, A., *Perennials for Trouble-Free Gardening* (London: Faber, 1960)

Bloom, A., *The Bressingham Story* (London: Faber, 1963)

Bloom, A., *Alan Bloom's Hardy Perennials* (London: B. T. Batsford, 1991)

Roberto Burle Marx

Cavalcanti, C., El-Dahdah, F. and Rambert, F. (eds), *Roberto Burle Marx: The Modernity of Landscape* (Barcelona: Actar, 2011)

Doherty, G. (ed.), *Landscape as a Way of Life: Lectures by Roberto Burle Marx* (Zurich: Lars Müller, 2016)

Eliovson, S., *The Gardens of Roberto Burle Marx* (Portland: Timber Press, 1991)

Montero, M. I. and Schwartz, M., *Burle Marx: The Lyrical Landscape* (London: Thames & Hudson; Berkeley: University of California Press, 2001)

Roberto Burle Marx: The Unnatural Art of the Garden (New York: Museum of Modern Art, 1991)

Silva, R., *New Brazilian Gardens: The Legacy of Burle Marx* (London and New York: Thames & Hudson, 2006)

John Brookes

Brookes, J., *Room Outside* (London: Thames & Hudson, 1969; rev. ed. 1979)

Brookes, J., *Gardens of Paradise: The History and Design of the Great Islamic Gardens* (New York: New Amsterdam Books, 1987)

Brookes, J., *Planting the Country Way: A Hands-On Approach* (London: BBC Books, 1994)

Brookes, J., *Garden Design* (London: Dorling Kindersley, 2001)

Brookes, J. and Price, E., *Home and Garden Style: Creating a Unified Look Inside and Out* (London: Ward Lock, 1996)

www.johnbrookes.com

James van Sweden

Christopher, T. and Van Sweden, J., *The Artful Garden: Creative Inspiration for Landscape Design* (New York: Random House, 2011)

Naito, T., *Wolfgang Oehme and James van Sweden: New World Landscapes* (Tokyo: Process Architecture, 1996)

Oehme, W. and Van Sweden, J., *Bold Romantic Gardens: The New World Landscapes of Oehme and Van Sweden* (Easthampton: Spacemaker Press, 2003)

Van Sweden, J., *Gardening with Water* (New York: Random House, 1995)

Van Sweden, J., *Architecture in the Garden* (New York: Random House; London: Frances Lincoln, 2002)

GARDENS OF PLANTSMANSHIP
William Robinson

Allan, M., *William Robinson, 1838–1935. Father of the English Flower Garden* (London: Faber, 1982)

Bisgrove, R., *William Robinson, The Wild Gardener* (London: Frances Lincoln, 2008)

Blomfield, R., *The Formal Garden in England* (London: Macmillan, 1892)

Robinson, W., *Gleanings from French Gardens* (London: Frederick Warne, 1868)

Robinson, W., *The Wild Garden* (London: John Murray, 1870)

Robinson, W., *The English Flower Garden* (London: John Murray, 1883)

Claude Monet

Holmes, C., *Monet at Giverny* (Woodbridge: Garden Art Press, 2014)

Holmes, C., *Water Lilies and Bory Latour-Marliac, the Genius Behind Monet's Water Lilies* (Woodbridge: Garden Art Press, 2015)

Joyes, C., *Life at Giverny* (London: Thames & Hudson, 1985)

Royal Academy, *Painting the Modern Garden: Monet to Matisse* (London: Royal Academy, 2015)

Russell, V., *Monet's Garden: Behind the Scenes at Giverny* (London: Frances Lincoln, 1995)

Gertrude Jekyll

Brown, J., *Gardens of a Golden Afternoon. The Story of a Partnership: Edwin Lutyens & Gertrude Jekyll* (London: Allen Lane, 1982)

Clayton-Payne, A., *Victorian Flower Gardens* (London: Weidenfeld & Nicolson, 1988)

Festing, S., *Gertrude Jekyll* (London: Viking, 1991)

Jekyll, G., *Wood and Garden* (London: Longmans, Green & Co., 1899)

Jekyll, G., *Colour Schemes in the Flower Garden* (London: Country Life, 1908)

Massingham, B., *Miss Jekyll, Portrait of a Great Gardener* (London: Country Life, 1966)

Vita Sackville-West

Brown, J., *Vita's Other World: A Gardening Biography of V. Sackville-West* (Harmonsdworth and New York: Viking, 1985)

Glendinning, V., *Vita* (London: Weidenfeld & Nicolson, 1983)

Nicolson, N., *Portrait of a Marriage* (London: Weidenfeld & Nicolson; New York: Atheneum, 1973)

Sackville-West, V., *The Land* (London: Heinemann, 1926)

Sackville-West, V., *V. Sackville-West's Garden Book* (London: Michael Joseph, 1968)

Scott-James, A., *Sissinghurst: The Making of a Garden* (London: Michael Joseph, 1975)

Mien Ruys

Abbs, B., *Gärten in den Niederlanden und Belgien: ein Reiseführer zu den schönsten Gartenanlagen* (Basel: Birkhäuser, 2000)

Ruys, M., Ruys, J. D. and Ruys, T., *Het vaste plantenboek* (Amsterdam: Moussaults, 1957)

Ruys, M., Ruys, J. D. and Ruys, T., *Die Stauden* (Erlenbach-Zurich: Rentsch, 1951)

Wilson, A., *Influential Gardeners* (London: Mitchell Beazley, 2002)

Graham Stuart Thomas

Thomas, G. S., *The Old Shrub Roses* (London: Dent, 1955)

Thomas, G. S., *Plants for Ground Cover* (London: Dent, 1970)

Thomas, G. S., *Perennial Garden Plants, or The Modern Florilegium* (London: Dent, 1976)

Thomas, G. S., *Gardens of the National Trust* (London: Weidenfeld & Nicolson, 1979)

Thomas, G. S., *Ornamental Shrubs, Climbers and Bamboos* (London: John Murray, 1992)

Thomas, G. S., *The Garden Through the Year* (London: Thames & Hudson, 2002)

Lelia Caetani

Attlee, H., *Italian Gardens* (London: Frances Lincoln, 2006)

Caracciolo, M. and Pietromatchi, G., *The Garden of Ninfa* (Turin: Umberto Allemandi, 1999)

McLeod, K., *The Best Gardens in Italy* (London: Frances Lincoln, 2011)

Marchetti, L. and Howard, E., *Ninfa – A Roman Enchantment* (London: Thames & Hudson, 1999)

Quest-Ritson, C., *Ninfa, the Most Romantic Garden in the World* (London: Frances Lincoln, 2009)

www.fondazionecaetani.org/fondazione.php

Rosemary Verey

Lees-Milne, A. and Verey, R. (eds), *The Englishwoman's Garden* (London: Chatto & Windus, 1980)

Lees-Milne, A. and Verey, R. (eds), *The Englishman's Garden* (London: Allen Lane, 1982)

Robinson, B. P., *Rosemary Verey, The Life and Lessons of a Legendary Gardener* (Jaffrey: David R. Godine, 2012)

Verey, R., *Good Planting* (London: Frances Lincoln, 1990)

Verey, R., *Rosemary Verey's Garden Plans* (London: Frances Lincoln, 1991)

Christopher Lloyd

Anderton, S., *Christopher Lloyd: His Life at Great Dixter* (London: Chatto & Windus, 2010)

Lloyd, C., *The Well-Tempered Garden* (London: Collins, 1970)

Lloyd, C., *Foliage Plants* (London: Collins, 1973)

Lloyd, C. *In My Garden* (ed. Ronan, F.) (London: Bloomsbury, 1993)

Lloyd, C., *Colour for Adventurous Gardeners* (London: BBC, 2001)

Lloyd, C., *Meadows* (London: Cassell, 2004)

Lloyd, C., *Exotic Planting for Adventurous Gardeners* (London: BBC, 2007)

Beth Chatto

'Beth Chatto', *Garden Museum Journal*, 21 (2008)

Chatto, B., *The Dry Garden* (London: Dent, 1978)

Chatto, B., *The Damp Garden* (London: Dent, 1982)

Chatto, B., *Beth Chatto's Gravel Garden* (London: Frances Lincoln, 2000)

Chatto, B., *Beth Chatto's Woodland Garden* (London: Cassell, 2002)

Chatto, B. and Lloyd, C., *Dear Friend and Gardener* (London: Frances Lincoln, 1998)

Piet Oudolf

Gerritsen, H. and Oudolf, P., *Dream Plants for the Natural Garden* (London: Frances Lincoln; Portland: Timber Press, 2000)

King, M. and Oudolf, P., *Gardening With Grasses* (London: Frances Lincoln; Portland: Timber Press, 1998)

Oudolf, P. and Gerritsen, H., *Planting the Natural Garden* (Portland: Timber Press, 2003)

Oudolf, P. and Kingsbury, N., *Piet Oudolf, Landscapes in Landscapes* (New York: Monacelli Press; London: Thames & Hudson, 2011)

Oudolf, P. and Kingsbury, N., *Oudolf. Hummelo* (New York: Monacelli Press, 2015)

Richardson, T., *The New English Garden* (London: Frances Lincoln, 2013)

www.oudolf.com

Steve Martino

Harpur, J., *Gardens in Perspective* (London: Mitchell Beazley, 2005)

Richardson, T., *Great Gardens of America* (London: Frances Lincoln, 2009)

www.stevemartino.net

www.stevemartino.blogspot.co.uk

SOURCES OF ILLUSTRATIONS

1 From Repton, H., *Fragments on the Theory and Practice of Landscape Gardening*, London, 1816; 2 Wellcome Library, London; 4–5 © Karin Fremer; 6 © 2006 John Hedgecoe/Topfoto; 7 Wellcome Library, London; 8 Photo RMN-Grand Palais (Château de Versailles)/Gérard Blot; 9 Paul Mellon Collection, Yale Center for British Art, New Haven; 11 © Philippe Huchez; 12 © Piet Oudolf; 13 Steve Martino; 14–15 Landeshauptarchiv Sachsen-Anhalt, Dessau-Rosslau; 17 © John Lander (www.asiaimages.net); 18a The Art Institute of Chicago; 18b Metropolitan Museum of Art, New York; 19 National Palace Museum, Taipei; 20 Metropolitan Museum of Art, New York; 21 © John Lander (www.asiaimages.net); 22 © Gordon Sinclair/Alamy Stock Photo; 23 Imperial Collection, Tokyo, Japan; 24 British Museum, London; 25, 26 © Alex Ramsay/Alamy Stock Photo; 27 Imperial Collection, Tokyo, Japan; 29 National Portrait Gallery, London; 30 London Borough of Lambeth, Archives Dept. Photo Alan J. Robertson, LBIPP; 31a Paul Mellon Collection, Yale Center for British Art, New Haven; 31b Devonshire Collection, Chatsworth; 32 Photo © roseov/123RF.com; 33 © Andy Malengier; 34 J. Paul Getty Museum, Los Angeles; 36–37 Courtesy Royal Academy of Fine Arts, Stockholm; 38 Paul Mellon Collection, Yale Center for British Art, New Haven; 39 Trustees of the British Museum, London; 41 Photo Jerry Harpur. © Harpur Garden Images; 43 Bildarchiv Heinz Fräßdorf , Kulturstiftung DessauWörlitz, Dessau-Rosslau; 44 Landeshauptarchiv Sachsen-Anhalt, Dessau-Rosslau; 45, 46 Bildarchiv Heinz Fräßdorf , Kulturstiftung DessauWörlitz, Dessau-Rosslau; 47 White House Historical Association (White House Collection); 48 © Thomas Jefferson Foundation at Monticello, watercolour of Monticello by Jane Pitford Braddick Peticolas, 1825; 49 American Philosophical Society, Philadelphia; 50 Collection of the Massachusetts Historical Society; 51 © Thomas Jefferson Foundation at Monticello, photo Leonard G. Phillips; 52 Photo © Werner Hannappel; 53 Photo Sam Rebben. By courtesy of The Estate of Ian Hamilton Finlay; 54 © gardenpics/Alamy Stock Photo. By courtesy of The Estate of Ian Hamilton Finlay; 55 Photo Sam Rebben. By courtesy of The Estate of Ian Hamilton Finlay; 56 Photo Michael Loudon. By courtesy of The Estate of Ian Hamilton Finlay; 57 Photo Sam Rebben. By courtesy of The Estate of Ian Hamilton Finlay; 59 Chris Barham/Daily Mail/REX Shutterstock; 60, 61, 62 © Jonathan Myles-Lea; 63, 64, 65 © Clive Boursnell; 67a Photo Ian Rutherford. Courtesy Charles Jencks; 67b, 68 © Charles Jencks; 69 © gardenpics/Alamy Stock Photo; 70–71 © Charles Jencks; 72 © Charles Jencks & Jencks Squared; 73a, 73b © Charles Jencks; 74 © Joan Sullivan; 75 Les Amis des Jardins de Métis Collection; 76, 77a, 77b, 78, 79, 80, 81 Louise Tanguay (www.louisetanguayphoto.ca); 82–83 Bibliothèque nationale de France, Paris; 85 Photo Château de Versailles, Dist. RMN-Grand Palais/Christophe Fouin; 86 Rijksmuseum, Amsterdam; 87 © Arnaud Chicurel/Hemis/Corbis; 88 The Getty Research Institute, 84-B21384; 89 Photo RMN-Grand Palais (Château de Versailles)/Gérard Blot; 90, 91 Nesfield Archives; 92 Photo courtesy Broughton Hall; 93 Royal Collection Trust/Her Majesty Queen Elizabeth II 2016; 94a From Morris, F. O., *A series of picturesque views of seats of the noblemen and gentlemen of Great Britain and Ireland*, London, 1880; 95 Photo © Philip Bird/123RF.com; 96 Edward Gooch/Getty Images; 99a RIBA Collections; 99b, 100 © Country Life; 101 © Michael St. Maur Sheil/Corbis; 102, 103 © Country Life; 105, 109 Photo Marcus Harpur © Harpur Garden Images; 106, 110, 111, 113 Photo Jerry Harpur © Harpur Garden Images; 114, 115, 116 The Garden Museum, London. Courtesy The Estate of Russell Page; 117 © Alex Ramsay/Alamy Stock Photo; 118, 119 RHS, Lindley Library/Courtesy The Estate of Russell Page; 120 Photo © Louisa Jones; 121, 122 © Philippe Huchez; 123 Clive Nichols/GAP Photos; 125 © Philippe Huchez; 127 © Sam Luke Walton; 128 Photo Jerry Harpur. © Harpur Garden Images; 129 © The National Trust Photolibrary/Alamy Stock Photo; 130 Photo Jerry Harpur. © Harpur Garden Images; 131 Photo Mick Hales/The New York Botanical Garden; 133 Courtesy Christopher Bradley-Hole; 134a © Andrew Lawson; 134b Photo Jerry Harpur. © Harpur Garden Images; 136a © Hugh Palmer; 136b, 137 Courtesy Christopher Bradley-Hole; 139, 140 Photo Jerry Harpur. © Harpur Garden Images; 141, 142a, 142b, 143, 144–145, 145b Courtesy Fernando Caruncho; 146–147 Drawing Edna Walling. Pictures Collection, State Library of Victoria, Melbourne; 148 Paul Mellon Collection, Yale Center for British Art, New Haven; 149 Private Collection/The Stapleton Collection/Bridgeman Images; 150 © Photimageon/Alamy Stock Photo; 152–153 © Pete Seaward/Blenheim Palace; 155 Tate, London 2016; 157 From Repton, H. 'Memoirs' (manuscript), *c.* 1814–15; 158 From Repton, H., *Sketches and Hints on Landscape Gardening…*, London 1795; 159a, 159b From Repton, H., *Fragments on the Theory and Practice of Landscape Gardening*, London, 1816; 161 From Repton, H., *Designs for the Pavilion at Brighton*, London, 1808; 162a, 162b, 163 From Repton, H., *Fragments on the Theory and Practice of Landscape Gardening*, London, 1816; 165 The Artchives/Alamy Stock Photo; 166–167 From *Thirteenth Annual Report of the Commissioners of the Central Park*, New York, 1870; 167 Michael S. Yamashita/Getty Images; 169a Brooklyn Museum/Brooklyn Public Library, Brooklyn Collection, 1996.164.2-1433; 169b Riverside Historical Museum, Illinois; 171, 172 Photo Edna Walling. Pictures Collection, State Library of Victoria, Melbourne; 173, 174 Drawing Edna Walling. Pictures Collection, State Library of Victoria, Melbourne; 175 Photo Edna Walling. Pictures Collection, State Library of Victoria, Melbourne; 176, 178a Thomas D. Church Collection, Environmental Design Archives, University of California, Berkeley; 178b Previously published by *House Beautiful* magazine, April 1951. Reprinted with permission of Hearst Communications, Inc.; 179 Thomas D. Church Collection, Environmental Design Archives, University of California, Berkeley. © 2016 Rondal Partridge Archive; 180, 181 Thomas D. Church Collection, Environmental Design Archives, University of California, Berkeley; 183, 184, 185, 186, 187 © Bloom Pictures; 189 Charles Allmon/National Geographic/Getty Images; 190 © Malcolm Raggett; 191 Photo Jerry Harpur. © Harpur Garden Images; 192 © Malcolm Raggett; 193 © Ricardo Aguiar/agefoto.com; 195, 196, 198, 199al, 199ar, 199b Courtesy John Brookes; 201 © Oehme, van Sweden; 202 Photo Jerry Harpur. © Harpur Garden Images; 203 © Roger Foley; 204 Photo Jerry Harpur. © Harpur Garden Images; 205a, 205b © Oehme, van Sweden; 206–207 © Piet Oudolf; 211, 212–213 Private Collection; 214, 215 From Robinson, W. *The Wild Garden*, London, 1881; 216 Yale University Art Gallery, New Haven; 217 RMN-Grand-Palais/Droits réservés; 218 Photo © Musée d'Orsay, Dist. RMN-Grand Palais/Patrice Schmidt; 220a © Pierre Choumoff/Roger-Viollet/Topfoto; 220b National Gallery of Art, Washington, D.C.; 221 Photo © Collection Jean-Baptiste Leroux. Dist. RMN-Grand Palais/Jean-Baptiste Leroux; 223 Photo © Sebastian Nohl. Image courtesy of The Lightbox Gallery and Museum; 224 Reproduced by permission of the Jekyll Estate and Surrey History Centre; 225, 226, 227 © Country Life; 228–229 Reproduced by permission of the Jekyll Estate and Surrey History Centre; 231 © Hulton-Deutsch Collection/Corbis; 232 From Morris, F. O., *A series of picturesque views of seats of the noblemen and gentlemen of Great Britain and Ireland*, London, 1880; 233, 234, 235 © Jonathan Buckley; 236 Photo courtesy Ellis & Co. (ellisbooks.co.uk); 237 © The National Trust Photolibrary/Alamy Stock Photo; 239, 240, 241, 242, 243 © Buro Mien Ruys, Amsterdam; 245 Courtesy David Austin Roses; 246–247 © The National Trust Photolibrary/Alamy Stock Photo; 248 RHS, Lindley Library; 249 © Becker/FocusOnGarden/FP/The Garden Collection; 251 © Russell/Alamy Stock Photo; 253, 254a, 254b, 255, 256, 257 Archivio fotografico Fondazione Roffredo Caetani; 259, 260 Photos Jerry Harpur. © Harpur Garden Images; 261 Andrew Lawson/FP/The Garden Collection; 262 © Country Life; 263 Photo Jerry Harpur. © Harpur Garden Images; 265 © Jonathan Buckley; 266 © Country Life; 267 Courtesy Fergus Garrett; 268 © Jonathan Buckley; 269 Photo © James McGrath (plinthetal.com); 270 © Jonathan Buckley; 273 Photo Helen Dillon; 274, 275, 276–277, 278, 279 Courtesy Beth Chatto; 281 Photo Karl Buhler. From *Oudolf/Hummelo*, The Monacelli Press, 2015. Courtesy Piet Oudolf ; 282 © Jürgen Becker; 283 © Jo Whitworth; 284–285, 286, 287 © Piet Oudolf; 288, 289, 290, 291, 292, 293 Steve Martino.

INDEX